Swim, Bike, Bonk

Confessions of a Reluctant Triathlete

Will McGough

Foreword by Gordon Haller

Guilford, Connecticut

An imprint of The Rowman & Littlefield Publishing Group, Inc.
4501 Forbes Blvd., Ste. 200
Lanham, MD 20706
www.rowman.com

Distributed by NATIONAL BOOK NETWORK

British Library Cataloguing in Publication Information available

Library of Congress Cataloging-in-Publication Data available

ISBN 978-1-4930-4162-6 (hardcover)
ISBN 978-1-4930-3639-4 (e-book)

∞™ The paper used in this publication meets the minimum requirements of American National Standard for Information Sciences—Permanence of Paper for Printed Library Materials, ANSI/NISO Z39.48-1992.

Contents

This book is an account of my experience as a participant at the 2017 Ironman Arizona and my experiences before, during, and after that event. The opinions and portrayals shared in this book are my own and are in no way affiliated with Ironman or the World Triathlon Corporation.

Some of the names in the book have been changed. In minor instances, events and interactions have been streamlined for the sake of storytelling. Overall, the major timeline remains true and intact, and all the accounts of the events, people, and places are genuine and my own.

Tempe Tourism granted me a media pass to compete in the 2017 Ironman Arizona. I have not been authorized, endorsed, sponsored, or licensed by, nor has content been reviewed or otherwise approved by, Tempe Tourism or the World Triathlon Corporation.

To my Mom and Dad
for always encouraging
me to be
no one but me

Foreword: Reflecting Back to the First Race in 1978

By Gordon Haller, the first Ironman

Will McGough has written a very detailed account of how he prepared for and participated in his first and possibly only Ironman Triathlon. His story includes the effects of Ironman training on his life, work, and relationships, as well as on his mind and body. He provides a taste of the history of the race and musings on the early years for the creators of the race. From the descriptions, we gain that there is a marked difference in how he and many others prepare now compared with the way we, the fifteen original competitors, approached the first Ironman Triathlon back in 1978. This is true. Not only did we train differently, but also the race itself was completely different.

I first heard about the Ironman two and a half months before the race while I was on O'ahu running in the Honolulu Marathon that December. I answered an ad in the newspaper and, because it was not a big thing at all, was swept up with fourteen other people on the organizing committee. Some of those names you might recognize: John Collins; Ian Emberson; John Dunbar. Together, throughout December and January, we created the framework for the Ironman leading up to the "race" on February 18, 1978.

Obviously, we didn't give ourselves much time to train specifically for the race, but we were all fitness enthusiasts, so we were in pretty good shape. In this way, Will's journey is probably more similar to our experiences back in 1978 than it is to today's journey, where people hire coaches and train twelve to eighteen months for a single event. But Will also had an advantage that we original athletes didn't: He had access to a lot of information on the Internet and social media about what others were doing to prepare for the race.

Iron-Man Triathlon: Haller leads 15

By DICK FISHBACK
Advertiser Sports Writer

If they ever need a stand-in for television's Bionic Man, the producers should quickly jot down the name of 27-year-old Gordon Haller of Honolulu.

Haller lays no claim to the mechanical man's title, but he went the fellow one better yesterday while winning the first Iron-Man Triathlon in a total elapsed time of 11:46:58.

It was run in a day marked by driving rain, some breezes; an event launched at 7:19 a.m. and finished by Haller about 7:06 p.m.

For those of you who may have missed the first report on this gut-buster, the events were these in this order: 2.4-mile ocean rough water swim, 112-mile bicycle race around Oahu and the 26-mile, 385-yard marathon run over the regular Honolulu Marathon course.

One of those is enough to do in most mortals. But except for some cramping in the back of his legs and a numbness of his posterior in the bicycle ride, Haller was amazingly fresh.

He finished roughly 33½ minutes in front of John Dunbar (12:20:27), a Chaminade University student who had led the pack by 13 minutes through the first two events.

They were the frontrunners among a field of 15, which had only one dropout early in the day. And the dropout—Ralph Yawata—retired because of his handler's car failure rather than because of fatigue.

When Haller ran out of the Aloha Tower checkpoint for the

See HALLER on Page H-7

Advertiser photo

Haller on the run

News clipping from the *Honolulu Advertiser* on Sunday, February 19, 1978, the day after the first Ironman, announcing Gordon Haller's victory. NEWSPAPERS.COM

We weren't thinking much about that. To us, there was no hype—it was just a fun race. My coworkers became my support crew. One of them became my support crew chief and organized my team of six to help guide me through the day.

MORNING OF RACE

Current races call for participants to arrive in the dark to get numbers marked on their arms and legs, to check their bikes, turn in bags. There are a lot of cameras and interviews going on. Loud music playing, bright lights. Helicopters in the air. Thousands of people moving about, competitors, families, friends, TV crews, reporters, race officials, and crews.

The first race was much different. The gray morning on the beach at the Diamond Head end of Waikīkī brought a few dozen people who quietly milled about waiting for the word to be passed about how the day was expected to go. John Collins gave a short speech about the rules. The rules were simple: Swim 2.4 miles, ride 112 miles, run 26.2 miles and brag for the rest of your life.

It was very casual. Everyone had their own support crew (sometimes, that was only a single friend). Each had a paddler on a surfboard, as there were no buoys to guide us. Drafting wasn't illegal, but I don't think there was any opportunity to do so. I had two bikes and that was OK. We could accept help from anyone. There were no aid stations on the run or bike.

SWIM

Of course, now there are very large orange and yellow buoys every 100 meters or so in most races. Kona has a cannon to start the race. Many Ironman races have wave starts due to the number of entrants, which now often top 2,500. There still are paddlers, but they are there for guiding and rescuing any and all. There are boats, jet skis, and scuba divers to ensure safety.

I don't remember if we had a starter's pistol or if they just said "Go." We went. Out to where our paddlers were. My paddler was eleven years old and a surfing veteran. He did a great job, as did all of the paddlers. The water was very calm and nobody got in anyone's way, and I never saw anyone after the first turn. After all, 2.4 miles is a lot of open water with only fifteen people.

TRANSITIONS

Transitions are perhaps the biggest difference between then and now. When we came out of the water, we walked up the beach to the Hale Koa military hotel, showered, and changed into dry clothes for the ride. I spent maybe 20 minutes at T1, though it wasn't called T1—we didn't have a name for it. For T2, I jumped in the fountain at the Aloha Tower, changed into my dry running kit, did an interview with the newspaper, got a massage, drank a Coke, and started my run. Probably another fifteen or twenty minutes. This type of dillydallying would horrify competitors today, who consider transitions part of the race.

BIKE

Will goes into a lot of graphic detail in his description of his bike training. For those not in the know, that may be too much information. But sooner or later all of us will have a similar experience regarding digestive disorders, some more so than others. His problems can hit anyone anytime. He tells us his thinking in his selection of fluids and nutrition. It is perhaps the most important part of race preparation. He nails it as his energy source, but something goes awry, so we get to see how he tries to solve that problem. As President Eisenhower once said, "Plans are useless, but planning is indispensable." Will did a lot of planning.

Unlike today, where you have an aid station every 15 miles or so, there were no aid stations back then, except what your crew could provide you with. We had to obey traffic laws, stop at stop signs (some Ironman events today are closed course, others are partially open). We had two support vehicles. One would follow along behind me, and one would go ahead. I had to be helped off the bike to go to the bathroom on the North Shore because I couldn't walk. I remember thinking, if I feel this bad halfway through, how am I going to feel at the end? As soon as I switched bikes I felt better. We could use two different bikes back then, a lighter bike to go uphill and then a heavier one to go down. At the end of the bike course I jumped into the Aloha Tower fountain and got a standing massage from my crew. There was a newspaper guy there who wanted an interview. Then I took off on the run.

RUN

A large variety of nutrition is now available at aid stations. What you take can determine the outcome of your performance. Nowadays you have aid stations every mile or two on the run course, with a large variety of nutrition available. We had to rely on our crews. I had two guys running the last five miles with me (this would be illegal today). One carried my water, one carried Coke. I wasn't feeling that great. I ran 3:27, slow because I was a 2:27 marathoner at the time. The finish was much different from today because there was nobody there.

FINISH

Those with any familiarity at all with the Ironman know what a celebration it is at the finish line. It runs the full range of emotions nowadays, with Mike Reilly shouting "You are an Ironman!" to all finishers as they cross the finish line. There is loud music and thousands of fans line the finish chute. As I approached the finish line in 1978, I could only see a single spotlight and a couple of guys sitting in lawn chairs. On crossing the finish line, one of them asked, "Are you in the race?" When I answered in the affirmative, he said, "Well . . . you're done." Not that I expected any fanfare, but it was a bit of a letdown. I had a few friends and my support crew there. It was still satisfying to have completed it.

EQUIPMENT

There was no such thing as a tri-suit. We wore Speedos—well, most of us. That required a wardrobe change after the swim. We required everyone to wear a helmet on the bike. The helmet technology was very limited, so we wore leather hairnet helmets. They wouldn't keep you from dying in a crash, but they would keep the mess in one place. I think I was the only one with real cycling shorts. The best we could do for pedals was running shoes with toe straps. No such thing as aero bars, and we only had ten speeds. We changed clothes for the run. Pretty standard running kits, though the running boom in the '70s had been going for some years, so the shoes had made pretty good advances.

RECOVERY

I don't know what the other guys did in 1978, but after the race, I waded in the ocean for half an hour, then went home and slept for twelve hours. I was very tired the next day, but not sore. After the 1979 Ironman, Tom Warren and I hit the Jacuzzi at the Nautilus Fitness Center before I went home to sleep for another twelve hours. I heard Tom just walked the streets for a while that night. Now, when I finish an Ironman, I can hardly walk and need to have someone get my things from transition and drive me home. I can get up in ten hours now, but I get real sore muscles. Lots of food with additional protein is still my main tool for recovery.

PARTICIPATION AND PUBLICITY

We had almost no publicity in 1978. A full-page article ran in the two Honolulu papers with photos, and a paragraph ran in the back of *Runner's World* magazine. I don't know if many noticed. Only fifteen of us took a chance participating in this new and unusual "non-competition." The next year, we were the same number of "competitors," but we made it a bit more of a race.

However, the progression of publicity grew from there. The first boom came out of an article in the May 14, 1979, issue of *Sports Illustrated*. The article brought a lot of growth—106 entrants in 1980. This was followed by the *Wide World of Sports* story of the 1980 Ironman: It featured the race as a part of the show each year until Julie Moss's 1982 performance earned her the "Agony of Defeat" symbol in the show's opening sequence.

Gordon Haller speaks to a crowd as part of Walmart's "Get Active" personal sustainably program in 2010. He has continued to be active in the triathlete community since becoming the first champion in 1978. He has competed in more than two dozen 140.6-mile events and, in 2018, he participated in the fortieth anniversary event at the Ironman World Championships in Kona. WIKIMEDIA COMMONS

After that, a full show was dedicated to Ironman. Eventually, Ironman got its own show and grew so that fans were able to watch all seventeen hours of the race on the Internet. The race is known throughout the world now, to say the least.

After seeing the growth in that 1980 race, we realized that if it grew more, we'd have to change the course drastically to handle the traffic and the less manageable number of entrants. It was decided at that point to move the race from O'ahu to Kona. It was a smart move as the number of entrants swelled to over 350 in 1981. Since then, the race has grown rapidly. To date, there have been over 700,000 finishers in the forty-plus years of Ironman. That may seem like a lot, but of the 7.53 billion people in the world, that's only 0.01%.

Where I live in the south, there has been exponential interest in and growth of triathlon. It seems like everyone I know is getting into it. It is easy for one to assume that is the case everywhere, but often, when I leave this little corner of the world, I still meet a lot of people who don't know what a triathlon is, much less an Ironman. There is still room for continued exponential growth.

Prologue

November 19, 2017
Tempe, Arizona
Mile 49 of 140.6

> *You can keep going and your legs might hurt for a week, or you can quit and your mind will hurt for a lifetime.*
>
> —Mark Allen, six-time Ironman World Champion

Both sides of my neck are bleeding. The wet suit brushed up against it so hard in the chaos of the swim that it's now cut, rubbed raw—it looks like I got a hickey from a prickly pear cactus. As I ride, the sweat drips from my hair and the side of my head, finding its way down my neck and into the abrasion. It burns like the Arizona sun, and it's been that way for most of the bike.

The silver lining is that it's been a welcome distraction. Something to complain about, something to take my attention away from the fact that my legs are tremendously tired, at times bordering on inoperable. Something to ease my paranoia about a third flat tire. In this sick, twisted way, the pain helps me stay focused on the present. Otherwise, I'd be thinking about how, nearly 50 miles in, I'm still not even halfway through the race.

I stand up on the pedals to stretch out my legs. The desert scenery is going by, just not as fast as it once did. My pace has slowed considerably the last two miles. If this is the end for me—if this is the "bonk"—then I'm about to meet my maker. I try my best to crank through. I try to forget the fact that my legs are tired. I try to forget the fact that I have diarrhea. I try to forget the fact that my penis is completely numb. The last time I stopped to pee, I had to twirl it around for fifteen seconds before the feeling came back. I change positions on the seat. I switch out my left butt cheek for my right butt cheek to get my circulation going again. Physically, my body is sounding every alarm.

I decide to pull into the next aid station for a bathroom break. A lot of my fellow competitors pee while they are riding—without stopping—but I haven't been able to bring myself to do it. I didn't practice it enough. Plus, my bathroom breaks right now are, unfortunately, not about peeing.

The Porta-Potties along the course are supposed to be stocked with toilet paper. Earlier, I learned the hard way that some have run out. Now, I keep my old energy bar wrappers in my pocket in case I need them to wipe myself.

I see the aid station up ahead on the right. Volunteers are lined up in a row for a couple hundred feet and hold out Clif Bars, Gatorade, water, and other snacks for riders to grab as they go by. I pedal all the way to the end where there is a row of Porta-Potties. A volunteer meets me as I pull in. She takes my bike and hangs it on a bike rack in front of the Porta-Potties. I step into one of them. I unzip my bike jersey and carefully take it off. I don't want the food in my pockets to fall into the pit. I lay the jersey on the floor. I pull down the shoulder straps of the leotard. I pull the leotard down to the middle of my thigh. The sweat makes everything sticky. It's a process. I sit down on the toilet. Bursts of gas erupt like a geyser, a strong blast with the force of a fully loaded whoopee cushion. Liquid discharge splatters the bowl below. I find half a roll of toilet paper on the floor. I wipe myself, stand up, and pull up my leotard. I pick the jersey up off the floor and put my arms through. I zip up the jersey. I reach for my head and realize I never took off my helmet. I put on my sunglasses, open the door, and step out. The door slams shut as I let it go and jog back to my bike.

I tear off the top of a package of Chamois Butt'r—Chamois butt paste and chafing cream—and squeeze it into my hand. It's the consistency of toothpaste, or sugary cake icing, bright white and smooth. I reach down the back of my bike leotard and spread it over both of my butt cheeks. I can feel the cool temperature of the paste on my hot skin, and it provides instant relief. Rubbing it in feels like a massage, soothing out the tension and putting out the fire. I refill my hand and apply a second coat to both cheeks.

The next handful goes down the front. I coat my penis, rubbing over its entire length, and then spread the paste across the circumference of both testicles. It feels . . . good . . . and it will help with friction. I bend my knees and extend my arm, reaching past my penis to apply a layer to my grundle. Thankfully, there are no children around.

I pocket the remainder of the cream and lift my bike off the rack. I notice the volunteer is staring at me. Maybe I had my hand down my pants a little too long. Her look tells me it's time to move on—and that next time she'll call the cops.

I grab a Gatorade and a water and mount my bike. I thank the volunteer and pull away from the aid station. I merge back onto the course and into the steady stream of bikers. My stomach still doesn't feel right—there will undoubtedly be more stops—but with the pressure relieved temporarily, I can carry on. Off I go up the road, up the big hill. The day is entering its hottest portion. The wind is blowing full force. The comfort of the cream lasts a couple of miles before the hill takes over and the misery returns.

Part One

Don't Do It

August 2, 2017
Waimānalo, O'ahu, Hawai'i
109 Days Until the Ironman

> *But there are men for whom the unattainable has a special attraction. Usually they are not experts: their ambitions and fantasies are strong enough to brush aside the doubts which more cautious men might have. Determination and faith are their strongest weapons. At best such men are regarded as eccentric; at worst, mad.*
>
> —Walt Unsworth, *Everest*

Today's the day I call my friends and family and tell them I intend to do the Ironman in Tempe, Arizona, on November 19. I figure telling them is a good first step to all this, to get it out there in the open, to get some accountability—and motivation—flowing in my direction. Once I tell people I'm doing it, there's no going back. In this way, talking about it makes it official.

I'm also interested to hear the reactions from people across the board: friends, family, athletes, nonathletes, strangers. I know I'm cutting it close in terms of how much time I have to train, but I believe I can do it. I know not everyone will share my confidence. After all, this is the Ironman, considered to be one of, if not the, most difficult single-day athletic event in the world: 2.4 miles in the water, 112 miles on the bike, and then a full marathon, 26.2 miles, to be completed in 17 hours or less. I know some people, especially within the Ironman community here in Hawai'i, where the race got its start forty years ago, will have doubts about my fate, given that many of them train for more than a year for the event, and I'm just now getting started.

But, come on. You swim for a bit, jump on the bike for a while, then give the run your best shot—walk a little bit, stop and grab a water and a snack, rest for a while and then, you know, keep going and get there in one piece. I am thirty-two years old. I am generally fit and active. I have experience in these sports, and in athletic accomplishment in general. I've climbed mountains in the snow. I've done long treks in the desert. I've done multiday bike rides at altitude. This will be another adventure to add to the list. And maybe by the end of it I'll be able to understand why in the world anyone would want to do it in the first place.

I start with my friend Bird. He's a few years older, and he's the big bro I never had. I went off to college with his advice in hand, celebrated my twenty-first birthday at his apartment in Philly, and crashed on his couch on Friday nights when I still lived with my parents after graduation. He's a casual runner, but has done a marathon or two in the past, including the Disney Marathon. He usually drinks a lot of beer after he runs. He's a good person to start with because while he's not overly insane about running, he does have some legitimate experience, and overall, he's a realistic person. He lives a stone's throw from where I grew up in Philadelphia—a place where people pride themselves on giving it to you straight—and we've known each other for fifteen years now.

When I tell him, he is a little concerned that I haven't started training. He thinks I need to get my tail in gear, considering the magnitude of the challenge. But for the most part, he's supportive.

"Oh man, it's a lot of work, Willy, big time obligation," he says, "but good for you. Your beanstalk gumby ass is built for it, so you might be all right."

Bird is referring to my six-foot-two, 170-pound frame. I've always been tall and long, going all the way back to high school and then college, where I played volleyball at Virginia Tech. I remember on the last day of tryouts, when they posted the final roster on a piece of paper on the gym corkboard. Everyone was listed under their proper names—except for me.

I was last on the list. Instead of my name, there was this descriptor: *Will, the lanky freshman.*

Bird recommends I touch base with one of his pals, Bmac (B-Mack). I know him—I've met him a bunch of times over the years. We've been at the same parties and in the same fantasy baseball leagues, but in reality, we only cross paths once a year or so. When Bird brings it up, I remember that Bmac's a triathlete, and I decide to reach out.

The last time I saw Bmac was a year ago. I was home for a visit, and a group of us were supposed to meet up in Philly for beers. We had a group text message going on about the developing plans, and also to give each other shit, the way longtime buddies will do. Someone wrote in the message that Bmac had to bail on the evening because he fell off his bike and hurt himself. We all laughed, thinking this was just another joke, throwing shade at Bmac for his obsessive workout regime that had prevented him from attending get-togethers in the past. But it turned out it really was true—he had lost his balance crossing a slippery bridge on a trail outside of Philly. When I saw him a couple days later, his face was nicked up, and he had a big scrape on his leg. He was living proof that you don't have to be seven to fall off your bike.

Contacting him now, given my situation and his background, feels like I've gone to the driving range once or twice and then asked Tiger Woods if he thinks I could win the Masters three months from now. Despite this, I decide it's best to throw myself to the wolf. I don't care if he thinks I'm crazy, and I'm not going to overexplain myself. All I want is his real reaction to my situation, his true thoughts about how the everyday person would fare at the Ironman. His reaction will give me an idea of what I'm up against. Maybe he will tell me I've got plenty of time, that the Ironman is overblown and it's really not that big of a deal. As long as you're in decent shape, you'll be fine, he might say.

Via text:

"Yo, Bmac, I just signed up for my first Ironman. Phoenix at the end of November."

"Bird told me. You're insane."

Yikes. Apparently, Bmac and Bird had already discussed it. Bird will later tell me that Bmac asked him if I knew what I was getting myself into. I'm not sure. I think I do?

"I'll be OK though," I half tell him, half ask him.

"Have you done a triathlon before?"

"No, never."

My phone vibrates and his text comes through:

"I'm not sure I know anyone that has never done a triathlon before that went straight to the Ironman."

It's a tough thing to read, because not only have I never done a triathlon before, I haven't taken part in any sort of organized race in well over a decade. So, on one hand, Bmac's raising some legit concerns, I guess. But he's also being a bit of a buzzkill, and it makes me wish he would fall off his bike again. What I need now, more than anything, is belief in myself. It doesn't matter what anyone thinks, so long as I believe in myself. Going forward, it's important that I view all advice as constructive, and prevent doubt from slipping in. The more triathletes I meet in the coming months, the harder and harder this will become. But for now, I still have my innocence, and I decide to keep telling Bmac the truth.

"The farthest I've ever run in my life is eight miles," I admit to him.

And I actually remember that day with a surprising degree of clarity. It was when I was on the cross-country team in high school. Most days, coach gave us two workout options, usually a short, 3- to 5-mile run and then a longer, 6- to 10-mile run. The best runners always did the latter, and those of us who were on the team solely to stay in shape for other sports—like volleyball—did the shorter runs and used the time to socialize, jogging side by side and catching up on the latest high-school gossip, music, movies, who we were going to ask to homecoming, whatever. I can't remember why, but one day six of us lollygaggers—all freshmen—decided we were going to "take it seriously" and do the longer run. We called ourselves the freshmen "six-pack," and we jogged the eight miles together. I remember it well, because at the time, it was a monumental run for me. I was a very average runner at best and eight miles was a long way back then. I guess it still is today, given that I have yet to run farther.

I do have one feather in my cap from my four years on the cross-country team, though. The way cross-country worked back then was that you could have a team of unlimited people, but only the top seven finishers from each squad scored points. In our case, the team had more than seventy runners. The top dozen or so were serious competitors in terms of their ability to rotate in and out of the top seven and impact the scoring. The rest of us were basically moral support, completely irrelevant to the success of the team. So you see, it sounds good when I say I ran cross-country for four years, and that each year, my team won the state championship. But in reality, I—along with sixty other teammates—contributed nothing to the cause.

Well, one day that changed. Sometimes, when we ran against another school that also had a big team, we split up into different groups to ease congestion on the course. On this day, the race organizers split us into two groups: The first heat was the top twenty runners from each team, and the second heat was everyone else. At this point in the season—I think it was my junior year—I was the number twenty runner on the team, in a virtual neck and neck tie with my teammate Dave in terms of our average times. For whatever reason—maybe Dave was trending a little better than me at that point—coach picked him to occupy the twentieth spot in the first group, which left me as top dog in the second wave of runners. I remember being excited for that race like never before. It was the first time I had ever stepped up to the starting line with a realistic shot of winning.

I wasn't in the lead for most of the race. I don't start races well, and I hung back for the first mile or so, letting a small group of my teammates lead the way. About halfway through the 3.1-mile course, the trail entered a small forest, where there was a series of turns. In cross-country, a red sign means turn left, yellow means turn right, and blue means go straight. I always thought the right on yellow and left on red should have been reversed, but hey, why not make things confusing? I turned the corner and looked up to see my teammates had taken a wrong turn—they had missed a sign in the brush and run straight through a right turn. I called out to them, but I didn't stop to wait. I yelled their names, got their attention, then made the right turn as they should have. I was in the lead! And I never looked back. None of them could catch me now that I had this turn of fortune, this head start. I crossed the finish line with outstretched arms and soaked in my first-ever cross-country "victory." I was the talk of the team, the guy who usually sucks that "won" the race, a meaningless member of the squad suddenly given the momentary spotlight. Poor Dave. He collected his things quietly. He beat my time by a good half minute that day.

I can tell that Bmac is frustrated, perhaps even insulted, when I reveal all this to him. We're texting back and forth, but I can hear him sighing, and I can picture him shaking his head at his phone. I guess I can't blame him a whole hell of a lot. He tells me I should e-mail him right away, and that he can pass on some advice and set me up with some training intel "should I decide to go through with it."

I take him up on his offer and send him an e-mail. In the subject line I write "Ironman." Then in the body, I ask him flat-out: "How screwed am I?"

While I wait for Bmac's response, I decide to break the news to the person my announcement will affect the most: my girlfriend. We spend a lot of time together, and I don't want that to change. Even though I'm taking a watered-down approach to training, I'm realistic about the amount of time I'll need to commit. I don't want her to get pissed off or feel like I've started to date someone—or something—else. I assure her that the training will be minimal, a couple times a week at most, and that it won't impact my social life.

"I thought you had to train a lot for these races," she says.

"Ah, I'm just going to do it! Hunny, don't worry, nothing will change."

"You can't just go out and run a marathon. You'll get hurt."

"Don't worry," I tell her. "I'll work up to it."

"In three months? What about the bike and the swim? You don't have a bike."

I wave her off. I tell her not to worry. We'll talk about it later, over dinner. I make the rounds to other friends and family. Most of them don't have much of an opinion because they don't know what the Ironman is. They know it's a race, or whatever, but don't know the specifics. They don't know the order of the sports, that you swim, bike, run. They don't know the distances: 2.4 miles, 112 miles, 26.2 miles. When I tell them the details, they aren't so much impressed as they are shocked that I would do such a thing. Or, they assume they misheard, or misunderstood.

"So . . . wait . . . you do all three back to back to back?" one asked, eyes wide.

Another squinted at me and said, "Jesus, Will, what the hell are you doing that for?"

I explained the Ironman to my ninety-three-year-old grandmother. "Oh my," she said. "Are you going to be able to do all that?"

"Well, that's the plan," I said. "I mean, I'm training for it now."

"OK, well . . . you . . . you be careful, you hear?"

The most common question from friends and family?

"Why?!"

And who could blame them? It's probably the most sensible thing to ask someone who tells you they are going to swim 2.4 miles, bike 112, and then run a full marathon all in the same day, without a significant break, for no reason, without being paid. And it's a question I'll ask over and over again leading up to the Ironman in an attempt to understand the rising popularity of these extreme athletic events, to understand why people are drawn to them, and to get an idea about why they're willing to spend a small fortune to, as many will put it to me, suffer.

Because for me, personally, it all seems a little extreme, a little unnecessary. Believe me, I'm all for athletic, adventurous endeavors that serve little purpose. Walking into the woods for a weekend with everything I need to survive on my back—backpacking—is my number one stress-relieving activity. I like to summit high peaks, I like to ski, I like to take scenic bike rides. But all these things are inherently fun to me—not just the payoff, but the activity and the process itself. I will come to find triathletes can't—and don't—say the same thing.

As I continue informing my friends over the course of the coming weeks, I find I am almost always disappointed by their reactions, regardless of what they are. Here I am, about to embark on one of the world's toughest single-day physical challenges, and no one even knows what the hell I'm talking about. Or, if they do know and understand, they don't congratulate me, they don't encourage me, they don't seem impressed by my efforts or honored to stand in my presence. Not one of them will say, "Hey Will, that's great! You're a real inspiration, you know?"

Instead, they say, "Why would you do *that*? You're a fucking idiot!"

They don't say that last part out loud, but I can see they are thinking it. It's not the reaction I want, and it's certainly not the emotional support I seek. When you're about to do something outrageous, whatever it may be, you want people to recognize the outrageousness of it. Having to explain how outrageous you are eliminates the satisfaction of being outrageous. It makes me wonder if I really am outrageous, or just an idiot. I will learn that this concept—deciding you're going to do something outrageous, and then learning that no one even knows what the hell you're talking about—is a touchy subject within the triathlete community.

I decide to call my sister to follow up on the e-mail I sent her (I sent a mass e-mail to my family explaining my intentions, asking them to save the date). I think she can give me some good, balanced advice. She's family, yes, but she's also an accomplished runner. Unlike me, she was a very good cross-country runner. She was state champion two years in a row, consistently one of the best runners in the region, and has qualified for and run the Boston Marathon twice. In 2015 she crushed it, setting a PR (runner's lingo for personal record) of 3 hours and 15 minutes, a pace of 7 minutes and 30 seconds (7:30) per mile. I know she understands the Ironman and the distance it entails, and as a lawyer in Washington, D.C., and mother of two, I know she'll be practical about it. She knows me and my work ethic, my passion. I'm thinking she can massage the apprehensions others have been manifesting and help turn them into a practical plan.

I FaceTime her. She's sitting at her kitchen table, playing cards with her husband, Stan, and my mom, who is in town visiting the grandkids. They prop up the phone so that we're in a diamond formation and I'm the fourth person sitting at the table. It's like a classic dinner scene from a movie, talking over each other. When I bring up the Ironman, my mom jumps in and asks me if I want her to come to the race in Phoenix. I tell her she might be bored, that I won't be much fun in the days leading up to the race, and that the race is literally all day, sunrise to past sundown. It won't be a vacation, I tell her. She looks perplexed, and I can tell she still doesn't understand what the Ironman is or what it entails. When this happens, my sister, who has been unusually silent throughout the back-and-forth, not saying anything, finally butts in.

"Mom, you *need* to go," she says. "He can't go alone. He's going to need someone to literally feed him dinner that night after the race."

My mom looks at her and, as a proper Italian mom, begins to worry. She cocks her head to the side. "Will, you're not going to be able to eat?"

My sister jumps in again. "Remember how I was after the marathon? Remember? Multiply that by a million, and that's what Will is going to be like after the Ironman."

Oh, how could any of us forget. I remember her coming out from the finish area wrapped in one of those shiny, aluminum-foil blankets, shivering, even though it wasn't cold. Well, I don't exactly remember the temperature. Stan and I had mapped out the course in terms of viewing areas that were in proximity to beer bars. We were feeling pretty good. But I'll never forget how all those runners looked as they climbed Heartbreak Hill, as they crossed the finish line. They looked miserable.

"Let's not be dramatic," I say. "I'm going to be fine." My mom swivels her head between my face on the phone and my sister at the table, trying to figure out who to believe. I can see Stan smile, sitting back and enjoying the show.

"Plus, he hasn't been training," my sister tells my mom. "Remember how hard I trained for the marathon?"

"Hey—I have been training," I tell them. "I started this week!"

"You are not well trained!" my sister fires back. "Mom, he has not been training enough! He's going to *die*!"

My mom turns to me, the look of concern grave now.

"Will," my sister says, on a roll, "how far have you run so far?"

"I did six miles the other day," I tell her. Shit. That sounds bad.

"Six miles? Six miles!" she says, turning to my mom and then back to me. "You know there are twenty miles to go after that, right?" She's looking right into the phone now. "And that you're going to swim and bike before that? You don't even own a bike!"

My mom turns to me with sad, concerned eyes. "Willard!" she says. "Is this true?!"

I see my brother-in-law smile and sip his vodka. I can't deal with it anymore and I hang up. My sister obviously recognizes the size of the dragon I'm trying to slay—which is refreshing—but I was hoping for a little reassurance from her, a vow of confidence. If my own sister doesn't believe I can do it, who will? It's frustrating, but I need to learn to deal with it. There's going to be much more doubt coming my way in the future.

Moving forward, I figure I should focus on talking with triathletes to get their perspectives, since they'll know exactly what I'm up against, and regardless of whether they believe in me, they can offer constructive advice. I leave a message for my friend Drew, who lives in North Carolina and has done two Ironmans, including the one I'll be doing in Phoenix. He will no doubt be a great resource for what's to come. I also send a text to my colleague Jon, who lives in Seattle, to tell him I've signed up for an Ironman in November. He's done a couple of half Ironmans—the same concept as a full Ironman only half the length, 70.3 miles instead of 140.6—and gets back to me right away.

"Dude, that's so awesome!" he says. "Since that is pretty soon, I would say from now until then your life will be training. But . . . you got this, dude!"

The exclamation point at the end sounds like it should be a question mark, but hey, I'll take the positivity. I pencil him in, alongside Bmac and Drew, as my three amigos of constructive, concrete advice going forward. Still, I think it's probably a good idea to get some straight advice from strangers, and more importantly, to open myself up to a variety of opinions and perspectives. Jon tips me off to an online resource: Ironman events have several online groups where competitors communicate and share motivations and tips. I find a few and post calls for advice as a first-timer.

> *"Hi . . . I got a late start on my training and this will be my first triathlon . . . so I'm happy to hear any advice from those of you who have done one before. Help a first timer out?"*

It doesn't take long for the comments to start pouring in, and the reactions vary widely. I try to be as objective as possible when reading them, taking each with a grain of salt, remembering that they don't know me and more importantly, I don't know them. I don't know where they are coming from, why they think what they think. They could be professional athletes. They could be trolls. Over the next few months, I will meet people on both sides of this spectrum. Some will assist me significantly. Some will annoy me greatly.

I start reading the comments in real time as they are posted. I turn the sound up so I can hear when someone responds. I can't help it. It's addicting, that feedback. When all is said and done, the comments break down into three groups.

Some are very heartfelt and helpful, but make it clear that what I'm attempting—doing the Ironman on only a few months training—is not recommended.

> *"Hey Will, 140.6 is really not the way to go for your first tri . . . just my two cents."*

> *"Hi Mr. McGough! It's awesome to see that you are going into the beautiful world of Triathlon! I am concerned that your first triathlon is an Ironman, which is a 2.4mi swim, 112mi bike, and 26.2mi run. This race is very physiologically demanding and requires a firm grip on race nutrition, training, and experience. As a medical volunteer for Ironman for three years now, I know (especially as a triathlete myself) the Ironman triathlon requires a lot of endurance and adequate race nutrition. The number one reason why athletes come to the med tent*

after they [did not finish] (or finish but have to spend a few hours in the med tent to recover) is inadequate race nutrition and endurance training. I am not trying to discourage you from ever competing in an Ironman, but in order to have a good chance in successfully completing your first one you really should start your triathlete career with a much-smaller distance race. Once you got a few sprints and Olympics under your belt, and have a good training plan plus race nutrition, then try a half ironman. Once you got a few halfs under your belt and have trained for the full adequately, then consider the full ironman! Definitely look into getting a race coach and nutritionist. Those are good keys in increasing your chances for better performances. I hope this helps!"

"You are not giving yourself a lot of time to train. Could be very difficult if you are not already physically strong. What I have learned is that you cannot cram like I did for my finals. It does take time to build up or you are risking injury. . . . especially as you get older."

"If you are serious, I'd hire a coach."

"Agreed on hiring a coach and don't miss a single workout for the next 3 months. Ironman distance need[s] to be built over a long period of time with gradual increases to avoid injury or overtraining. Yours will have to be MUCH more rapid. Hopefully you have good baseline fitness."

"I am sure that you will do fine on race day . . . it's the days after it that will make you pay. I am thinking that you will [be] out of commission for a few days . . . good luck!"

Other commenters aren't as diplomatic. Some sound like they're sucking on sour grapes. Others seem to have bike seats up their butts.

"Don't do it. Seriously. But if you want to my advice is open water swimming 3x per week with 2x more in a pool. Then comes the biking.

You need to be able to avg 14mi per hour on a bike. And that's 8 hours. I wouldn't run at all because it's doubtful that you will run more than 4–6 miles. When you leave the main area and are in the dark, it's cold, maybe raining, you are most likely not going to have the ability to mentally push yourself. So now you have 6.5hrs to go 26.2 miles. That's a 14:30 ish pace. Go walk that and see what it's like. I'm sorry for being hard on you, and you gave no background on your abilities, but you do not respect the distance. Harsh sure, but true. I was in tris for a few years before my first IM. Even then my training was not where it should have been. My plan was overshadowed by ego, then there was the 20mph winds and hail."

"Do you have experience at any of the three disciplines? It's a little crazy to have a full IM as your first triathlon. You know they have shorter distances as well. Seriously, look at any IM results and you will see hundreds that did not finish. And most of those training for 6 months to a year. I know I was one of them last year when I failed to finish my first—after doing triathlons for 3 years and completing [two half Ironmans]."

Yikes. Now, it would be easy to write these people off, chalk them up as Internet trolls. But I can't do that at this point. I need to take all opinions seriously. That doesn't mean I can't latch onto particular ones, however. Doubt does me no good. There is a final category of people whose advice serves my purposes. Turns out a small underbelly—and I will come to find out that it is very small—consists of people who take things a little less seriously. Finally, at the end of a long day of digging, I find the small ray of hope I'm looking for.

"I will not start training until September. People train too much and overthink this race. It's mostly mental. I'm not saying you could be completely out of shape but if you pace yourself right and stick to a good nutrition plan during the race you will have no issues. Don't listen to these people saying it can't be done because this will be my fifth and I never start training till September."

"Attitude is everything. Get up every day and do some kind of training. If you're not a strong swimmer, start by getting yourself to where you can swim 3000m without stopping. You'll have just over 2 hours to complete the swim, so that should be your first goal. Biking is an easy skill, just get on your bike and ride. Put in the hours and do at least one long ride a week. Get used to pacing yourself and taking in nutrition. Don't worry about the run. You'll likely be walking most of it anyways. Any able-bodied person can finish an Ironman if you have discipline and patience."

August 3, 2017
Waimānalo, O'ahu, Hawai'i
108 Days Until the Ironman

I intend to live forever or die trying.

—Groucho Marx

Last night, I drove down to Ala Moana beach park to run during the sunset. Ala Moana is on the south shore of O'ahu, and there's a nice, meandering path along the water for runners. The evening is a good time to go because it's cooler, you have a line of sight to the west to see the sun go down, and there are more things to look at—you can see teams of paddlers come in and out of the harbor, and boats going out for the golden-hour sail. It's a good place to have a beer on a bench. The relaxing setting did me well, because that's all I was trying to do. I wanted to jog at an easy pace, get my legs moving, nothing too crazy.

I officially started my training a couple days ago on July 31, when I stepped out of my apartment and ran six miles in 47 minutes and 3 seconds, a sub-8-minute per mile pace. I created a training log in Excel to keep track of all my workouts. It's very basic: Date, Exercise, Distance, Place, Time, Notes. In the notes section, I plan to keep track of how I felt and what I learned.

The six-mile run looks like a great start in my training log across the board—solid distance, decent time—until you get to the notes, the part

I kept from my sister yesterday when telling her I ran six miles: *Had to stop three times, felt awful at times, felt like puking at end, probably didn't eat enough, back was tight, road was sunbaked and it dried me out.*

This was a classic example of "going out too fast," pushing myself a little too hard. The first two miles didn't feel great, but I take a while to loosen up. I get stronger as I go. I did the first two miles in 16.5 minutes, then finished the third at what seemed like a furious pace. I looked at my watch and saw I did it in less than seven minutes—I had crushed the third mile, and I felt great. It went downhill immediately after that. A few minutes into the fourth mile, I had to stop to catch my breath and slow down my heart. It was pounding in my chest. I power walked for 30 seconds, then tried to get going again, but I couldn't regain my rhythm. That third mile, as good as it felt at the time, had ruined me. Why did I do it? I don't know. I didn't mean to. I felt good and let my body do what it wanted. This is a very common and menacing mistake for racers. Pacing is one of the most important aspects of long-distance competitions. But I don't run a lot, so I have no idea what my pace is or should be. Quite honestly, at this point, I don't have any concept of how to reliably monitor it throughout a race of a couple of miles, let alone twenty-six.

Upon returning home, I thought I was going to deposit my stomach all over the dirt driveway. This got me discouraged. If I'm feeling this way after six hard miles, what am I going to feel like for an entire marathon, when I've already swam and biked? Am I already pushing myself too hard? Maybe my girlfriend is right. If I go too hard too soon, I'm bound to get injured.

The quandary sends me to the Internet looking for answers. The first article I come across is entitled "8 Reasons Triathletes Get Injured" on Triathlete.com. The first reason on the list entices me to sigh.

You go too far, or too fast, too soon.

What's more, that same article references a five-year study from Great Britain that found 72 percent of triathletes sustain some sort of injury. While I anticipate minor issues like sore knees and ankles are bound to pop up, I did not expect the list of six dozen injuries that I later found. According to one article on Physioworks.com, these injuries fall under the "likely to occur" category for triathletes: calf muscle tear, degenerative disc disease, facet joint pain, heel spur, neck headache, plantar fasciitis, sciatica, shin splints, pinched nerve, tarsal tunnel syndrome—just to name a few. I have no idea what a neck headache is but . . . it sounds bad.

In another article, *Men's Health* identified the five most common triathlon injuries as iliotibial (IT) band syndrome, Achilles tendonitis, patellar tendonitis, stress fracture, and rotator cuff tendonitis. To read about these injuries and the reasons they are likely to occur is scary, considering my late start makes me a prime candidate for each and every one.

I begin to further question myself when I read another grim article: I'm surprised to learn that not only do triathletes get injured a lot, they also die on occasion.

Long-distance endurance events, including the Ironman, have a mortality rate. The *Daily Mail* reported a seasoned fifty-four-year-old man, who had previously completed six Ironman events, died during the swim of a Houston-area competition in April 2017. A few months later in August, a sixty-seven-year-old cyclist died of cardiac arrest during Ride-London, a 100-mile bike race.

About a year before these two incidents in May 2016, the Daily Beast released a report that tried to answer the question: "Why Do So Many Middle-Aged Men Die During Ironman Competitions?" (That was the exact headline.) According to the article, 109 people died during amateur triathlons between 1985 and 2015. The majority of the deceased—85 percent—were men around the age of fifty.

ESPN weighed in on the same data, noting that most deaths occur during or shortly after the swim: The majority—seventy-six deaths, or 70 percent of the total—occurred during or upon exiting the initial swim leg. The bike leg accounted for another nineteen deaths, mostly in crashes. The remainder came during the running leg, which is last in the event. About half the total fatalities were in shorter "sprint" triathlons, which attract more newcomers to the sport and more participants overall.

If you don't die during the race, you could die after. A 2015 *Runner's World* article dives into the debate over whether long-distance running—and thus long-distance training in general—is good or bad for your heart. It references a few studies that found scar tissue on the hearts of lifelong endurance athletes. The results are still unsettled as far as a cause-effect relationship, though the article does conclude: "People who run an occasional marathon and spend the rest of their lives staying fit with 30 to 60 minutes of exercise most days of the week are not likely to be affected. A percentage of people who spend a lifetime training hard for marathons and other strenuous endurance events may be at risk for some heart-muscle scarring."

A related article from Active.com ("The Risks and Benefits of Long-Distance Running") discusses the clash of long-term benefits and long-term pitfalls associated with endurance racing. "Running generally has profound benefits," the article states. "It has been shown to decrease the risk of diabetes mellitus, cardiovascular disease, and depression while improving bone density and supporting weight control." But it also talks a lot about the side effects, some of which could be long-term: inflammation; muscle collapse; muscle overuse; osteoarthritis; and cardiac events.

Oh, and get this: It is even said that the first person to run a marathon died from the exertion. That same article explains that the "26.2-mile race got its name from the legend of Pheidippides, who ran slightly less than 26 miles from Marathon to Athens to announce the Athenian army's victory over the Persians. Once poor Pheidippides arrived and proclaimed, 'Rejoice, we conquer,' he is said to have fallen over dead."

I stand up from my computer and make a drink. I better get them in now while I can, while I'm still alive. Imagine, sitting there realizing you've signed up for an event that leaves you with a 72 percent chance of injury and the possibility of death. Some people call that suicide.

I check my e-mail and see that Bmac has gotten back to me with a long, list-like questionnaire filled with logical and legitimate questions about my ability and any planning I've done. It's extremely useful at times, and incredibly annoying at others—annoying in the sense that I'm beginning to think he's right. His questions reveal how unprepared I am compared to most people competing in Ironmans. Here we are, just three months out, and I don't even have the obvious things taken care of—like owning a bike—let alone the lesser-known aspects of gear, nutrition, and travel planning.

On August 3, Bmac wrote:

Hopefully not screwed at all, but you are certainly cramming for an Ironman being only 3.5 months out.

First off:

1. *Do you have a bike (if so, what kind) and have you set up transport to AZ?*
2. *Do you have a wet suit?*
3. *Have you made hotel arrangements?*

Those are some important things for the actual IM itself.

Next:

4. *Did you swim competitively growing up and can you swim a mile comfortably?*
5. *What's the farthest you've ever run?*
6. *What's the farthest you've ever biked?*
7. *Have you been regularly biking, swimming, or running prior to signing up, otherwise known as, do you have a "base" that you're starting at?*

If you answer those, you can help me gauge where you're at in terms of fitness and where you might want to focus much of your training. For example, I grew up a swimmer, so swimming comes easily to me and I typically get in pretty good shape by just swimming 2x/week during training, and then doing a few 2-mile swims as the IM gets closer. If you also swam growing up through high school, college, etc. . . . and have swam pretty regularly since then, you should be good, and therefore you can focus most of your attention in biking and running (the two events where you'll be spending most of your time on the course).

You've picked a pretty flat course, which is good, so you don't really need to focus on any hill training. My bike and run training typically consists of a few 45-minute to 1-hour "trainer rides" during the week, and a couple runs, no longer than 6–7 miles, and can be as short as a 1–3 mile run after your bike session. The longer training sessions are on the weekends (your work schedule might dictate otherwise). By long sessions, I'm talking your 10, 13, 16, 18, 20-mile runs, and your 30, 50, 60, 80, 100-mile rides. You should get one 20-mile run under your belt, and two 100-mile rides before the IM. You should also have one bike/run that is around a 70-mile ride with a 16-mile run after before the IM. No real reason to do anything longer than that. If you do a 100-mile ride, you should definitely run a little after, 3–5 miles, but no reason to go any longer than that.

To me IM is 10% your physical fitness and 90% your mental fitness. The above training summary prepares you for both. IM training is long, boring, and often painful, and you need to stay sharp and focused. You also need to feed your body and maintain good nutrition. You can't necessarily "wing" an Ironman if you truly want to finish it.

Things I would recommend:

- *Buying an indoor bike trainer (CycleOps mag trainer is a good and not too $$$ one) and using a program like TrainerRoad (what I use). Set it up in a room where you can watch Netflix or whatever, you'll spend a lot of time on this. Trainer workouts [in my opinion] are better than outdoor ones, especially for your 45–90 minute training sessions. Your longer ones will have to be outside.*
- *If you don't have a tri bike, I would recommend getting one or at least having a bike shop install some aero bars on whatever road bike you might have.*
- *Get yourself a GPS watch of some sorts, possibly one that will track your bike too.*

- *Sign up for some Tris—Sprints and Olympic*[*]*—do as many as you can before the IM—you need to understand what it is, and you need to be comfortable on a course riding with other people and more importantly swimming with a lot of people, it's fucking mayhem in the water (kicking, elbows, dunking, etc. . . .).*

Just a few things that will make training and the IM more comfortable.

I'll have plenty of race day advice as it gets closer, but this should be a good start. Let me know about the above questions and we can continue this.

A bit overwhelming, but it's not all bad. Almost as important as what he does say is what he doesn't. For example, even though he knows I've never run farther than eight miles, he didn't say, "You have no chance, don't even try." His tough-love approach forces me to really think about my abilities, what I've done in the past that might prepare me for what's ahead. And it turns out, I do have some things going for me.

For example, Bmac says he grew up a swimmer, and because of that he can take a shortcut on his swim training. I could do that, too, if I have a history with one of the sports. He already knows I haven't done much running, but previous experience on the bike or in the water might allow me to redirect my efforts to my two weakest sports, he says, instead of trying to master all three.

Though they might not qualify as triathlon equivalent endeavors, I do indeed have some history on the bike and in the water. For the bike, I have two things to brag about. In 2016, I rode across Nicaragua from west to east, from the Pacific to the Caribbean Sea. The total distance was approximately 450 miles, much of it in 100-degree heat and on rocky, dusty, unpaved farm roads. I made it without major incident, only a few fits of frustration here and there at the hands of the hellish heat. The kicker—and

* Sprint triathlons are typically 400–500 yards of swimming, 12–15 miles of cycling, and a 3.1-mile run. Olympic triathlons are typically double those distances. Both are used as training vehicles for the Ironman.

reason I fear Bmac might not think it's legit—is that the 450 miles was broken down over nine days. And we had beer at the end of each day.

My other claim to fame on the bike is a 100-mile ride from Estes Park to Steamboat Springs over Trail Ridge Road in Colorado, which tops out at more than 12,000 feet above sea level in Rocky Mountain National Park. Apparently, it's the "highest-elevated continuously paved road in America." That ridiculous description is the product of shameless marketing efforts, but I repeat it here just to say, you know, this was quite a road. And the distance is close to what I will have to do at the Ironman. Yet again, this ride was over the course of two days, not one, which means it might not do much for Bmac.

Still, the experiences give me hope that my time on the bike—the longest portion of the event—won't be complete torture. I didn't train much for either of those trips beyond a half-dozen days at the gym on the stationary bike. I got in shape on the Nicaragua ride as I went, feeling stronger as the days passed. In Colorado, I remember feeling like hell the second day going over Rabbit Ears Pass because I didn't eat enough. I can learn from that. The bigger picture is that I enjoyed the time on the bike, the good with the bad, seeing the sights and scenery. I think I'll be happy on the bike while training for and doing the Ironman.

This was, of course, before I saw that Bmac recommends most of my bike training be done indoors, in front of the television—yet another head-scratching twist in an already strange tale. In his e-mail, he suggests buying a device called a trainer that will allow me to convert my bike into a stationary bike. This way, he says, I can set up the bike in front of the television and watch Netflix while I train. Seriously?

Whether I decide to ride inside, outside, or upside down, my experience in the pool will forever be my most valuable asset. I was on the swim team for more than seven years as a kid, and I was quite good. I still hold the nine- and ten-year-old age group record for the 50-meter freestyle at my swim club in Gibbstown, New Jersey (twenty-two years and counting!). Although swimming is the smallest portion of the race by far, it is the most daunting segment for most racers, without question. Everyone knows how to ride a bike. Anyone can run. Swimming is a different beast. You have to be comfortable in the water, obviously, and you also have to know the proper technique, otherwise you'll exhaust yourself. It is not something that comes easily to everyone. The swim portion of the triathlon, I will learn, is what causes the most people the most anxiety. It's a foreign language to a lot of athletes.

For me to have a background in swimming might be a game changer. I figure this is something that will really impress Bmac. He wrote in his e-mail that the race is 90% mental and 10% physical. Originally, I was a little annoyed by this—everyone's lecturing me on how I need to be in amazing shape and yet it's only 10% of the race? But I'm putting that aside for now to focus on something I'm doing really well, something I've been working really hard on already, something everyone's been trying to ruin with their skepticism: the mental edge. From an outsider and newbie perspective, I don't see how you would go through such a thing without times of great struggle. I feel like that's unavoidable. How you deal with that struggle, it seems, determines your fate. My plan is to take optimism to a new level.

I pump out responses to his questions and send it back his way. Hopefully, it won't piss him off too much.

August 6, 2017
Wichita, Kansas
105 Days Until the Ironman

When you gotta go, you gotta go.

—*Jurassic Park*

Bmac's words loom large in my head, but they will have to wait.

I'm in Kansas to do a story on Wichita's beer scene, and I've spent the past three days bellied up to bars. I went on a run the first day I got here—a moderately paced 41-minute run—but otherwise I've been making the rounds and visiting the different breweries, drinking steadily from the early afternoon on through the late night. There are six breweries and counting in Wichita and familiarizing myself with them is part of my job, something I need to do to research and write the story.

Seriously! I'm not trying to be funny here. My job is without question one of the biggest hurdles to my training. I'm constantly on the go as a travel writer, quite literally a week or two a month, and I've always struggled with holding down a regular routine for any component of my life, much less a workout regime that calls for sharia law-style consistency. And, beer aside, my trips involve eating out two to three meals a day, or worse, heating something up in the hotel room. This typically does not lead to a feel-good, exercise-friendly diet.

Though it's hard to train on trips, especially ones that involve so much beer, I've always been good about staying in shape—sneaking in an hour at the gym between appointments, walking instead of taking cabs, doing push-ups in my hotel room, doing stories that involve active travel, taking the stairs instead of the elevator. Swimming and biking are unrealistic on a work trip, but you can run anywhere, and there's no excuse for not doing it.

On that first morning, before the beer bender began, I went on an early-morning run before breakfast, forty minutes of evenly paced jogging. It is amazing how good even the smallest workout can make you feel mentally. To take a shower before breakfast knowing I had already completed my training for the day was an unbelievably empowering feeling. That I was going to drink beer and eat pub food all day could be ignored. With the workout done, it was justified.

Throughout this first week of training, I've run more in a couple days than I had the previous 50 weeks combined. After my 6-mile, 47-minute run on July 31 (the near-puke incident), I ran 4 miles in 36 minutes on August 1, a little more than 3 miles in 26 minutes on August 2, and then the aforementioned 41-minute run a few days ago on August 4th.

Even though it was only 41 minutes, it was a big run for me because it was the first time in as long as I can remember that I ran or worked out in the morning. At no point in my life have I ever been a morning workout guy. For me, mornings are about waking up slow and drinking coffee, writing, easing into the day. But that's not the Ironman way. Talk about being up and at 'em: The gun for the Ironman Arizona will go off before 7:00 a.m. By November, my body needs to be able to get up to speed quickly.

I can't repeat the same productivity in the days that follow. Today marks my second day off in a row. There are no excuses except, of course, for all the excuses I can come up with. It's not my fault I drank beer all day yesterday and now I feel too hung over to run today—it's my job's fault. Besides, in my haze, it's been easy to look on the bright side. I have more than a hundred days to get ready, and a tempered start might be shrewd in the end.

Considering everything I've read about injuries, I can say now, after a couple days off, that I think the break has been good for me. Running punishes your body like few other athletic activities, and I have already begun to feel small aches, pains, and sore spots. Most are reassuring, the "good kind" of sore, when you wake up and feel like you did something the day before, like you put your body up to a challenge and succeeded. Things like burning thighs, where it feels good to stretch and there's a sense of accomplishment in your fatigue. Others are not so encouraging. There's been a small pinch in my knee that stings every once in a while, and an ache in my foot from all the pounding. I probably need to get new shoes. What I'm wearing have been my everyday walking and traveling shoes for the last two years.

I'm wearing them again as I arrive at Wichita's first craft brewery, River City Brewing, which opened way back in 1993. From the outside it looks very Wild West, boxy in shape with wood banisters and a big front porch, like a cowboy might pop out the front door. Inside, I meet the head brewer, Ryan, who walks me through the lineup of beers—he twists my arm, and I end up trying samples of them all. Because this is a small town, friends of his come in and out throughout the night, saying hi, staying for a beer or two and then moving on. One of them is named Tommy. He is the town's most prominent muralist, I'm told. He's covered in tattoos—both his arms have full sleeves—yet one sticks out like a sore thumb on the back of his calf: a small, square-shouldered little red man, the Ironman brand icon.

Holy shit—an Ironman tattoo. I blink twice. You've got to be kidding me? An Ironman tattoo? This blows my mind. Oh my god. Is this real? Wait, yes. Yes it is. I remember reading about this. People who have completed an Ironman get a tattoo of the logo as a tribute and as a sign of reverence, to remind them that anything is possible. Or, alternatively, as others may see it, to brag, and to advertise the accomplishment. To me, it's completely outside my realm of understanding. The idea of putting a company's brand on my body permanently does not compute. At all. Why would someone do that?

Of course, I don't say this to Tommy, because he's really fit, and he's got a lot of tattoos. Instead, I offer to buy him a beer.

I'm excited, because I know Tommy will be a great resource for me. Any dude who gets an Ironman tattoo is certainly not screwing around. That also makes me nervous, because this guy ain't screwing around. Up until now, the only people I've consulted in person have been those who know me. Now here I am, talking to someone who felt strongly enough about the Ironman to get a tattoo in its honor, and he is literally right here in front of me, and I'm going to tell him that I'm doing the Ironman, and when he asks how my training is going, like I know he will, I'm going to have to tell him the truth—that I'm winging what seems to have been one of his life's signature accomplishments.

"Unfortunately," I tell him when he asks, our beers half empty now, "I really haven't started training yet. I've just done a few runs this week."

He stops drinking his beer and looks at me, holding the glass in front of his face. He's partially balding, his head thin like the rest of his body, the tattoos running down his arms. I'm looking past all that, trying to read his face, to see what's behind his eyes. Is it anger? Is it hatred? Is it annoyance?

No. It's pity.

"Holy shit man," he says, his voice full of concern. "You're going to be hurting."

Tommy is a nice guy. He's also insane. He has done two Ironmans in the past couple years. He spent eight months training for the first one, only to come down with a gastrointestinal issue on race day. He had to go to the bathroom a lot, threw up on the course, and was unable to keep down any food, his body deprived of nutrients and energy—the infamous "bonk," as triathletes call it.

An article on Active.com explains: "You may have heard people say, 'I totally bonked on that long ride' or 'I got the bonk on my run.' Often, people associate the word 'bonk' with 'hitting the wall' during endurance events. For endurance athletes it is a sudden and overwhelming feeling of running out of energy. You were running or riding along at what seemed like a manageable pace, then seemingly without warning your legs turned to cement. With heavy legs, a body-wide feeling of fatigue and sometimes dizziness, you are forced to stop."

Amazingly, despite "bonking," Tommy was still able to finish the race before the cutoff time, an accomplishment you can only attribute to the size of his balls. He goes on to tell me how angry he was, how he couldn't see the bright side in what he had accomplished. All he saw was a year of training down the drain, a failure to perform and compete as he had longed to do. Despite the hardships he had overcome, he crossed the finish line in a state of defeated frustration. His wife, who greeted him proudly with a big hug, took the bulk of his disappointment.

"I was so rude to her, I was pissed off," he admits. He tells me he isolated himself in the athlete area, unable to face his family and friends.

"Then my training partner came and pulled me aside. He reminded me that my wife had just spent fifteen hours on the course cheering for me, and that she had supported my training the previous eight months. I felt bad, but still, this had been something I'd worked so hard for."

Tommy says he apologized to his wife but ultimately did not make her happy when he signed up for another Ironman, and another year of training, the following year.

"Wait wait wait," I say. "Gastrointestinal problems?"

"Yeah," he says. "It was a mess."

I look at him, reading between the lines. "Are you saying you crapped yourself?"

"No, not really," he says. I look at him, not saying anything—an old journalism trick. Then he backtracks.

"Well, I guess, yeah." His face is calm. "I went a little bit in my pants."

"Holy shit man, are you serious?"

Tommy gives me a wide-eyed, rosy-cheeked smile and asks me if I want another beer. I look at my watch. I can't. I've got an early flight in the morning, and it's already late. I exchange e-mails so I can keep in touch with him.

When I get back to my hotel room, I can't stop thinking of Tommy limping through the marathon portion, one hand behind his back holding his butt cheeks shut. I wonder how many other people have had this problem. I scoot over to my computer and google "ironman poops himself." What comes up in the search is shocking. There are a variety of articles and videos. These are the real headlines and I have not made them up:

Top 15 Athletes Who Pooped Their Pants During Competition

Olympic Athlete Poops His Pants, Finishes Race

5 Athletes Who Shockingly Pooped Their Pants While Competing

Here's A Man Who Shat Himself At The Florida Ironman Last Weekend

The Runner Who Pooped His Pants

Wow. Just . . . wow. That is an impressive collection of headlines. Fascinated, I continue down the rabbit hole, clicking on stories and links within the stories. Chalk up "pooping while running" as one of the world's great problems I had no idea about. And there has apparently been no shortage of money thrown at finding the solution. In 2016, *Shape* did an article entitled "Why Does Running Make You Poop?" that explains to runners "how to reduce the likelihood of a mid-run poop." I laugh out loud at the photo art for the story: a woman running away, her cute little butt front and center. The author quotes a gastroenterologist to explain that "up to 80 percent of runners experience GI disturbance, including abdominal pain and bowel dysfunction."

Eighty percent? That seems impossibly high. If that were true, I feel like I would see people pooping all over the place at the high-school track. I read on. The article is weak on its explanation of why this happens to people, so I dive back into the bowels of the Internet to find out. I come to another article, this one in *Competitor*, which introduces me to the concept of runner's diarrhea.

In an effort to point out that it can happen to anyone—"it" being a strong urge to poop while running—the article explains the famous case of Paula Radcliffe, the women's marathon world record holder who, in 2005, on her way to winning the London Marathon, "was forced to stop on the side of the road and take a dump in front of thousands of fans."

Those are the exact words from the story.

"Contributing factors likely include the physical jostling of the organs, decreased blood flow to the intestines, changes in intestinal hormone secretion, and pre-race anxiety and stress . . . What is clear is that food moves more quickly through the bowels of athletes in training," Dr. Stephen De Boer, a registered dietician with the Mayo Clinic who has studied this topic, told the magazine. I'm guessing this is not the type of research Dr. De Boer had in mind when he daydreamed as a kid.

But hold on, can we talk about Ms. Radcliffe for a second? She was so far ahead that she could stop, poop on the side of the road in front of thousands of people, and still win? I had to know more about this, so I did a search for the incident. There is also a video of it online,* because of course there is. It shows Radcliffe, skinny like a pole with blonde hair, darting off to the side of the course next to the metal gates, squatting down, and relieving herself. Don't think fiber-induced coils—think a blast of watery discharge that splatters down onto the pavement. The video is zoomed in on her, so you can't get a sense of how many people are around, or if there's a grandstand nearby. But you can see a couple people standing behind the gate, a few feet from where she squats.

There are others like her, too. Go ahead and google the plight of Swedish distance runner Mikael Ekvall. In 2008, he crapped himself during a half-marathon in dramatic fashion, and a photographer captured it on camera. The river of feces that flows down his legs in the photo is something he's never lived down. Publications circulated the photo. Memes were created from it. Unfortunately, the photographer had no gripes about cashing in on the photo, despite the embarrassment it no doubt caused Ekvall. I guess that's life in an Internet-driven, click-obsessed media. The photo went so "viral," and Ekvall became so "legendary," that Gawker felt compelled to track him down seven years later, in 2015, to chat about it.

* The video is mislabeled as Ms. Radcliffe stopping to pee.

According to the story, Ekvall continued to run after he pooped himself despite the mess. After the race, he was asked if he ever considered stopping to clean himself off.

"No, I'd lose time," he said. "If you quit once, it's easy to do it again and again and again. It becomes a habit."

I love this so much. Dude, come on, you crapped yourself. You're not a philosopher, OK? This wasn't part of a greater plan or a test of determination. I'm wondering if the reporter, misunderstanding Ekvall's Swedish accent, mistook "quit" for "shit."

"If you shit once, it's easy to do it again and again and again." That sounds more like it.

Ekvall persevered through this incident and went on to continue his running career. He set a Swedish record at the 2014 Copenhagen half-marathon, and represented Sweden at the European Athletic Championships. The article tries to romanticize a happy ending. The author writes, "Ekvall's story is truly an inspirational one: Never quit. If you can live down running around in public with your own feces streaming off your bare legs, you can live down practically anything."

I haven't run far or hard enough to know whether gastrointestinal issues will be a problem for me. I'm crossing my fingers that I'm in the 20 percent. But what if I'm not? Is there anything I can do to decrease the chances of public humiliation?

Runner's World published an article in 2017 called "How to Avoid Pooping During the Race." Most of the advice revolves around understanding how your body reacts to certain foods and implementing those findings into your diet. The article recommends keeping track of what you eat and "how that correlates with your bowel movements." Training is the time to try out different foods and see how your body reacts, it says.

All right, I'll be sure to keep track of my bowel movements. Because that's what I signed up for. Right. I will experiment with food, but it won't happen this week in Wichita, where the beer is surprisingly good. Plus, there's more pressing issues to handle before I begin messing around with food choices. I need a bike, and before I buy one, I need to learn about bikes. I need new running shoes to ward off any more knee problems. I need to go for a swim, to make sure I am still as good a swimmer as I think I am. I need to come up with some sort of training plan, even if it is a loose one. And I need to keep shaking hands with triathletes who have done the Ironman, keep turning over these mysterious stones. I never thought crapping myself would be something I need to worry about.

It begs the question: What else am I missing?

August 7, 2017
Waimānalo, O'ahu, Hawai'i
104 Days Until the Ironman

If you really want to do something, you'll find a way. If you don't, you'll find an excuse.

—Jim Rohn, American entrepreneur

It is with a full belly that I return to Hawai'i, and I can't say I feel much like working out or training. I spent all of yesterday on a plane, I'm tired from my trip, and I have a lot to catch up on workwise. Errands to run. Laundry to do. Friends to touch base with. Etc. The last thing I want to do is go out for a run. I don't have a bike yet, so that's out. I thought about going for a swim, until I realized I don't have goggles. I guess there are a few more errands to add to the list this week.

As a substitute, and in an effort to leave me feeling productive and accomplished, I am doing activities and chores that make me feel like I'm training. For example, I went for an hour-long surf today to loosen up the shoulders (no goggles required!), and I did a lot of up and down movement when I was pruning my tomato plants and lilikoi vine. Just a few minutes ago, I carried my coconut palm container—which I set out in the open to be exposed to rain while I was gone—back under the awning, outside my front door. I carried it all the way from the other side of the yard.

I know this indulgence to diversion will have to change in the very near future. There's only so long I can let this slide. After all, I am to compete in the world's toughest single-day triathlon, and I probably shouldn't spit in its face. At least not directly. I know I have to take it more seriously. But I don't want this to hijack my entire life. I need to be able to have days like today, where I rest and get myself together after work trips. More importantly, I don't want training to prevent me from casually hiking, hitting the beach, drinking beer with friends, cooking dinner, making wine at home. I don't want to wake up every day and feel like I *need* to train.

In time, I will look back on these thoughts and find them very foolish.

Of course, I *need* to train for the Ironman. But I can feel myself being held back by a couple of things. For one, I mean it when I say I want to stay true to my current lifestyle. I don't want to become a one-dimensional person, where all I have to say for myself is how far I ran or biked that day. The more I learn about triathletes, the more concerned I become about getting along with them. I found an article on the official Ironman website entitled "Ten Things Not to Say to a Triathlete." The subhead of the article sets the tone for its defensive nature: *10 things triathletes are sick of hearing, and how to respond.* It's angry and bitter—and extremely revealing—right from the start. Consider thing #1 you shouldn't say to a triathlete, and the author's response:

> *1. "All you ever do is workout, don't you have a life?"*
>
> *Why yes, I do. Nothing makes me MORE alive than bringing back childhood through swimming, biking and running while enhancing them with the competitive spirit.*

Hmm. My childhood memories of bike riding don't include riding on a trainer inside, watching Netflix. Also, notice how that question was answered. Do you have a life outside of training? *Yes, I do! I swim, bike, and run! And it reminds me of my childhood!* All right . . .

But, whatever. Fine. These people are into working out. I can relate to that. Like I said, I have a lot of athletic experience. There's a lot I could converse about with these people, I think. But thing #8 makes me wonder if that's true.

Imagine you are at a party and you are introduced to someone. They reveal to you that they are a triathlete and have done an Ironman. You have not done anything close to that physical challenge, but as a way to relate and connect with this person you just met, you decide to offer up an experience you had at another event, like a half-marathon or mud run or multiday trek.

According to the article of things you are not supposed to say, this would be a huge mistake.

8. "I'm doing the Warrior Dash, Spartan Race, Tough Mudder . . ."

Here's the thing: It's not that we don't appreciate the challenges of a good obstacle course. It's that it's often brought up it [sic] *in a way that seems "one uppy" in conversation. We mention a seven-hour brick workout on a Sunday morning, then we hear about someone climbing into a dumpster of ice during a 5K.*[*] *Once. On the weekend. And then there's free beer. I'm betting I'm not alone when I say that I only WISHED there had been a dumpster of ice in the last 5K of an IRONMAN race or any of my scheduled long workouts. And I'll take the beer, too.*

First off, yes, that is the actual response in the article. Basically, if you didn't do a seven-hour brick workout—the triathlete term for biking and then running afterward (more on that later)—then you better keep your mouth shut. Any mention of another athletic endeavor is immediately regarded not as a conversation starter, but as a challenge to their abilities. They are the ones who are doing the toughest things, not you. Who cares if you did something cool . . . was it seven hours? Did you feel like you were going to die? In this way, it seems unlikely that my interactions with these people are going to go well. It seems like they are really into themselves.

Which leads us to thing #4 on the list. It confirms a suspicion I've held from day one: Triathletes take it personally that people don't understand what the Ironman is or what it entails, much less why anyone would want to do it.

4. "Triathletes are in love with themselves."

* A "5K" refers to a five-kilometer (3.1-mile) run. It's a very common race distance in the running world. For your reference, there is a glossary in the back of this book with other common terms.

If it seems like we talk a lot about what we do, it's partly because we're often forced to explain what an IRONMAN race actually is (see #3). We're excited by our goals and our accomplishments, and many of us got into the sport because we were inspired by hearing stories about it from others. The love is everywhere—and yes, it makes it [sic] *for a stronger self-esteem and sense of self-confidence—but that's not a bad thing.*

Sounds like a fun crowd!

Aside from having to mingle with triathletes for the next three months, another thing I'm concerned about is the toll this is going to take on my body. So much of the initial advice and insight I received makes the Ironman sound more like something people are forced to do at Guantánamo Bay than a fun, healthy activity engaged in by rational people. So much of what I'm hearing from people includes a large amount of mental and physical pain and suffering, including injury and, of course, diarrhea.

I'll be honest, the idea of doing the Ironman sounds a lot better than actually doing it. Envisioning myself doing it was easy; now I actually have to do the workouts, and that doesn't sound like much fun. Thinking about the hours and hours of training I have to do doesn't intimidate me, but it does discourage me. Especially considering the lack of clarity I have about what it means to train in the first place. The last thing I want to do is start training, and then find out what I've been doing is counterproductive, or not enough, or too much. I don't want to get injured. I don't have time to waste. Bmac advised me to start running and biking, but how far? And how much? I need to look into workout plans to figure out exactly what I should be doing, specifically, to better understand what I'm up against.

I start with the Ironman's own website. I punch in a bunch of topics in the search field, and end up coming across a FAQ with the question: *What is the average time it takes an Age Group* triathlete to prepare for an IRONMAN?* Perfect. This is exactly what I'm looking for, some advice right from the horse's mouth. When I read the answer, my face falls and my eyes refuse to blink.

* Age Group triathlete = nonprofessional/amateur triathlete.

Triathletes train an average of seven months for the IRONMAN World Championship. The average hours per week devoted to training for the IRONMAN World Championship generally falls between 18 and 30-plus. Average training distances are:

- *Swimming miles per week: 7 (11.3 km)*
- *Biking miles per week: 232 (373.3 km)*
- *Running miles per week: 48 (77.2 km)*

I get up and walk away from my laptop. I look back at it from a few feet away. My hands are on my head, like I'm catching my breath at the top of a hill. The numbers are so big they seem like a joke. Two hundred thirty-two miles of biking a week? Forty-eight miles of running? That's not going to happen. No chance. This is stupid. This is dumb. Two hundred thirty-two miles? I'd have to ride around O'ahu like six times.

I immediately drop to the floor and bang out thirty push-ups. I don't know why—maybe it's a physical reaction to combat the mental discouragement of reading those workout recommendations. I pace around my apartment, breathing deliberately, pumped up from the push-ups. OK, get it together, man. I take a deep breath and sit back down at my laptop. This is the recommended amount of training for someone taking part in the World Championship, not necessarily someone looking to simply finish an event. I go back to the site and this time search for first-time Ironman plans.

Turns out, there's a lot of advice under the category "Ironman 101." It's a little better, but ultimately, what I find is every bit the reality check, every bit as discouraging.

Most kits and guides I read, on the Ironman site and on other sites, are centered around a workout plan of eight to sixteen hours per week. The first number, eight hours, is meant to be what you start out with, and sixteen is what you eventually get up to a few weeks before the race. While most plans agree that this range of hours is appropriate, they all differ in how they see the buildup—that is, how far out they recommend you start training, and how quickly they advise you to increase the duration and intensity. In terms of avoiding injury, this is important for me.

One plan, for example, suggests that Ironman training is a twelve-month process, echoing the e-mail lecture I got from Bmac. Then there are other plans that are less rigid, making the claim that you can get there in just six months. Less frequent—but in existence—are plans that focus on what you should do when you're twelve weeks out, which is approximately where I'm at right now (I'm closer to fifteen, but who's counting). At first glance, this seems great, just what I'm looking for. But upon further review, I see that there is an underlying assumption built into these few-and-far-between plans. They figure you have a solid base to build on, and that you aren't tying to go from zero to hero. I'm not sure what my base is yet. I know my background, but I don't know my current base, or how quickly I can recover and build endurance. To know that, you need to—get this—start training.

I come across one strategy in particular on the Ironman site that piques my interest. It lays out a plan for a successful race with "just" ten hours of training per week. The author introduces the concept of "performance in context." If you want to be a professional athlete and compete for podium spots and sponsors, then yes, you need to put in 14, 16, 18, or even 20 hours per week. But if you're a regular person trying to finish, then just ten hours is all you need.

Just ten hours a week, eh? Just a measly 1.43 hours per day? Compared to 232 miles on the bike and forty-whatever on foot, that sounds reasonable. But ten hours a week still figures to be the most dominant activity on my schedule. I try to think of the things I do for at least ten hours a week currently. Do I spend ten hours a week eating? I write ten hours a week and I sleep ten hours a week, for sure. That's two right there. I'm not a big TV guy, maybe an hour per week. None of my life maintenance responsibilities (errands, bill paying, cleaning my apartment, showering) or current hobbies (socializing, hitting the beach, hiking, exercise) take up that much of my time individually.

If I pick up training for an Ironman, what am I going to remove from my life? It's important to point out that those ten hours are workout hours and do not include warm-up and cooldown times, stretching, gear maintenance, or transportation time to and from the point of workout. It also doesn't include the state of fatigued indifference I am sure to find myself in post-workout. It's not a stretch to think this ten-hour plan will end up taking up closer to fourteen hours per week, or two hours a day.

There's got to be something else, something lighter, a way to weave it all together. I'm a child-free, self-employed person and I'm balking at ten hours . . . what about the athletes that have families? Nine-to-five jobs? You know, real responsibilities. What do they do? I read up on it and find that the solution for most is to stack their workouts by doing short, concise exercises a couple days during the week—thirty-minute to one-hour swims, runs, or rides—followed by longer, more elaborate workouts on the weekend—four- or five-hour bike rides, for example.

As if this couldn't get worse, the solution to reducing my workout load is now to dedicate my weekends to it. That doesn't bode well for my desire to keep up with my current hobbies. I am intrigued by this idea of stacking workouts, though. Maybe I could pencil in one or two big workouts per week, sprinkling in general exercise along the way, and get by that way. Maybe I could start out by doing two two-hour rides per week and then move up to a four-hour ride once I get in better shape, then five, six, and so on. Or, I could set aside time once a week to do all three sports back-to-back-to-back, and rack up the hours that way, all in one day. That approach gives me the chance to take a few days off and have balance in my life. Basically, I'd be ruining one or two days to have the others free. Then again, those big days will be *completely* shot, rendering me useless for the rest of the day. And, should I miss that one big workout for some reason, I would really set myself back.

For a second I consider hiring, or at least talking to, a coach. Ironman has its own "Ironman U" division—short for Ironman University, I'm guessing—that allows coaches to become certified through the organization, and for athletes to consider the coaches reliable. It's a business move by Ironman. It makes them the expert certifiers of coaches, and puts them in a position to collect some of the mega-bucks that get thrown around between athletes and coaches. Prices vary widely depending on whether it's a one-sport or multisport coach, whether you want individual or group sessions, how often you want to meet, etc., but from what I saw on a couple of forums, people are spending, generally speaking, anywhere from $100 to $300 per month on their coaches and classes. I don't think this is for me. I can't afford that, for one, and even if I could, I hate the thought of inviting a coach into my life.

I look over at the clock and two hours have gone by in a flash. Shit, I'm late. It's been a less-than-inspiring morning, yet it comes at a better-than-usual time. I'm on my way to a doctor's appointment. It's meant to be a simple meet and greet for a prescription refill. As a travel writer living in Hawai'i, I take a lot of red-eye flights, and I've become a big fan of Ambien. The drug has been a reliable way for me to get some rest on flights—to time travel, if you will. So far, I have not done anything ridiculous. I haven't woken up raiding the meal cart or anything. But because it's a controlled substance, I have to go in every time I need a refill. The visit today coincidentally provides me an opportunity to ask my doctor what he thinks about the Ironman. How concerned should I be about injury? Is hard-core endurance training bad for your heart and long-term health? Is this something I should put my body through? I have a feeling he's going to tell me to run for the hills.

They call my name and I get my blood pressure and pulse taken. I'm at 62 beats per minute. Not bad. I would say I'm about to improve on that number with my upcoming exercise, but after this morning's research I'm not so sure. Perhaps I'm on the path to cardiac arrest.

I'm sitting on the examination bed, on top of that white crinkly paper, when the doctor knocks and comes in. He remembers me. I'm pretty sure I'm the only drug-taking travel writer he knows (although I could introduce him to a few more). He asks me how the writing is going. I tell him I have a new project.

"Doc, I have to ask you. The Ironman . . . have you ever heard of it?"

"Oh yeah," he says. "Those people are . . . " He searches for the right word. "Intense."

"Right? What do you think of that? All that exercise?"

"I think it's great," he says.

"Really?" I'm surprised to hear this.

"Yeah, sure," he says. "Why not?"

"Well, I was doing some reading today . . . " I tell him about what I read, about all the injuries and the people who have died. He pulls the chair out from the desk and sits down with his clipboard on his lap.

"Look, will extensive endurance training give you early arthritis? Sure, but you're going to get that eventually anyway." I look for a smile and wink, but he remains serious. He looks down at his chart and flips up a page, to look at the one underneath it. "Will it hurt your knees long term? Sure, but everyone has knee problems when they're old."

"So . . .," I say, "you actually think I should do this?"

"Yeah, why not?" he says. "I can't be a hypocrite. I'm training for the Honolulu Marathon in December. My wife and I are doing it." He tells me he and his wife work out together every night.

Oh boy. I've heard about these kinds of couples—triathletes, marathoners, and bikers that shack up together. In the online communities, people often mention that they are training with their wives or husbands, sometimes even running the same events together. I'm quickly learning that being a triathlete is a lifestyle, not a hobby, and perhaps even more life-defining than a career. The amount of time it requires, and the patience needed from your partner, is extraordinary. I will learn this firsthand soon enough.

I exhale and lean back on the exam table. The white paper crinkles underneath me. Figures, I get the one doctor who doesn't secretly smoke cigarettes. I get Mr. Marathon who thinks this shit is fun. Why worry about your knees when you're young . . . you won't be able to walk when you're older anyway! Real funny, Doc. He looks at me lying there on the table.

"When do you ramp up your training?"

"Tomorrow, I guess," I say. "No thanks to you."

He looks at me. I laugh so he thinks I'm kidding.

August 8, 2017
Kailua, O'ahu, Hawai'i
103 Days Until the Ironman

Why fit in when you were born to stand out?

—Dr. Seuss

Now that I'm actually going to go through with it—there was a shimmer of hope the doctor would direct me not to—I have to start getting things together. This morning, I went over to the whiteboard and wrote down the heading, "I Am Ironman?" I drew a line underneath it, then took a few steps back and looked at it. I thought writing it in the form of a question lacked confidence, so I erased it, and replaced it with an exclamation point: "I Am Ironman!"

Under that headline, I'm now making a list of all the things I need to get:

- Running shoes
- Swimming goggles
- Swimsuit
- Wet suit
- Bike

I step back to look at it. Fuck. The list is literally everything you need to do an Ironman. Don't let the fact that there are only five items fool you, that list is very dense. Buying a bike is not something I can go out and do in a day. In fact, it should probably be broken down into a dozen items. I have to buy the bike, and then I have to customize the bike. There are thousands of bike models and a million accessories to consider, and I have about a fifth the budget I need to buy a serious bike. Oddly enough, I do have everything I need clothing-wise as it relates to the bike. I have a basic helmet, bike shoes, and a bike leotard, padded-butt bottoms and a zip-up top. I got them as part of a media event* a few years ago.

In light of the costs associated with doing an Ironman, and in competing in triathlons in general, I'm thankful for every piece of equipment and clothing I already own. You would think the sport would be relatively cheap, since swimming and running require minimal equipment. That's true to a point. Except the little equipment you do need, as I'll soon find out, is expensive. And bikes! Bikes can cost thousands of dollars, plus thousands more dollars for fancy tires, a digital GPS, pedals, and the

* We rode from Estes Park to Steamboat via Trail Ridge Road and Rabbit Ears Pass. The two-day media event was sponsored by Moots.

obligatory outfits. From my initial research, I've gathered that the cheapest bike I can hope to get that will be reliable and comfortable for that distance will be somewhere in the $600 to $800 range, before accessories. I'm going to have to bite the bullet and do it—I can't realistically ride 112 miles on a bike from Walmart. I need a certain level of quality. Hopefully, I can reduce my costs elsewhere between what I have, what I can borrow, and what I can find on the secondary markets. This is not so much a problem for most Ironman participants: In 2014, *Fortune* reported their average annual household income to be $174,000. For me, that's more like a seven- or eight-year income.

One thing there is no getting around for budget-oriented triathletes is the Ironman entry fee. To register for the Ironman Arizona, it costs a whopping $850.* That's not a misprint. If their workout routines don't convince you triathletes are serious about their sports, perhaps the money it costs to participate will. All the entry fee includes is entry—not the transportation to the race, or the equipment. I have to cover the flight from Hawai'i to Phoenix as well as the nights of lodging before and after the race.

For the swim, I need goggles and a racing suit. All I have now are board shorts. They definitely have too much drag for a race. I'll also need to buy a wet suit at some point. Believe it or not, the water temperature in Arizona will be in the low 60s, 20 degrees colder than Hawai'i. From what I've read, a few people have attempted the swim without a wet suit to various degrees of success—a few ended up in the hospital with hypothermia. Not sure why the Arizona water is so cold, but it is.

Sign me up for some new running shoes, too. As much as it pains me—last thing I want to do is spend a couple hundred dollars on shoes—it's probably a good idea, considering what lies before me.

I think the best way to dive in is to go down to the local triathlon store and poke around, ask some questions. "Tri stores" are basically bike shops on steroids. They specialize in gear for all three sports and attract athletes of all disciplines. For me, it means one-stop shopping.

* This was the entry fee at the time. By the time you read this, it will have undoubtedly increased.

That's right, baby. Today is going to be an Ironman day. I'm going to get geared up, and I'm going to hit the gym. I did some thinking last night. For all the blabbering I did about wanting to adopt an official plan, I have decided to go with my own plan. My takeaway from yesterday is that there are a bunch of ways to do this, and I'm going to carve out my own. I learned a lot, the biggest thing being that there's no right or wrong way.

Instead of rearranging my life and succumbing to online pressures, I'm going to start working out and I'm going to listen to my body. I'll use what's left of August to see where I stand, and then, if necessary, come up with something more formal for September, October, and the first half of November. To hell with Bmac and everyone else. The only thing that matters here in August is that I start building my endurance in a responsible way, and I start collecting information about where I am. Instead of following some plan written by some guy or gal who may or may not know what they're talking about, I'm going to let my body tell me how far to go and what to do.

So far, I've done four official workouts. There was that first six-mile run I mentioned. Remember? *Had to stop three times, felt awful at times, felt like puking at end, probably didn't eat enough, back was tight, road was sunbaked and it dried me out.* That was on July 31. I did two, slower-paced jogs on August 1 and 2, about thirty minutes each. Then, in Wichita on August 4, I did a forty-minute run, where I felt the pinch in my knee.* I haven't done anything for the last three days, but I'm going to make up for it today by tackling my first "brick workout."

A brick workout is a combination workout in which you run after you've biked. Even the most anti-routine athletes, from what I've read, suggest that these be taken seriously. Running after you bike on a regular basis prepares your legs for the bike-to-run transition, which is despised for very obvious reasons. When you get off the bike, your legs are going to be wobbly, like you've had five tequilas—you can walk, just not very well. The idea is that if you practice this transition, and you can "get used" to

---

* I'll try not to list every single workout from here on out, for fear of annoying you. For your reference, you can find my training log in the appendix of this book.

running after biking, you will not be mistaken as drunk in public on race day, when you dismount after 112 miles of hard riding and head out on a 26-mile run.

I'm not sure why they call them brick workouts. The Internet has a number of theories: 1) because the workouts are stacked one on top of another like bricks; 2) because the workouts are named after world duathlon champion Matt Brick, who employed them in his training and thereby made them famous; 3) because of the way your legs feel the first time you try to run off the bike; 4) because you feel like you've been hit by a ton of bricks when you're done; 5) because it's an analogy for laying down your triathlon fitness foundation brick by brick; 6) because the workouts are hard like bricks; 7) because no one wants to do a "vinyl siding workout"; 8) because only someone dumb as a brick would want to do them voluntarily; and 9) because a brick is what you shit after you're done with the workout.

Before I hit the tri store, I'll hit the gym. I've decided to join . . . drumroll . . . the YMCA. Considering I don't have a bike yet, a gym is my only option for bike training. Yes, I *will* get a bike. Hopefully I'll get the ball rolling on that later today. For now, and until I get a bike, I need a place to pedal. More importantly, I need a sanctuary, somewhere I can go and get after it. The Y in Kailua is ten minutes from my apartment and has a pool, making it a place I can do all three sports in one shot. Plus, it's a decent deal for me. I found out that YMCAs offer membership deals based on your income. You can print out your social security earnings report, and they'll make you an offer.* I was able to get a membership for $28 a month, when it's usually $47 a month. Not sure I like what that says about my income status but, whatever, I'll take it.

It's been a while since I went to a local gym. Last time I can remember was a couple months ago, in early July. I was in Montreal on an assignment, and the hotel I was staying at had a partnership with a gym nearby, so I went for a workout. That's not very typical. Hotels usually have their own gyms, and that's where I've logged most of my hours the past few years.

* This is true. You should try it.

The YMCA in Kailua is not exactly state of the art, and it's small. The room is in the shape of an L. The cardio section, where I'll be spending most of my time, is at the top of the L, up a small staircase. Four stationary bikes sit at the top of that staircase. Only two of them, the ones on the inside near the staircase, have a view back over the weight room. The other two face that direction, but the wall is built out to meet the staircase, and those two bikes stare right into it. The five treadmills are in worse position, just behind the bikes but facing the other way. When you use them, you stare directly at a stone wall, your back to the rest of the gym. It's not the most scenic place in the world. At least it's air-conditioned.

I hop on one of the bikes with a view of the floor. One of the things I love most about coming to the gym is people watching and seeing all the different characters. Most of the clientele here are middle-aged, just regular people doing a regular workout, hopping on a cardio machine for twenty or thirty minutes and then doing a circuit on the various weight machines. There's a big free weight rack, but just a handful of adjustable benches. There's only one full bench press setup, and it's tucked in tight between a bunch of other, smaller machines. This attracts an older, subdued crowd. Right now the most entertaining person is the middle-aged, dark-haired man who is over-embellishing his movements on the elliptical. He's rolling his shoulders dramatically as his hands go back and forth. It looks like he's doing it as a joke and it's funny because he's not.

I start pedaling. I have no micro-goals for this workout session—only to go where I've never gone before. I'll bike for one hour, then try to run a few miles. This will be the first time I've ever done back-to-back sports like this, and I'm interested to see how it feels. I can't remember the last time I biked and ran in the same day. If you're not an eleven-year-old kid riding your bike to soccer practice, and you're not a triathlete, then why would you?

Despite the gym's bare-bones nature overall, the cardio machines themselves are relatively modern, and each has a personal TV screen attached. This intrigues me. I don't have a TV at home, and because I rarely watch it, having the option here at the gym is interesting. It's actually not a bad compromise—if I'm going to watch TV, it has to be here, at the gym, while I'm exercising.

Flipping through the channels, it's like I'm being reintroduced to the modern world. I can't believe the number of shows I've never heard of before. Mostly, it's a bunch of daytime TV melodramas, and a couple channels of sensationalized, provocative, hot-button gossip disguised as news. *Next, a 91-year-old man says that for years he's been mistaking a dog-poo disposal bin in a nearby park for a mailbox. None of his letters have reached their desired recipients, reportedly costing him hundreds of dollars in wasted stamps. Authorities say post office employees are authorized to collect mail from official USPS postboxes only. But is that fair to the elderly? We're on location after the break . . . dun dun duuuuuun.* I try ESPN for a few minutes, but it's not the channel chockful of highlights that I remember. There are a lot of commercials. I unplug my headphones from the TV and into my phone to listen to music.

I've been so absorbed by the absurdity of the TV that I've gone three minutes over on my warm-up. It's time to start ramping it up to speed. I want to ride for an hour, as hard as I can, and see how it feels, get a gauge of how far I can pedal and for how long. Bmac told me that riding at 90 rpm—revolutions per minute—is a solid, sustainable effort. I shoot for between 80 and 90. How hard I have to pedal depends on the resistance setting of the bike.* I find a setting in the middle of the road where I can pedal at 85 rpm comfortably without feeling overexerted.

I look over at the woman next to me. She's probably in her sixties. The bikes are close enough that we can see what the other is watching on our personal TV screens. I look over to find she's watching a medical show. A patient is undergoing some kind of stomach surgery. There's a lot of blood. I can't stand blood. It makes me want to curl up into a ball. A couple years ago, my girlfriend cut her foot on a metal storm drain as we were walking through San Luis Obispo. Blood poured all over the sidewalk and ran over the edge into the storm drain. I kept it together long enough to call an ambulance and get her to the hospital, but later that night, as she sat icing her stitched-up foot, happily pumped up on pain pills, I sat in the corner with my knees to my chest, rocking back and forth. I *hate* blood.**

* On a real bike, it would depend on the gear you are in.

** My mom was a nurse and my dad was a homicide detective. Go figure.

Who is this woman? What kind of person watches this stuff? I need to move bikes or find a way to get her to change it. She sees me peering over, looks at me and smiles.

"Are you a nurse?" I ask.

"No," she says. "Why do you ask?"

I point at her screen. "They're taking someone's insides out on the show you're watching."

"Oh, it's just an operation." She looks back at the television. "I love these medical shows. I find them fascinating."

"Cool," I say. Hopefully I don't cross paths with this lunatic in the parking lot. I can tell she wants to say something else. She keeps swiveling her head between my bike and her screen. She leans over and whispers to me.

"I just wanted to tell you, the last person who used that machine didn't wipe it down after. You might want to spray it down." She motions over to the bottle of cleaner hanging under the towel dispenser. Her face is relieved, as if she had been holding in this secret for a long time.

"I had a friend who picked up a bug from a gym," she tells me. "It spread to her eye and she had to have an operation. She was fortunate that they were able to save 85 percent of her eye."

I could spend a couple pages going through all the germs and diseases you can pick up at the gym. *Men's Fitness* has a list* of the "seven grossest," for example. But I'm not going to do that, because I'm not a germaphobe. Still, I feel obligated to go over and get a paper towel and disinfectant. She pedals and smiles with delight as I wipe down my machine. It must be nice to be enjoying your workout.

I sit down and try to settle in. Enough fidgeting around. I put my earphones on, turn up the music, put my head down, close my eyes, and work hard for the next twenty-five minutes. I ride nearly eight miles in the first thirty minutes.

Suddenly I sense that someone is standing behind me. Right when I pass the thirty-minute mark, he taps me on the shoulder. He points to the sign on the wall that says there's a thirty-minute time limit on all cardio

* Do an Internet search for "gym germs."

machines. He asks if he can take over. I look around. There are treadmills available, and low-seated bikes. But he wants this upright bike. The woman on the bike next to me has been going for longer but, OK. I'm not about to start an argument with the guy. He's in his sixties or seventies.

"Sure," I tell him.

I hop off the bike and wipe it down with a paper towel. He swings his leg over the seat and I notice he's wearing flip-flops. The fact that he's wearing flip-flops—which is against the rules of the gym—and then going around enforcing other rules annoys me. But it's my first day and I'm trying to be a good boy. There's a low-seated bike open on the other side and I jump on to finish my workout. Another one of the signs stares me in the face: *There is a 30-minute time limit on all cardio machines.* This could pose a problem for my workouts here.

I complete another thirty minutes, again covering eight miles. In total, it was an hour-long, 16-mile ride. Sixteen miles per hour. I'm very pleased. At that pace, it would take me seven hours to complete the 112-mile course. That's about where I want to be. Granted, the pace is by no means anything to brag about, nor am I currently capable of sustaining it for another six hours. But I walk away feeling confident. With the hour-long bike finished, I'm ready to get on the treadmill and complete the second half of my brick workout. I set the treadmill to an eight-minute mile pace and start running. My feet are pounding hard on the treadmill—it sounds like I'm stomping. I look around and no one seems to notice. I stay with it. I try to get into a rhythm. I can feel the fatigue in my upper legs, especially my left leg. Each time it pounds the treadmill I feel a jolt come up through it, from the bottom of my foot to the top of my thigh. Before long it feels dead, tingly like it's falling asleep. I compensate by leaning on my right, pushing through. I'm trying to train with the understanding that sometimes you need to push through things. It doesn't look pretty, and it's not easy. It's like I have exchanged my legs for two wooden logs.

With my pride top of mind, I clobber through the workout, gritting my teeth. The result is 3 miles in 26:04 for an average pace of 8:41 per mile. I'm not even going to calculate what that would mean over the course of 26 miles because my legs would have given out well before mile

26. It's nearly a full minute slower than the pace of my first run—the one I nearly puked after.

It's not the way I want to end the workout. It leaves me worried about injuries, not only long term but of the nagging variety that seem guaranteed to show up over the course of the next three months. I try to stay positive. I'm sure I'll have good days and bad days as I build my base. I rode a good bike session, and I tackled my first brick workout. A sub-nine-minute per mile run pace is nothing to be embarrassed about. It has become very clear, though, that I still need to find my footing.

By the time I get to my car, my legs feel loose again. The pain today, and in Wichita, could have been the result of any number of factors. Perhaps my running shoes are not up to par. Perhaps I'm pushing myself too hard too early. Maybe I'm not eating or drinking enough. Time will tell on the latter two. Today, I can fix the former.

There are a couple tri shops on the island, and I arrive at one in the late afternoon. I drive past, looking for parking. I see a bunch of guys out front standing around their bikes. They look like they're in their forties. One has his bike standing straight up, the back wheel on the ground and the front wheel head high. It looks like he's examining part of the frame. The other guys are standing around with a hand on the seat or handlebar. They're decked out in full bike leotards, tight pants with tight jerseys up top. Some are bright red and white, others are lime green and black. They're all rocking sunglasses and stylish helmets, really streamlined, seemingly designer, round in the front with a long tail in the back. I've never seen helmets like that before.

I'm still in my gym clothes, an old bathing suit with a tight, quick-dry athletic shirt. The bathing suit is sea-foam green and the shirt is bold blue. I'm not as stylish as the biker gang standing out front, and there's a good chance I never will be. I brush past them into the store. There's no employee immediately available, so I start to browse around. Though the store is split up into sections—some swim stuff in that corner, running shorts over there—biking is the most dominant presence. It's a working shop, with mechanical equipment, bike mounts, and tools spread out in the middle of the store. Hanging from the ceiling is a circular rack of bikes. Each bike is hanging upside down, the tires on the ceiling and the handlebars and seat toward the ground, a foot or two above my head. Price tags hang from most of them. The cheapest one I can find is around two grand. Let's hope they have a bargain bin in the back.

I make eye contact with one of the employees, and he signals that he'll be with me in a few. I continue my lap around the store. They have branded bike jerseys in the pattern of the American flag, made by some company called Jakroo. I've never heard of them. Must be nice, though, because it costs eighty dollars just for the jersey. I'm amazed by some of the other things I see. There's an entire section of water bottles, many of them skinny and oblong. One in particular catches my eye—it's called the RZ2 System by Profile Design. It's a flat, triangular-shaped, aerodynamic water bottle that's built to sit on the frame of the bike, behind the stem. The price is close to fifty dollars. For a water bottle. Wow. How much difference could this water bottle actually make?

I head over to the helmet section. The model the guys are wearing outside cost $200. I bought mine, a standard bike helmet, from the Goodwill in Kailua for five dollars. As far as I know, it protects the same. So why pay that much for a helmet? The packaging boasts about its aerodynamic qualities that will make you ride easier, and ultimately, faster. But again, how much difference could this possibly make? While I wait for an employee, I pull out my phone and search for the answer: *How much time does an aerodynamic helmet save?*

BeginnerTriathlete.com says:

> *Aero helmets typically save 30–60 seconds for every hour of riding. The actual time saved for a triathlete depends on how well the helmet smooths the airflow from the helmet to the middle of the back. This time can be broken down by race distance as:*
>
> - *Sprint triathlons—15–30 seconds*
> - *Olympic distance triathlons—30–60 seconds*
> - *Half Ironman distance triathlons—1.5–2.5 minutes*
> - *Ironman distance triathlons—3–5 minutes*

Cycling Weekly says:

> *A properly-fitting time trial helmet compared to a standard road helmet is worth about a minute over 40km . . . For slower riders the gains can be even bigger.*
>
> *A fully-vented normal helmet is the least aerodynamic thing in the world you could put on your head . . . It's about as aerodynamic as a sombrero. It's designed to swirl air around your head, it's designed to create turbulence. You're better off without a helmet at all. And you're certainly better off with a cloth cap.*

Well, I guess you can sign me up under sombrero. I'm not spending $200 to save five minutes, and I don't need anything else to worry about. According to the articles, the rider must hold his head in the proper position to gain optimal results. Aero helmets also reduce ventilation, meaning you can overheat on a hot day if you're not careful. Sort of ironic. Nothing like turning a piece of safety equipment into a dangerous accessory.

It becomes clear that money is going to be a huge issue for me. Everything is expensive, seemingly for the sake of being expensive, for the sake of saving a couple minutes over the course of an entire day. Frankly, I don't care about saving ten minutes. I'm not vying for the podium. I'm not going on a world tour here. Even if I wanted to, I wouldn't be able to, not at those prices. My budget for the bike, including all accessories—pedals, aero bars, water bottles, pumps—is somewhere in the vicinity of $700. For that price, from what I'm seeing here, I can buy either a third of a bike or fourteen water bottles.

The employee finishes with a customer and comes over to me. His name's David. He's short, skinny, and Asian. Not that any of that matters but now you know what to picture. I tell him I want to buy a bike.

"What are you looking to do? Commute around town?"

"No," I say. "I'm doing an Ironman in November."

"All right," he says. "So, what's up with your other bike?"

I look at him. "My other bike?"

"Yeah, the one you've been training on. Did you wreck it, or are you just looking for a different style?"

I bite my lip. I'm embarrassed about what I'm about to say. I know I shouldn't be but I can't help it, here in the tri shop, face-to-face with the professionals.

"I don't have a bike," I admit. "I've actually just started to train for it."

He just looks at me and doesn't say anything.

"That sounds bad, doesn't it." I don't frame it as a question.

"Kind of," he says. "I hope you have a good base."

"Me too," I say.

"OK, well . . . Do you know what size you want?"

"I have no idea what I want," I say.

This doesn't surprise him. "I can give you a fitting."

He leads me into the back room of the store. I have no idea how they fit you for a bike. Maybe it's like going to a tailor. Maybe David is going to measure my inseam and my arms. The closest I've ever come to a bike fitting is getting on the bike and riding it around the store to see how it feels. You know, when I was in grade school.

In the back, among the work benches and tools, there's a mechanical bike positioned in front of a television screen. It looks like a video game, similar to those boardwalk-style arcade games where you ride the motorcycle and your movements correspond to what happens on screen (Manx TT Superbike). David tells me it's called the GURU Fit System. Via the computer, you can customize the fit by changing the height of the seat, the position of the handlebars, and the length of the pedals. These measurements can then be used to find the bike frame size and style that will fit best. Because you can actually pedal while these measurements are altered, you can feel the consequences, good or bad, of small alterations. The mechanical bike can mimic any make, model, and size of bike so you can "ride it before you buy it."

I watch as David browses through a selection of preset bike models. This is the starting point for the fitting. He runs through a series of models and asks me how each feels. To me, there's not a significant difference between them. A little lower position on one, slightly higher on the other. They all feel comfortable in different ways. David is most concerned with the seat and handlebar heights. He moves the seat up and down a few times, leaning down to see the bend in my knee.

"How's that feel?" he asks.

I look down at him kneeling beside me as I pedal. "It feels fine."

That's about as deep as I can get. It feels . . . like I'm riding a bike. Nothing is uncomfortable or out of the ordinary. There was a big change when he moved the seat significantly—four or five inches—but now we're tinkering around, a half-inch up, a half-inch down. I don't feel a significant difference between those small amounts. David tells me that I will feel the difference over time, as I ride more.

"The seat height is important for efficiency," David tells me, encouraging me to take it seriously. "You want to be able to max out your threshold power without putting too much stress on your knees."

"OK," I say. I have no idea what he's talking about. Threshold power. I'll look it up later. For now, I nod my head. I feel the seat move ever so slightly underneath me.

"How about now?"

"Yeah," I say. "Whatever you think."

He asks me to get down in the aero position. I bend forward and set my forearms over the handlebars and grab the aero bars, my hands over my front tire. It looks like I'm riding an antelope and grabbing the horns. He checks the angle of my back.

"Do you have any back problems?"

"Sometimes," I admit. "I herniated a disc ten years ago and sometimes it gives me trouble."

He turns and plugs an alteration into the computer. "OK, we'll move you a little closer, to take the pressure off your back." He tells me that the farther back I sit from the handlebars and aero bars, the farther I have to lean over, and the more pressure it will put on my back. The mechanical bike hums and drones as the handlebars move closer, bringing my elbows toward my body. "How's that?" he asks me.

"Feels fine," I tell him. He nods. David's been patient, and I appreciate it. He seems down to earth and calm. Maybe he can give me some advice about biking. He tells me to start pedaling and watches my form. I start to pedal and say, "I take it you're really into biking?"

"Yeah," he says. "For the past couple years."

"How much do you ride?"

"Between commuting and training, I ride about four-hundred miles a week," he says.

I correct him. "Forty miles?"

"No, four hundred," he says. I can tell the number doesn't mean much to him, because his face doesn't flinch. He's modest about it.

"Four hundred miles *a week*?" I say slowly.

"Yes, but that's only this time of year. I don't do that all year."

He tells me he's training for an event of some sort, I forget what.

"So, you must have done a bunch of Ironmans, then," I say.

"Nah," he says. "They're not for me."

David explains that he rides in local events. He says he has mixed feelings about the Ironman. He likes triathlons but thinks the Ironman has become too trendy. It's now less about the ride and the enjoyment of that ride, and more about people checking a box and getting a tattoo, he says. He tells me he'd rather ride in lesser-known events where it's strictly about the passion.

Oh Jesus, I think. This guy must think I'm a joke. I come in and say I'm doing an Ironman, that I haven't trained, that I don't know shit about bikes. I am one of these box-checking people he is talking about. I'm . . . *one of them*.

"Oh," I say, trying to save face, "I'm just, you know, giving it a try. I hear so much about it, I want to see what it's like."

As I say it, I realize I'm literally saying, word for word, what he said he doesn't like about it. He smiles at me. He's a nice guy. I'm pretty sure he doesn't want to be my friend. But maybe he'll sell me a bike. I change the subject back to business.

"Do we have a verdict on the size?"

"Looks like you need a sixty-centimeter frame," he says.

The measurement means nothing to me. "Cool. Do you have any of those?"

He walks me back into the main room. We stand underneath the circle of bikes hung from the ceiling. He points at one of the bikes. "This one is a fifty-eight centimeter, but I think it might work for you if we . . ." He goes on to say something about how we can adjust this or that. I'm not listening. I'm blinded by the price tag: $2,400.

"I appreciate it, but here's the thing. This bike costs $2,400, and my budget is much less than that."

"How much do you want to spend?"

"About $700."

He wasn't expecting this. Based on the price of water bottles, he's used to customers with deeper pockets. When a cocky dude comes in and says he's planning on doing an Ironman he hasn't trained for, David probably assumes he's got some coin to throw down.

"OK," he says, "I don't have anything like that in your size here on the floor. I can take a look around and give you a call later this week."

I thank David for his help and ask him where they hide the running shoes. He tells me they don't carry running shoes anymore. He says part of the reason is because he doesn't want to compete with the store down the road. He says they are the ones that have the shoes. We walk over to the checkout counter, where I give him my information so he can call me about the bike. Lined in front of the checkout counter are a variety of food items. There's a selection of energy bars and packets of gel. I grab an assortment of them. David sees me grabbing them and tells me he likes the Bonk Breakers at the end of the rack. I add one to the collection on the counter.

While he's ringing me up, a man comes over and says hi to David. This man cares little that I'm here, or that he's interrupting my transaction. He doesn't look at me. He engages David in small talk, about his day. David introduces me to the man, Richard. Richard completed an Ironman last month and is also going to compete at the Ironman Arizona in November.

I shake hands with Richard. He's middle-aged, probably in his late forties. He doesn't look like an Ironman. Most notably, he has a significant beer belly, flabby up top in his chest with the bowling ball pushing out his belly button. Hey, all good. I like to party, too. I introduce myself and tell him that Arizona will be my first Ironman. Looking at his chubby face, I realize what a good resource he could be for me. Unlike Bmac and Tommy, he is not a physical specimen. He seems like a regular, good-timing dude who did an Ironman or two. He could be an excellent source of down-to-earth advice, perhaps even a training partner. I tell him I'm just getting started on my training for Arizona.

"Maybe we could take a ride together sometime," I say.

"You're just getting started, huh?"

"Don't worry. I won't hold you back," I say, thinking that reality is very obvious, given our body types. "It would just be nice to ride with someone here and there."

"Hmmm," he says, looking anywhere but into my eyes. "I'm not sure about that."

I'm confused by his comment. Is he saying he's not sure he can ride with me because, like, he lives far away? Or is he saying he's concerned I will hold him back? It couldn't possibly be the latter. I'm not ripped or jacked by any stretch of the imagination. However, compared to this guy, I'm Arnold Schwarzenegger.

I ask him, "Do you like to train alone or something?"

"Well, it's not that," he says. "It's just . . ." I swear to God he said this! "I'm actually on another level right now, having done a race this summer. You're not there yet, and honestly I don't know if you'll ever be there. So . . . it's probably best we don't ride together."

Wow. I look over at David and he's trying his best to pretend like he's going through the cash drawer, like he didn't hear Richard say it. I am stunned by his comment. It's as if I've been hit over the head with a frying pan. You're on another level? Why? Because you bought more expensive gear than I did?

"Wow, another level?" I say, patronizing him. "You must be really good."

"I'm OK," he says. He still hasn't looked me in the eye.

"Well, good luck then," I say. "See you on the course."

"OK."

I thank David for helping me and leave the store. Thinking about Richard annoys me. He's not the first doubter, and he won't be the last. But good god, *I'm on another level?* I make a pledge to remember this day. I will see this guy's face in my training. I will repeat that mantra to myself over and over. *I'm on another level.* Yeah buddy, you sure are.

I drive a half mile down the road to the shoe store. I'm not sure when the last time you bought running shoes was. It's been a while for me. Not only are there many brands to choose from, there are many styles within each brand. The store has a color-coded system to help you find the pair for you. You have to value the importance of weight, sturdiness, and padding.

I am staring at the wall of shoes like I've just smoked a blunt. I am mesmerized by all the options and the color-coding system. This blue shoe has a yellow marker, which I like, but the red shoe is labeled green. Hmmm. The employee comes over. I tell him I'm having a hard time figuring out which pair to get. He asks me if I have measured my pronation. I tell him I haven't heard a word like pronation since grade-school math. He says I'm thinking of protraction, not pronation. He makes me take off my shoes and walk in a straight line across the room. He watches me as I do it. It feels like I'm taking a sobriety test. I walk back and forth until he tells me it's enough. He's watching to see if, and how much, my foot rolls when I walk.

Based on what he observes, he's able to narrow down my shoe options. He says I don't have pronation, so I don't need to worry about going overboard with sturdiness. I decide to go with an average shoe, an equal mix of lightweight material and long-distance support. A pair of blue and yellow Asics catch my eye. The shoes cost $159.99, which seems like a bargain next to other pairs that cost more than $200.

The employee asks me if I need anything else. I tell him I need running socks. We walk over to the sock section together. I see a pair that are green and white and yellow and have "Hawai'i" written across the ankle. Socks are socks, but I like the idea of that. It would be cool to wear them in Arizona to represent the islands. They are very soft. I look at the price tag and a three-pack costs $19.99. That seems like a lot for socks.*

"What's so special about these socks?" I ask the store employee. He turns over the packaging and points to the back of it.

"They have superior venting and are engineered to give you max arch support," he says. He's right. At least, that's what's written on the back of the box, with a tagline of "Engineered Fit and Performance."

I'm skeptical of getting carried away on the performance capacities of socks—it's a sock for Christ's sake. But these are substantially softer than

* Come to find out, this is very cheap for socks.

any of the old pairs in my sock drawer. I am sure they will fit better and reduce the likelihood of blisters. He rings me up and I pay. I'm getting on the freeway when I realize I forgot to buy swim goggles. I also still don't have a bike. Oh well. There's a lot of other stuff to think about, specifically the bars and gels I bought, and race food in general. It's an important thing to think about, what I'm going to eat. I've heard far too much about what can happen when you don't get your diet right. But for all that can go wrong, it stands to reason a lot can go right. I want to learn what to avoid, but I also want to learn what to embrace. What's going to give me the most energy? What's going to help me avoid cramps? These are things I need to know.

It's a half-hour drive back to my side of the island, so I take the chance to reach out to Drew again. We've been trying to catch up ever since I left him a message last week. I roll up the windows and put him on speakerphone.

Drew's in North Carolina, winding down before bed. He's completed two full Ironmans, most recently the exact one I will do in Arizona. Even though I'm doing the same race he did, we approach it from two different angles that bring about two different types of stress. I'm trying to figure out how I'm going to finish, how I'm going to survive. Drew didn't have to worry about that. He's been an active triathlete for years. He was going to finish. His stress came from having advanced expectations of his performance. His goal was to finish in less than ten hours.* I can hear the frustration in his voice as he retells me the story. He missed it by four minutes, finishing in ten hours, four minutes and change.

Because of the intensity with which he competes, I expect Drew to be up in arms about my short-notice pursuit. To my surprise, he isn't as concerned as Bmac. In fact, he encourages me by assuring me that my swimming background is a huge advantage.

But what about the bike? And the run? I ask.

"Look, you have seventeen hours to finish the thing," he says. "Will it be the most pleasant experience of your life? Probably not. But once you're done, it will be pretty awesome."

* I didn't know it at the time, but "breaking ten hours" is a common goal among repeat Ironmanners.

The way he frames his response flashes me back to the doctor's office. "*Will extensive endurance training give you early arthritis?*" "*Will it hurt your knees long term?*" Sure, but . . . There's always a "but."

Drew and I go way back. His brother and I have been best friends since high school, and the first time I got drunk was at his apartment at Villanova. When I mention the bars and gels I just bought, he asks me if I know about the fourth leg of the Ironman.

"Swim, bike, run . . . kill . . . kill yourself?" I have no idea, I tell him.

In Drew's opinion, hydration and nutrition are the biggest factors in race outcome. More than fitness or competence in any of the individual sports, the fuel you give your body, and how much you give it, will make or break your day. If the pros are off on their nutrition even *they* can't finish, Drew explains. It's not just about eating before the race, it's about eating during the race. What I eat during the race—not only the specific foods but the amounts—is something I need to learn over time, with experimentation. Drew tells me I need to practice eating while I'm working out. Eat a peanut butter and jelly sandwich while I ride, for example, and try out different energy bars.

To understand my hydration needs, Drew says I can measure my "sweat rate"—how much water I lose while working out—and use this to calculate how much I need to drink. He says he can send me a spreadsheet with the mathematical formula. What I need to do is weigh myself before a workout, keep track of how many ounces I drink during the workout, and then weigh myself after to see how much liquid I lost via sweat. Something like that.

Although I know measuring my sweat rate is something I'll never, ever do, I listen intently. Drew is so calm and collected about this extreme advice that you get the sense he is reflecting on a previous life. Still, I know there is passion in his blood. Like Tommy in Wichita, Drew has an Ironman tattoo. Yet you would never guess he once held that level of intensity as he delivers his hard-nosed insight with great bedside manner.

He says the most important thing to remember is that I am training for an event, training for performance. I am not exercising to lose weight. I need to move past the commonly held mentality that says if you work out and eat less, you'll get into "good shape." While this may work for people who are following casual workout plans—thirty minutes a couple of times a week—it is the exact opposite of how I need to approach my endurance training. I am not trying to get skinny. I am trying to finish the world's toughest triathlon. My body needs more fuel, not less. I'm going to be exercising so much, so often, and so intensely that it will be impossible for me to eat more than I burn. Rest assured, I will be skinny. But I need to be strong, too.

Looking back, I'm beginning to realize that my debacle on that first six-mile run had more to do with my food intake than it did with my physical ability. I went out on the run after a few cups of coffee and a green smoothie—my usual breakfast—and didn't eat or drink anything during the run. A green smoothie is part of a healthy lifestyle, but not exactly rocket fuel.

I ask Drew the kind of stuff he used to eat while racing. He mentions some of the items I bought at the tri shop—the gels and energy bars of the world—as good places to start. "Real food" is also an option, things like peanut butter and jelly sandwiches and pretzels. The main thing, he says, is that I need to figure out what works for me.

An article on Active.com I read later expands upon this: "Different Ironman nutrition plans work well for different people. One person swears that they can only drink fluids during an Ironman race while another can comfortably eat a slice of pizza before the marathon run. Another person does fine on one small water bottle of fluid per hour, while another person needs two large bottles to do well. Yet another person swears by electrolyte tablets, several per hour, and the person next to them declares with confidence that these tablets are unnecessary. The bottom line is what works for your best friend may not work for you; you have to figure out what works for you."

Another article on Ironman.com confirms: "There can be a lot of confusion around what kind of fuel is best for a triathlon—and for good reason. The market is flooded with sports nutrition products, and if we asked 100 triathletes what they use, we'd probably get 100 different and successful fueling plans. What works for one athlete doesn't necessarily work for another—all the more reason to make sure that by race day, you've found an ironclad plan that works for you."

Drew says that for his second Ironman, in Arizona, he did a liquid diet. I should experiment with both, he says—many top athletes prefer a liquid diet for its ease of digestion. Regardless, the two main things to replace during the race are carbs and sodium. Proteins, generally speaking, should be kept to a minimum during the race, because they are harder to digest. Fiber should be avoided, because, you know, you don't want anything to slip out. Ironman.com advises that a person should eat "at least 0.6 grams of carbohydrate, per hour, per pound of body weight, on the bike and half of that on the run."

I'm 170 pounds at the moment, meaning I need 102 grams of carbs per hour on the bike, and 51 grams of carbs per hour on the run. Let's put this in perspective. A 12-ounce serving of Gatorade has 21 grams of carbs, and a slice of whole wheat bread has approximately 12 grams of carbs. So, each hour, I could drink 24 ounces of Gatorade and eat five slices of bread, for example. Obviously, eating that much bread on a bike is unreasonable, which is where alterative options, like energy bars, come into play.

While consuming carbohydrates makes logical sense, the idea of sucking down sodium took more convincing. After all, excess sodium is a leading cause of health problems for millions of people. But sodium, Drew says, is absolutely, 100 percent, no-room-for-negotiation needed during endurance events and is one of the most important nutritional elements of the while-exercising diet. You lose an abundance of it when you sweat—Ironman.com estimates that "most athletes lose between 800 and 4,000 milligrams of sodium per hour." If you don't replenish it, you will suffer cramps, digestive issues, and muscle fatigue that will certainly, without discrimination, end your day.

Finally, Drew brings up a non-essential but very helpful "nutrient": caffeine. It may seem counterintuitive. I mean, drinking coffee gets my blood pumping, but not usually in an athletic way. My morning cup(s) stimulates me to write and be creative, and to poop, but to run? Sweat? Not really. The closest I've experienced would be when I drink too much coffee and become anxious and shaky. Some of the gel packets I bought contain caffeine, so I tell Drew I'll let him know how it goes.

Is there anything I should avoid? Drew says, believe it or not, that water is something triathletes heavily debate. Too much "plain water" can actually deplete your sodium levels and leave you short of electrolytes. Yikes. I'll have to look into that more later on my own. Drew's got to jet, and I'm about home anyway.

It was a very insightful conversation, one that leaves me feeling more unprepared than ever, and also more confused than ever about the long-term outlook of endurance training. At this point, though I still don't have enough experience to fully understand what motivates triathletes to put themselves through all this, I do have enough information to know it's not for health reasons.

The jury is out on the physical effects of long-term endurance training on the body, and if that is not enough food for thought, this idea of "nutrition," as I'm beginning to understand it, seals the deal. The word itself is extremely misleading. "Nutrition." Though triathletes may (or may not) eat well outside of workouts during regular meal times, the food that fuels them through training and events is by no means healthy. Make no mistake about the word "nutrition." No one is pulling over to eat a salad. In truth, many triathletes fuel their workouts—especially the carb component—with a variety of sugar-based, processed foods. At this diet's core is the energy bar.

Energy bars have established permanent residency in grocery stores across America. Even if you're not an athlete, you've no doubt eaten one as a snack at some point. Of all the prepackaged, processed food consumed in the racing community, energy bars are the most familiar to non-racers because their appeal extends beyond endurance training and into everyday life (as compared to gels, which do not). Clif Bar is probably the most widely known brand. The bars have been around since the early nineties, are sold in almost every grocery store, and reach the everyday consumer base as a granola-bar alternative. But are they a granola bar alternative? Or are they closer to a candy bar?

As one article* put it, "While nutrition bars can be part of a busy, healthy lifestyle, there are a few good reasons they're not stocked next to the kale and blueberries at your grocery store. Many are made with cheap, low-quality ingredients and are hiding tons of sugar and additives that can cause digestive distress and prevent absorption of important nutrients."

* The Five Best and Worst Nutrition Bars; wellandgood.com.

In another article, Spoon University noted a marginal difference between the nutritional value of a Clif Bar and a Snickers, concluding you might as well indulge in the Snickers. Yet, despite these similarities, there does remain a big difference in the way the bars are perceived by consumers. One is an energy bar. Another is a candy bar. That's marketing. Take Clif Bar for example. There's a fit guy on the front of the package climbing a steep rock overhang. Some packaging promotes organic oats, or organic peanut butter, and some include the message, "Nutrition for sustained energy." The language used gives off a "Hey, I'm not terrible for you" vibe. You won't find that kind of stuff on a Snickers bar.

The same type of comparison could be made for Gatorade. It sounds healthier than soda. Probably is. But that doesn't make it a healthy option on a daily basis. It still contains large amounts of sugar and sodium.

This is an aspect I'm having trouble with. I know athletes need fuel. I know they burn sugar and lose sodium and it must be replaced. I know things like energy bars and Gatorade make it easier to do so, and are welcomed by the body during moments of depletion. I'm just not sure what it adds up to in the long run. Regardless of whether or not you burn it, you are what you eat. You're still living on a diet that relies on large doses of sugar. I think about it as if I was starving. Sure, Doritos would be a welcome thing. They've got fat and carbs and salt. In that individual moment, my body would be happy about them. Does that make them healthy in the long run? What all this tells me is that, if it does indeed turn out that I need to eat lots of energy bars and drink lots of Gatorade these next few months, I have to be extremely diligent with my diet otherwise.

That starts tonight. It's been a long day—I'm tired from the brick workout, and I'm hungry. I bake a chicken breast and a potato, with broccoli on the side. I drink lots of water. And I do one other thing. I look up Mr. I'm on Another Level. I'm able to find out that he did his last Ironman in a time of fifteen hours and fifty-one minutes. It took him more than seven hours to do the marathon. He competed in the 50–54 age group, so he's older than I thought.

Far be it for me to compare myself to a fifty-something dude, but spite can be a powerful drug. There will be thousands of people in the race, and I already told Drew—and everyone else—that I'm just trying to finish. That's not entirely true anymore. Looks like there's one person I need to beat after all.

August 15, 2017
Waimānalo, O'ahu, Hawai'i
96 Days Until the Ironman

Start where you are. Use what you have. Do what you can.

—Arthur Ashe, champion tennis player

I returned home after four days in the Alaskan wilderness with forty pounds of fish. Mostly silver salmon, but also some king salmon and halibut. The guides made it real easy for me. Each day when I came back to the lodge, I tossed the fish I caught into a big plastic bucket on the dock. At night they would bring all the fish inside, cut it into filets, vacuum seal it, and freeze it. At the end of the trip they packed it all up into a refrigerated box that could be checked as airline baggage. There was a storm on the last day and we could not take a seaplane from the lodge back into town. We had to take a boat and it was very rough and very rainy. We took the boat about an hour across the channel to where it was calmer and the seaplane picked us up from there. When we arrived in town we had coffee and sandwiches to warm up.

The timing of the trip* was good. I arrived back on O'ahu on Sunday. I used what was left of the day to get organized, and yesterday I hit the ground running. I went to the YMCA and biked seventeen miles, then ran four miles. It seems the rest in Alaska did me good. I increased my biking time by a whole mile per hour, and I did the run at a 7:47 per mile pace. I'm happy to see I still have room to grow on the bike and that I responded well on the run. There was no dead leg this time. However, it wasn't without concern. That same pinch I felt in Wichita returned, on my left leg, just below the knee on the outside corner. It didn't hurt at the start of the run, but by the second mile, it felt like I was being stabbed just below my knee, on the outside part of my leg. It hurt to the point where

* I went fishing as part of an adventure travel story assignment.

I considered stopping halfway through. Then I thought: *Do Ironmen stop when it gets tough?* They probably do, if they're injured. But I was able to push through and still move at a good pace. I am sure my legs need time to adjust to this whole bike-run brick combo thing. I ate a peanut butter and jelly sandwich during the ride and then one when I got home after the run. It sat well on both occasions.

David from the tri shop called while I was away. They don't have a bike in my size. Even worse, he doubts anyone in Hawai'i will have my size. He told me—and I swear he said this—that people in Hawai'i are short, and large bike sizes are hard to come by. I called a few other shops and did a quick search on Craigslist and confirmed he was right. The only bikes in my size are cruiser types. The bikes I found on Craigslist came with complications—the primary one being that I have no idea how to judge the value, condition, and quality. David said he could order me a bike but that it could take up to a month or more for it to arrive. I can't wait that long. Another option, he said, would be to buy a bike online. That might be my best option and I'm going to look into it.

Putzing around my apartment, I debate my options for today. I ran yesterday, and I don't want to push my knee. I still haven't done a training swim yet, so I could head to the Y and do a swim-bike workout. Only I don't have goggles—remember, I forgot to get them at the tri shop last week.

Well, that's not entirely true. I do have goggles—just not racing goggles. They're the big, blockish ones that you use for snorkeling and scuba diving. I pick them up and examine them. They're huge and dorky, something Scuba Steve might wear, only instead of being sleek and black, they're lime green and square. They are not ideal for swimming laps by any stretch of the imagination. But is that going to stop me from training? If I let a lack of proper gear hold me back, I wouldn't be biking either. No, I can't let myself make excuses that easily.

I change my clothes and put my bike leotard into a backpack. I'll swim first, then bike. I have never done a workout that combines the two sports. It will be a good chance to feel out that first transition. In the spirit of creating extra drag, I wear the baggiest board shorts I have—those green ones.

The pool at the Y is outdoors and receives full sun most of the day. It's a clear, hot day, so I need protection. I decide to wear a surfing-style, tight-fitting, long-sleeved, red-colored rash guard. Between that, the board shorts, and the snorkel goggles, I'm not going to get any extra points for style. I put a dab of regular dish soap in each eye of the big goggles, rub it around, and then rinse it out in the pool. I sit down on the side of the pool and put my legs in. There are only two lanes open for lap swim, sandwiched between a slow-paced water aerobics class and a kids' swim lesson. The kids are yelling and screaming between laps. I assume this annoys the older folks doing the slow-moving, methodic, warm-up portion of the aerobics class.

I look up and see the lifeguard is looking at me. I smile at him and he stares at me, sunglasses covering his eyes. Despite all that's happening around me, it's easy to imagine how I'm the oddball in this situation. I slide in so the water passes my waist. The sun is strong enough that the water feels refreshing. Standing there in the shallow end, adjusting my rash guard and tightening the goggles, memories of my swim career come flooding back. It was usually the opposite of this. I remember waking up at the crack of dawn for practice, standing beside the edge of the pool in warm-up pants and a long-sleeved shirt, postponing entry into the chilly water. I remember we used to put on our caps and goggles before we would take off our long-sleeved T-shirts and warm-up pants. By afternoon it would be hot, but in the morning it was breezy and cold. At least that's how I remember it.

The weather is good here in Hawai'i. Almost too good—I'll have rosy cheeks by the end of my first couple laps. I drop below the surface, place both feet flat on the wall, and push off. I put my hands above my head in streamline position and shoot through the water like a torpedo. I surface like a submarine and bring my right arm out of the water. I stretch my arms out and reach as far as I can to get loose. I flutter my feet for a small kick and a small splash. At the opposite end of the pool, when the lane line turns red, I go for my first flip turn. I have not done one in years. I take my final stroke and pull down hard in front of my chest. My head follows my arm. I curl up and whip my legs over top, finding the wall with my feet and pushing off as I corkscrew back into a stomach-down position. I surface, take a stroke, and head off on lap two. I can feel the resistance of the big green goggles as they push through the water, like I'm pushing an umbrella.

Though I have not swum competitively in a long time, I have never stopped swimming, and it doesn't take me long to find my rhythm. It feels natural. A couple laps in, I'm immersed in a world I knew twenty years ago. I remember the practices and the meets. I remember the feeling of wrapping my toes over the edge of the starting block, going all-out on a 50-meter butterfly or a 25-meter freestyle. I remember all the summer mornings and winter evenings of training. Oh boy, talk about an ostracizing activity! Of all the sports, swimming is among the loneliest. Being in the water puts you in a bubble. All I can hear is the sound of my breathing, of the water moving past my body. Meditative? Not exactly, considering the effort involved. There aren't any distractions and there's nothing to look at. I stare at the bottom of the pool, follow the black line until it ends, do a flip, then follow it back the other way until it's time to do a flip again.

After ten minutes of continuous laps, I stop to rest in the shallow end. I have no idea how many laps I have done. I tried to keep count but lost track after eight or nine. Not that it matters. Today is all about getting in the water and knocking the dust off. I feel good. Those first laps were nice and easy. My cardio felt good and so did my form.

The water aerobics class is now ramped up. There's music playing and everyone has their arms out of the water, over their heads. They're twirling around. On the other side of me are the kids. They've finished their warm-up and the teacher is talking to them about proper hand form—specifically, how far apart to keep your fingers when you pull your hand through the water. There are more than a dozen kids between the two lanes and some are paying more attention than others. I look at the kids. Two of them in the next lane look at me. One of them points to the goggles that rest on my forehead.

"Those aren't the right goggles!" he shrieks. I have no idea what to say. He's right. The teacher looks over at me and frowns. "Zach," she says to him, "look over here. Pay attention."

I push off the wall and get going. I swim for ten more minutes at a relaxed pace, then stop for another break. For the last ten minutes, I go hard. I swim as fast as I can. One-two-three-breathe. One-two-three-breathe. The water starts to feel hot. My breath gets away from me going into and out of the flip turns. It only makes me work harder. When the ten minutes are up, I decide to do four more laps as fast as I can. I finish strong, stabbing the wall with my outstretched hand at the end of the last lap.

I hop out of the pool and head for the locker room. In the mirror, I can see the veins popping out of my upper chest below my shoulder. I remember that happening when I was a kid, too. I take my pack from the locker and sit down on the bench. My breath is caught, but I'm still feeling the effects of those last laps. I feel distant. My mind is outside my body, not quite making a connection. My body droops toward the floor as a rush of fatigue flows through me. It's like someone flicked a switch that shut down half my system. I pause and sit up. Where is this fatigue coming from? I'm a good swimmer!

I take a few deep breaths and continue getting dressed. I move methodically to take off my bathing suit. I step into my bike leotard, feeling it wrap tight around my thighs. I pull the straps up and over my shoulders. They snap down when I let them go. The leotard squeezes my waist and thighs like a compression sock. I zip up the jacket, then sit back down. The humidity in the locker room is thick and it makes it hard to put on my socks. The struggle leaves me out of breath.

I still feel lightheaded when I sit down on the bike. I start pedaling and crack open a Gatorade. It's Fierce Grape. I take down half of it in the first couple of gulps. I can still taste the chlorine of the pool. It feels good to wash it down and replace it with the sugary taste of the sports drink. It seems I may have underestimated the swim-to-bike transition. Just because I'm a good swimmer doesn't mean I'm good at biking afterward. I pull out one of the GU Energy Gel packets I bought at the tri shop. Called "GU" for short, they are by far the most awkward race food I've come across. Snotty in texture, they come in little packets about the length of your finger. They're like little penis packets. I tear the top off, wrap my hand around the base of it and squeeze. When the slimy goo spurts out the top, I cover it with my mouth, rubbing my fingers from the bottom to the top—the same way you might a nearly empty tube of toothpaste—until the packet is empty and no more comes out. I can feel the sticky residue left on my tongue and the back of my throat. GUs are packed with sugar (maltodextrin and fructose) and sodium and are marketed as being easily digestible energy. Some have caffeine in them for an extra boost. I swallow and immediately reach for my Gatorade to wash it down and clean out my mouth.

I allow my mind to become distracted by the TV, and after ten minutes, I feel better. The Gatorade and GU are coursing through my system now, and the shock of the swim has worn off. My legs feel fine. I crank out sixteen miles in the hour. It's one mile per hour less than the day before. I chalk it up to the swim. I'm starting to get the feeling triathlons are convenient like that. You can blame a lot of things on a lot of things.

The next day, after two straight days in the gym, I decide to move my workout outdoors. The idea of moving the swim into the ocean sounds like a good plan. I live in Hawai'i, after all. Hopefully, it will combat the boredom I felt in the pool yesterday. Instead of staring down at a black line, I can look down on the ocean floor, maybe see a fish or a turtle. That would certainly make my goggles feel more appropriate.

I drive out to Sherwood Beach. It's another bright, clear, beautiful day. I park in the lot. The tall trees of the ironwood forest rise up and I can hear the wind going through their needles. I undress down to my board shorts. I take my goggles and leave my flip-flops. I walk shirtless on the path through the trees to the shoreline. The wind is blowing and there are some small waves. It doesn't look too rough. The small waves break on the shore and shoot water up onto the sandy beach. I bend down and rinse out the goggles in the water as it recedes. I put them on and wade out into the water. I dive over the first wave that comes at me and start swimming. I don't have a complicated plan. I will swim parallel to the shoreline for thirty minutes, then swim to shore and run back to where I started.

I swim with purpose and power to get past the break, then slow down and swim south toward the Makapu'u Lighthouse. I'm bobbing up and down with the current. The swell is bigger than it looks from land, and the wind makes the water choppy. When the pulse of the wave comes through and charges toward the shore, it lifts and lowers me as it passes. It's like I'm swimming parallel to the back wall of a wave pool. My plane of existence rises and falls as the waves come in and run toward the shore. Up and over and down, up and over and down. I can feel the current pushing me toward shore. I have to make a conscious effort to ensure I'm not being pushed too close to the break. I breathe on my right side, opposite the waves. I get salt water in my mouth from time to time. The current is pushing and pulling the sand, stirring up the water. I'm in seven or eight feet of water and cannot see the bottom. I pound on for twenty minutes down the coast, looking up with every breath to insure I stay on course.

Then, I start to feel strange. I feel a rumble in my stomach. I feel something in the back of my throat, a strong sensation to swallow. I feel seasick. No, really, I think I'm going to throw up. I stop swimming and tread water. I frog kick my legs and move my arms like a conductor as I tread water and float up and over the waves. I stare at the shore as a point of stationary reference. I catch my breath and the feeling passes. I had no idea you could get seasick while swimming. I did not think it was possible. But as soon as I put my head down and start swimming again, the feeling returns. In an instant, I feel like I'm on the verge of passing out, my mind softening as I look down into the opaque underworld of the blue water and the golden sand. I can see myself sliding side to side with the current. The dizziness sets in, the vertigo.

Fuck this shit. I come out of swimming position and tread water again. I do above-water breaststroke toward the shore. I let a set of waves pass before I make the final push through the break. I stumble through the knee-high water and reach the beach. I look at my watch. I swam for twenty-seven minutes. Back on solid ground and out of the water, I immediately feel better. Time to fight through. I start into a slow jog, my bare feet landing in the soft, wet sand. I splash through the water when a wave breaks and the tide shoots up. Lining the beach, I can see the small cottages and the trees, a couple of tall palms. Halfway through, I remember the goggles are on my head. I take them off and hold them in my hand. I make it back, without incident, to where I started in seventeen minutes.

I return home in a weird mood. It's a humbling experience to have your supposed best skills neutralized. It makes me feel helpless. I can overcome a lot of things. Seasickness might be one of those knockout punches. Arizona is a freshwater swim, but that doesn't mean the water won't be choppy. There will be thousands of people swimming in the same channel. A sickness like that could ruin my day. It's especially annoying because it's such a dumb thing. I've been hanging near the ocean almost my entire life. I used to own a sailboat. Really, seasickness is going to be what gets me?

I go online and read a couple of forums about seasickness, specifically about people who have experienced it during open-water races. It happens to a lot of people, and there are various over-the-counter solutions. One is to put wax in your ears. A major cause of seasickness is that your orientation gets thrown off, and plugging your ears fixes that—so it says. That's something I could try. Another idea is to fight the side effects—aka the nausea—by taking ginger before the swim. The ginger is said to settle the stomach. I guess the takeaway here is to be careful what you wish for. I wanted out of the pool, and now I have to deal with the ocean.

The next ten days are jam-packed with workouts. I avoid open-water swims but continue to build my base on the bike. One day, I ride for two hours (32.8 miles) and then run two miles (16:17). Though I'm able to complete the two miles, my knee gives me trouble and strongly recommends that I go no farther. I decide to rest my legs. When I resume action a few days later, I make a big mistake. I ride for an hour (16.46 miles) and then run three miles (23:09). The run feels incredible. I have no pain in my knee, and I'm able to do the three miles at a sub-8-minute per mile pace. I leave the gym in a great mood, oozing confidence. Finally, my knee feels better. Finally, I can start gaining some ground in the running department. I decide to take advantage of the good vibes by going for another run when I get home. In my mind, it's the right thing to do. This race is all about pushing yourself. I felt great at the gym. Why not go for a couple more miles?

A mile into it, I feel a slight curiosity in my left knee. A few strides later, it buckles and I go down. I catch myself with my hands, push myself right back up, and start to walk it off. I'm limping. I try to switch over to a jog and am met by sharp discomfort. I stop. So much for my great day. So much for my knee being better. I walk for the next five minutes, stopping to stretch my quad. I pull my heel up to my butt a few times. I can feel the muscles in my leg settle down as I walk and stretch. After a few minutes I can walk normal again. I move back into a slow jog. With each step I can feel the aggravation building. I decide to walk the rest of the way.

I put a big bag of ice on it when I get home. The fact that I could coax down the injury is confusing. How can it hurt so bad in one moment, and not the next? Why is it only during some workouts, only after a certain amount of running? Why isn't the pain consistent? I jump online and it clues me in to the source of the pain: It's not my knee, it's my iliotibial (IT) band. The sharp pain is the result of the IT band—which connects your hip to your knee—being inflamed or aggravated. That manifests itself in a point of pain below the knee, the Internet tells me.

That puts my mind at ease knowing its nothing structural, but the more I read about the IT band, the less lucky I feel. It's amazing to me that one weak muscle, a seemingly small injury, can entirely shut me down from running. IT band issues are extremely common in the running world, and, unfortunately, one of the peskiest injuries to curtail. Opinions on how to treat it are split. I find articles that suggest rolling out the IT band with a foam roller. I find other articles that say a foam roller will only make it worse—the argument is that foam rolling further irritates the inflamed tendon. Instead, I should work on strengthening the muscles around it.

The gluteus medius—sister of the gluteus maximus—plays a big role in IT band health, I read. It runs from your upper buttocks to your hip on either side and helps stabilize your hips when you walk or run. A weak gluteus medius sets off a chain reaction that causes your pelvis to shift and your knees to compensate. This can lead to problems, including IT band syndrome. Basic exercises, such as side-laying leg lifts and clams, can help strengthen the gluteus medius and alleviate IT band pain.

Worst case, there is a product called KT Tape that a lot of runners and triathletes use. It is basically expensive duct tape designed to be applied topically to the skin and provide support for weak muscles. In this case, I could run a strip from my IT band to my gluteus medius that, in theory, will provide extra support for those muscles. Given that relying on pieces of tape to get me through the next few months doesn't sound like the best idea, I will use it only if it is absolutely necessary—a last-minute Hail Mary should I not heal up in time.

Taking a week off of running seems like a better place to start. I substitute the elliptical for run workouts as a way to keep my legs in motion. I spend the rest of the time on the bike. Bike bike bike. I had done hour-long rides almost exclusively, but one day the gym is not crowded, and I am able to do a longer ride on the stationary bike—40 miles in a little less than 2.5 hours. Almost exactly 16 miles per hour, right in line with where I want to be. I can feel I'm making progress—a 40-mile ride is nothing to sneeze at. Then again, I rode 40 miles . . . the Ironman is 112. Long, long, long way to go.

Bmac had advised and encouraged me to look into smaller, "sprint" triathlons happening locally as practice for the Ironman. He said it would be a good way to get familiar with how it feels to take part in a race, the jitters and pacing and transitions and the push to the finish. I don't disagree with him, in theory. It would be good practice, if not the worst way to spend a Saturday. A search reveals that there are several multisport events upcoming on O'ahu, including a triathlon that starts on one side of the island and finishes on the other. That's kind of cool, if we're looking for a break in the clouds. But my eyes turn to saucers when I see the price of entry—$180. Ugh. I can't do it. I won't do it.

I begin looking for single-sport events. Perhaps they will be cheaper. I see an advertisement on one of the event pages for the annual Waikīkī Roughwater Swim, a 2.4-mile open-water event on September 4; Labor Day. It's the exact distance of the Ironman swim. In fact, it was *the* swim for the very first Ironman back in 1978. The cost is less than a hundred dollars. Hmm. I don't necessarily need to focus on swimming, but it would be a good litmus test here in the beginning, to figure out whether I can really skip out on swim training, and to experience what it's like to swim in a pack of people, flying elbows and all. Plus, I could relive and discover some of Ironman's history here in Hawai'i. I decide to sign up.

Registering and paying for the long swim isn't like buying tickets to a baseball game. There's no joy in it. There's no excitement. For me, it has the feeling of signing up for the SATs or something. Now I'm locked into taking this really exhaustive, really hard test. Great . . . awesome. I guess that means I should get down to the store and buy some goggles.

The tri shop is chill in the early afternoon. There is no work being done on bikes, at least not here in the front part of the store. I don't see David. I go over to the goggle section to look at options. It's pretty straightforward. Some pairs have tinted lenses, some don't. The shapes of the eye cups vary slightly. From my experience as a swimmer, goggles are all the same, so long as they don't leak and don't fog. In that sense, I don't need to spend a lot of time comparing them. I do like the idea of tinted lenses to cut down on sun glare. I decide on a pair from TYR. The cost is $21.25. Not bad.

I grab the box from the shelf. An employee comes over and asks if he can help me with anything. I tell him I'd like to buy the goggles and also need a pair of basic jammers. He takes me over to the swimsuits.

"I'm doing the Waikīkī Roughwater," I tell him.

"Oh yeah?"

"Yeah, and I'm doing an Ironman in November."

"Oh really?"

"Yeah."

He doesn't say anything. We look at the bathing suits. I ask him, "Have you ever done an Ironman?"

"I used to do them," he says. "Way back in the day."

I can tell he has more to say on the matter. Here in Hawai'i, though, you really have to pry to get people to say something controversial.

"Why did you stop?" I insist. "Did you burn out?"

He shrugs his shoulders. "I didn't like it anymore. It became . . . a thing."

He likes to do other races now, he explains, less popular ones. It's almost as if he's trying to say he doesn't do them anymore because of people like me. It's almost exactly what David said to me the other week. *I used to do it back in the day, before it got popular, before you showed up.*

"Yeah, it's a huge thing now," I say. "I . . . just want to see what it's all about."

He doesn't say anything. He rings me up without raising his eyes from the register. He puts the goggles and jammers into a bag. He hands me the receipt and closes the cash register door. Finally he looks up.

"Well," he says, nodding towards the bag on the counter, "good luck."

I leave the store feeling judged. Is he upset that I'm doing the Ironman? Is he sad the Ironman isn't "cool" anymore? Am I just another lemming in a popular movement? Is he . . . a hipster triathlete? I'm not sure. But I'm going to find out.

August 28, 2017
Waimānalo, O'ahu, Hawai'i
83 Days Until the Ironman

> *Being a little crazy is like being a little pregnant—you can only hide it for so long.*
>
> —Unknown

Today I learned a terrible, horrible, very bad thing. It's the worst news since hearing that I was going to have to do the Ironman in the first place. Turns out, per official race rules, you cannot wear earbuds—i.e., listen to music—at any stage of the event. This means you must go 112 miles on a bike and then 26 miles on foot without the aid of a single Deadmau5 or Boy Pierce beat. Hell, I'd even take a Phish jam or a Queen sing-along. Anything but the pounding of my feet on the pavement, my laboring breath, or worse—my own thoughts.

The idea of going that far without any music is a crushing blow. Literally, every workout of my adult life has been aided by music, my energy elevated and my mind distracted. I think the last part is the key part—distraction. That's what Bmac recommended, after all: that I watch Netflix while I train. I've taken his advice. In fact, watching television at the gym has become the cornerstone of my workouts. By going back and forth between music and a television show, I've been able to break down my workouts, at least mentally, drifting off into a state of distraction and daydream by staring into the TV when I'm trying to cruise at a steady pace, and then using music to get me pumped up when I'm pushing my pace to a sprint. All along, I've thought this mental practice would help me through training, and perhaps even be useful on race day, specifically the use of music.

Now that's going to have to change. I won't quit cold turkey—I can't—but I have to start mixing in some workouts where I don't listen to or watch anything. Obviously, the best and ideal way to accomplish this would be to do more workouts outside. Biking outside in Hawai'i would be a nice thing to do—there's so much to look at, so much natural beauty to help distract. Except I don't have a bike yet.

Maybe this is a wake-up call. Music is only one of the many diversions I've used during training. So many of the things I've done to distract myself—listening to music, watching television, looking straight down and closing my eyes while pedaling, sitting up straight on the seat and letting go of the handlebars—most of these are things I will not be able to do on a non-stationary bike during the race. But they are things I have done each and every workout thus far.

An idea comes to mind: What if I could keep the distractions without sacrificing the integrity of the workout? What if I picked the most dreadfully boring songs and shows? This way, I'd be cheating and training at the same time. Try, for example, to imagine biking full speed, sweat pouring down your face, while listening to Celine Dion's "My Heart Will Go On" or Whitney Houston's "I Will Always Love You." Or imagine watching a slow-paced television drama, like a daytime soap opera, while running full speed. The contrast between the mind and body would be extraordinary. Maybe that's something I can try later today at the YMCA.

Or, maybe I should just forget about the distractions and get to work, because today is going to be a big day. I'm going to tackle my first mini-triathlon and do all three sports back-to-back-to-back: An open-water swim of thirty to forty minutes at my local beach, an hour-long ride on the stationary bike at the gym, and then a one-mile run on the treadmill.

When it's over and I get home, I want to make a drink. I got seasick during the swim again, and the pain in my IT band returned on the run. And, of course, there was a bit of an unofficial break in the fifteen minutes it took me to drive from the beach to the gym in between the swim and the bike. Still, there's reason to celebrate the completion of my first (mini) triathlon. Swim-Bike-Run: 30:28 (half-mile swim); 60:00 (17 miles bike); 8:20 (1 mile run). Not bad?

I take a glass from the cabinet and stack it as high as I can with ice. I go over to where I keep the bottles of booze. I call it a liquor cabinet, but it's more like a liquor shelf next to the oven. I don't have much, just gin, some Southern Comfort someone brought over and left here at some point, two bottles of baijiu, some rum, vodka, whiskey, mescal, and tequila. I take the gin and pour some into a glass with ice. I look in the fridge and can't find any traditional mixers. I could have sworn I had soda water. I look for a lemon or lime and cannot find one. This is not good. Gin is not something I want to drink on the rocks. I move the containers of leftovers around like a game of horizontal Tetris. Behind everything I see the top of a Gatorade bottle. It's lemon-lime flavored, half full. I don't remember when it's from. It looks fine. There are no floaties or anything like that in it. I twist off the cap and pour it into the gin. I bring it right to the tippy top of the glass. I lower my head and lips to the rim of the glass and slurp off the top layer. I wrap a paper towel around the outside of the glass and put it on the coffee table. I retrieve my foam roller from beside the desk and sit down on the floor. I lay the foam roller flat on the floor, perpendicular to my body. I put it under my right leg and rest my hamstring on top of it. I put my palms on the floor beside my hips and push my butt off the floor. I lean into my leg on the foam roller and spin it underneath me. I can feel it steamroll the muscles on the underside of my leg. When my arms get tired of propping me up, I lower myself and reach for my drink. I take a sip, put it back on the coffee table, and switch the foam roller to the other leg.

This has become an all-too-familiar sight. Not the foam rolling—I should do more of it—the Gatorade. In the last month, my life has been taken over by the famous sports drink. There are now, at any given time, three to five bottles in my apartment. There are bottles on top of the fridge, tucked in between liquor bottles in my liquor cabinet, in the door of the fridge. Hell, I found one in the trunk of my car the other day.

Indeed, the notorious sports drink has become a big part of my life. The last time I remember drinking it in these quantities and with this frequency is when I was a kid in the midst of soccer season or playing summer baseball in the corn fields of South Jersey. I also went through a short phase in college when I mixed Gatorade with vodka. But since then—I swear—I haven't touched the stuff.

Now I won't lie to you: I'm loving it! I find myself looking forward to the Gatorade aisle at the store, browsing the flavors, seeing if they have anything new. The other day I found a mango-flavored one, which I had never seen before. This piqued my interest very much, because I thought it might be a special flavor only offered in Hawai'i. Unfortunately, they sell it all over the country, and the mangos are not grown in Hawai'i, because there are no real mangos in it.

So far, my favorite flavors are melon, green apple, and grape,* but I have not tried them all yet. Not even close. I was surprised how many different types there are, not just flavors but styles of Gatorade. Under the main umbrella of Gatorade, the family tree branches off into sub-categories: Regular, Low-Calorie, Fierce, Frost, and Flow. The latter three come with taglines. Fierce is "Bold and Intense," Frost is "Crisp and Cool," and Flow is "Smooth Finish." My three favorites, melon, green apple, and grape, all fall under the Fierce flavor line. I am finding I like the "boldness," I guess.

Otherwise, I've had fruit punch, orange, and lemon-lime, which are the three most traditional flavors under Regular. Flow tends to be combinations of fruit flavors. I've had Kiwi Strawberry and Blackberry Wave. They were all right. At some point, it all becomes the same. It's not like it's real fruit and you're getting a sense of strawberry season.

Frost offers many of the most artificial-sounding flavors, things like Glacier Freeze and Riptide Rush. I definitely remember having both of those as a kid. I can't remember whether they were branded by the Frost thing yet.

I haven't tried Low-Calorie. It doesn't seem like something an Ironman would drink.

If you're wondering, there is no difference between Regular, Flow, Frost, and Fierce from a nutritional standpoint. Each, regardless of branding and flavor, has 140 calories per serving and 36 grams of carbohydrates. Low-Calorie is obviously different.

It's a weird thing to welcome a new beverage into your life. I went from never drinking Gatorade to drinking it more or less every day. I know some of what Gatorade offers me is beneficial, like the calories and electrolytes that replenish what I lose during workouts. Yet at the same time, it's just another high-sugar, high-calorie food item that comes along

* I read that Gatorade discontinued Fierce Grape, along with twenty-five other flavors, a few years ago. But I still find Fierce Grape with regularity.

with being an endurance athlete. I'm torn about it. I highly doubt it is very good for me over the long haul. But, whatever, man. I'm just trying to make it through the next few months.

I sip the gin and Gatorade. It's honestly not that bad. I drink it fast and pour myself another. I put the drink down on a coaster next to my computer and sit down at the desk. I told Drew about my bike dilemma and he pointed me to a website called BikesDirect.com. It's an online warehouse of bikes and he said they are sure to have my size. It's a janky-looking website, to be sure, but according to everything I've read, it's a legit place to buy a bike. I click on the tab for road bikes and start eyeballing through them. I'm looking for one in the seven-hundred-dollar range, including shipping. I see a Triathlon tab in another heading, and I click it.

Only three bikes come up. Two are way over my budget: One is twelve hundred and another is eight hundred, without shipping. The final one catches my eye because it's listed at five hundred, discounted 60 percent, down from $1,299. It's the Motobecane Mirage Tri, 24-speed with aero bars included. I copy and paste "Motobecane Mirage Tri" into a Google search. All reviews conclude that it's a fine choice for an entry-level rider. I suppose that's me.

I check to ensure they have my size in stock and they do. Could this be it? I write up the details and text them to Drew to get his opinion. He gets back to me almost immediately with a thumbs-up. He tells me it's not the best bike in the world, especially compared to what I will see others riding in Arizona. He thinks it's a solid value for me, though, given my small budget and limited options here in Hawai'i.

I don't get through reading half his text before I reach for my credit card. I'm ready to be done shopping for the bike. Shipping costs $150 for a grand total of $649.99, fifty bucks under budget. This is exactly what I was looking for. Two weeks late, but exactly what I was looking for nonetheless. I buy the bike and get an e-mail that estimates it will arrive late next week. I make another celebratory cocktail with the last of the Gatorade.

There's a knock at the door and it's my girlfriend. Her arms are full of bags and she's hopping up and down. She splashes them on the bed before bouncing into the bathroom. She comes back out.

"Sorry, I should have peed before I left!"

It's OK, I tell her. "Do you want a drink?" We stand in front of the liquor cabinet and look at the bottles of booze.

"What are you having?"

"Gin and Gatorade."

"Gin and *Gatorade*?"

I smile. "I have to stay hydrated, hunny."

"Ew," she says. She reaches for the whiskey and pours herself one on the rocks.

That night I eat like a college student coming home for Christmas. I cook salmon and halibut filets from my fishing trip to Alaska. We kick back on the couch and catch up. She's been very supportive of my training thus far, and I'm grateful for it. It's been a great couple of weeks. One month down, two and half to go until the big event. But, I feel bad about what's coming for her.

September and October figure to be pretty brutal. I will have to invest even more time than I am now. The farthest I've ridden is forty miles. The longest I've run is six miles—and that was the very first day of training. Since then I've barely been able to run a couple miles without pulling up in pain. I have a long way to go and it's only going to get more demanding. It all kicks off on Monday, with the Waikīkī Roughwater, a 2.4-mile swim race.

But, there's no reason to go down a dark road tonight. I have battled through seasickness. I have had my IT band bring me to my knees. I said at the beginning of this month that I would use it to find out where I stand, and then go from there. Well, here is where I stand: Between August 14 and September 1 (nineteen days), I did thirteen workouts. My two longest were both more than two hours long; my average was well more than an hour; and I did my first "triathlon" today. Now the bike is on the way. There's gin and Gatorade. My girlfriend is here. It's Friday. I have the next two days to rest up and recover before my first big swim test. Life is good, for now.

Part Two

Is This Really My Life?

September 4, 2017
Waikīkī, Hawai'i
76 Days Until the Ironman

I'm going to make you so proud.

—Note to self

The alarm goes off at six in the morning, two and a half hours before the start of the race. I must say I did not sleep well last night. Today's the day I get my first taste of a modern-day, pay-to-participate sporting event, and I'm anxious about it. Not only will the outcome affect me mentally in either an encouraging or discouraging way, I will get to experience the mess of a mass swim start—the flying elbows, perhaps—and see what it feels like to compete in a pay-for event. The only previous sport-related event I can remember paying for is paintball. I guess this endurance race stuff is just like playing paintball, if instead of trying to shoot the other team, you shoot yourself in the face the whole time.

It's the annual Waikīkī Roughwater Swim, and I have paid $91.03 ($85 entry plus $6.03 processing fee) for the privilege of participating. It's a 2.4-mile swim from Kaimana Beach to the Hilton Hawaiian Village, basically from one end of Waikīkī to the other. Today is my tape measure, a chance for me to see where I stand in my swim training. If I'm able to complete the swim without a problem, in a reasonable amount of time—less than two hours would be OK, less than an hour and a half would be ideal—then, as Bmac suggested, I can concentrate on biking and running.

There's a vast difference between the Roughwater swim course and the one I will tackle in Arizona. The Arizona swim is held in a freshwater canal (more on this later). The Waikīkī Roughwater is an open-water swim, subject to the conditions of the ocean. The direction of the currents and the height of the waves play a big role in the performance of the participants. Last year, the current was pushing against the grain, from the finish at Hilton Hawaiian Village back toward Diamond Head and the start at Kaimana Beach. The year before that, the race was canceled because of the current.

Hawai'i may be a paradise, but it is no place for rookie swimmers. A study by the Honolulu nonprofit news organization Civil Beat found that between 2012 and 2015, approximately one tourist died a week in Hawai'i. A majority of the deaths occurred in the ocean. Make no mistake, they don't call it the Roughwater for nothing.

Aside from my individual goals and the chance to size up an Ironman-length swim, I'm also in for a broader perspective on the Ironman and its roots. The first-ever Ironman took place right here on O'ahu in 1978, with the Waikīkī Roughwater serving as the swim leg. This is where the Ironman craze began, forty years ago.

As the story goes—and let me go on record here as saying I take creation stories with a large grain of salt because they tend to get refined over time—the concept of the Ironman was first discussed at an awards banquet in 1977 on O'ahu. The banquet brought a bunch of local competitors together—swimmers, bikers, runners—who were always crossing paths at events and apparently always at odds with each other about which sport produced the greater athletes. Long story short, a man named John Collins took the lead on combining three existing events—the Waikīkī Roughwater (2.4-mile swim), the Around-O'ahu Bike Race (115-mile bike), and the Honolulu Marathon (26.2-mile run)—into one single-day monstrosity.* Apparently, John Collins said, no doubt in biblical fashion,

* Collins and crew decided to shave three miles off the Around-O'ahu Bike Race, which was a two-day event at the time, to allow the course to start where the Roughwater left off and end where the marathon began. That's how the seemingly arbitrary distance of the 112-mile Ironman bike route came to be.

"Whoever finishes first, we shall call him the Ironman." Lightning struck, the name stuck, and he convinced fourteen other people to give it a shot with him. They kicked off the inaugural event on February 18, 1978, right here on the shores of Waikīkī in the shadow of Diamond Head. A couple of years later, before the race of 1981, the Ironman moved to Kona on the Big Island due to concerns about the congestion on O'ahu. In reality, the Waikīkī Roughwater was only a part of the Ironman for three years, thirty-seven years ago. But today, for me, it holds a much larger legacy. This *was* the swim portion for the first Ironman. Everything about this swim is Ironman-caliber. Today, I get to see where I stand.

As I drive over the Pali Highway from the windward side and begin the descent down into town, I am crossing my fingers for a relatively calm swell. Between my lack of long-distance swimming experience and my newfound tendency to get seasick swimming in the ocean, I could be in for a pretty awful day if it's choppy. If it's too crazy, it won't be an accurate barometer of my progress, or a good feel for the distance. A choppy, seasick-tainted swim would leave me with one thing: an excuse. I don't need any more excuses. At breakfast—I had a big bowl of oatmeal with bananas and some coffee—I popped a couple ginger pills. They're supposed to be non-drowsy and help settle the stomach.

I park adjacent to Kapi'olani Park—close to where the finish line was for the first Ironman—and walk along the beach path toward Kaimana Beach with my back to the Waikīkī skyline. Looking out, I can see the big yellow buoys a few hundred yards offshore, beyond the break. They run parallel to the shore so far down into Waikīkī that I can't see the last one. Damn. I don't think I've ever had this perspective on how far 2.4 miles is—it's a long swim. To date in my training, the farthest I've swum is one mile. I don't need to tell you how unprepared and foolish that sounds. Standing here now, in the face of it, looking up and down the beach at the buoys coming and going, rising and falling as the waves come in and break on the reef, seeing how small that guy in the kayak looks as the horizon stretches on forever, it's startling to remember that I'm relying on my swim experience from twenty years ago to get me through.

Kaimana Beach is a cool place. It's not much of a beach, small and often congested. But it's a nice place, accessible from Waikīkī, yet tucked away on the edge, out of the spotlight. They've built a bunch of condos and a couple of hotels down here, but compared to Waikīkī Beach, it's in the country. My favorite thing about it is that it's right next to the old Natatorium, a saltwater pool that draws water from the ocean.* It opened back in 1927 as a World War I memorial and a major community centerpiece—it was even used by the Hawai'i Department of Education for its elementary school swim programs. Lucky kids. Unfortunately, its heyday didn't last long and it was shut down in 1979 after thirty years of neglect. The state of it today is nothing short of bizarre. There was momentum in the late nineties and early 2000s to restore it, and a budget was received to fix the facade, redo the locker rooms, and eventually reopen the pool itself. But funding was pulled on the project before it could be completed. Only the facade and the bathrooms were redone. Now there's a set of nice bathrooms on the outside of a refinished building that's still closed indefinitely. From inside the men's room, there's a barred-up doorway that leads to the old pool. It's cool to peer through at the cracked concrete and imagine how wonderful the place must have been back in the day.

My daydream comes to an abrupt end when the locker room becomes crowded. People have poured in to take their pre-race poop—which I thankfully managed to do at home this morning. The line is three-deep for the stalls. From the sounds that echo through the locker room I can infer one of two things: Either people are very nervous, or they all went to the same all-you-can-eat Chinese buffet last night.

There's still thirty minutes before the start of the race. I find the check-in desk, pick up my timing chip, and get body marked. The timing chip is pretty cool. It slips on your ankle and immediately gives you a sense of purpose. The body-marking station sounds a lot cooler than it is. It's a gal with a Sharpie, who writes your race number on your arm. I'm 219. I thought I'd have the opportunity to throw some war paint on my face or a tattoo on my bicep, but apparently you have to do those things on your own at home. Good to know.

* You might remember hearing on the news about a baby seal that got stuck in the pool for a few days in 2017.

I take off my clothes and stash them. I'm wearing my blue jammers. Think of really tight, elastic booty shorts for dudes, the boxer version of traditional swim briefs (or weenie benders, as we used to call them). I stretch out, touching my toes, windmilling my arms. I sip on Gatorade. I have a GU packet with caffeine in it that I'll eat right before the race. It's a beautiful day here on the beach in the early morning. Some people are doing warm-up swims in the surf, swimming up and over the waves toward the break, then turning around and coming back, nice and easy. I'm considering going in when the race director comes on the PA. He tells us the tide is low, and there's only a small channel in the reef deep enough to get us up and out over the break. Go too far left, or too far right, and you could be cut on the coral, he tells us. The waves aren't huge—just a couple feet—but they're there, he says. I decide against the warm-up swim in favor of continued stretching. I swing my arm up over my head in a big circle, like a pitcher warming up for a game.

The race director comes back to announce that we're just a few minutes away from the start. He advises us to be careful getting out over the break, but says the current is much better than last year. Slightly in our favor at best, an even drag at worst, he says. I tear open the GU pack and suck it down. It's Vanilla Bean flavor and has twenty milligrams of caffeine, much less than a cup of coffee (ninety-five milligrams). Still, combined with the sugar, it goes straight to my veins. When I hear the first group called to the starting line, my heart begins to pound. Any hints of nervousness are currently being converted into rocket fuel. I'm ready to go. It's like I'm on the front line of the war, ready to charge into the crashing waves and go nuts on them, go through them if I have to. That imagery comes to life as I hear the gun go off and see the first heat run and dive into the water, meeting the waves head on, like Braveheart or something. One more group, and then mine. Tom Petty was right—the waiting is the hardest part. By the time I get to the starting line, I feel like jumping around, banging my chest. But I do neither. I stand still, next to my fellow swimmers. It's a variety of ages, from college kids with chiseled bodies to older men who look like they would fit in well at the YMCA. With swim caps on, we all look like coneheads. There's not much time to get a sense of who these people are. When the gun goes off, I sprint out ahead and dive into the surf in attack mode.

In my peripheral vision, I can see bodies everywhere. Arms thrashing through the water, legs kicking as hard as they can. Adrenaline surges through my system, inviting me to break away from the pack. I'm not going to push it too hard—I want to be conservative, considering I have to cover far more distance than I ever have. But I do want to get out ahead for the sake of space. I want to make sure I can stay in the middle of the channel, and that I don't get sucked up into a slog of people in the back. Or worse, catch an elbow or foot to the face.

It turns out to be a good decision. The waves, which looked small from shore, crash into us as we try to plow out past the break. Ahead of me, I see swimmers get knocked backward. Looking down at the bottom, I can see myself going backward at times. A wave breaks on top of me, the whitewater barreling into my outstretched arm as it comes over my shoulder. I can see and feel myself rising up several feet as each wave passes, one after another as the set comes in. The space to maneuver is the vehicle, but the adrenaline is the gas. My heart beats hard and I breathe with intensity as I power up and over the waves.

A string of yellow buoys leads me out and over the break. There, I encounter an orange buoy. There are two orange buoys on the course, one here and one down at the end where you turn into the beach at Hilton Hawaiian Village. All the buoys that guide the way are yellow. The race director announced that the only other out-of-ordinary buoy was anchored at the halfway point. It's a yellow buoy with a hot dog raft attached to it. Yes, a hot dog raft at the halfway point. Reaching halfway was already going to be a good thing; now it's going to be a great thing.

I'm past the break, out in the open water with plenty of space to maneuver. It's time to go on autopilot. For me, the stroke rhythm is one-two-three-breathe, one-two-three-breathe, one-two-three-breathe. Before each breath, I lift my head from the front and sight the course before turning to the side to breathe. It's all one quick, fluid motion and it doesn't disrupt my rhythm. It's a lot of breathing—I'm not pushing my lungs—but it's the way I want it. There's a long way to go. I look for the hot dog every time I sight, even though I know I'm nowhere close to it yet. The halfway point is farther away than my farthest swim, in fact. But it gives me something to do, mentally, looking for the hot dog at the halfway point.

The water is deep, and I cannot see the bottom. This helps tremendously with the seasickness. In shallow water, when I can see the bottom moving in relation to myself, my brain becomes aware of the side-to-side movement caused by the current. In deep water, it's harder to perceive those movements. Maybe that's a big reason why I'm feeling good. Or it could be the ginger. I'm not sure. The only thing I know is that I'm being constantly reminded I took it. With every gas bubble that escapes as a burp, I taste a spoonful of ginger. Better than bile, I guess.

I'm not wearing a watch, so I have no concept of time. My lack of experience at long distances also means I have no mental estimation of how far I have gone, or how much time has passed, or how long I can swim at my current pace. With the adrenaline of the start behind me, I'm swimming steadily in a calm state. The sounds of the water as my body churns through it are a melodic symphony in my otherwise muted, underwater bubble. At times I feel like I'm holding back for fear that I don't have the endurance to go hard the whole way. My mind definitely wants to play it safe. Better to walk away knowing I had more to give, than give it all and not have enough. Mentally, that makes sense to me. Physically, I crave more. I know I can go faster. I just don't know for how long.

I stay in neutral. I'm not drumming my heart rate. I'm being about as boring as you can be, and it's lulling me into a state of indifference. There are long stretches of open water between packs of swimmers. My mind wanders. Looking down, I can see nothing—about twenty feet of clear water followed by endless, dark blue abyss. Every ten minutes or so I come up on a pack of swimmers. I feel a rush of competitiveness and weave my way through, exiting out into the next open patch of water. Then the monotony returns.

But then, finally, the hot dog! It's just what they said it would be: a raft that looks like a hot dog tied to one of the yellow buoys. The hot dog halfway point. This changes things. Now I'm going downhill. Now I have a judge of how much farther I have to go. The thought gives me a jolt of energy. I know I can turn it up. I bury my head and snarl.

I push hard for what I judge to be the next fifteen minutes (remember, no watch to know for sure), then settle into a comfortable yet still aggressive pace, a couple ticks below full speed. With each passing buoy, I'm motivated. I can't wait to be done with the swim. It's not that it's hard—I can swim and I'm doing fine. It's the boredom that's getting to me. You've been reading about this race for five minutes—I've been swimming for an hour. My only break from the physical stress is to listen to my mind wonder whether I have the physical strength to make it. There are moments of excitement at the start and then again when you see the hot dog and maybe when you feel a cramp come and go, but otherwise you're just staring down into the deep, dark depths of various blue colors and frantically moving your arms and legs so you don't drown. Time moves slower with your head in the water and saving your own life isn't as exciting as it sounds.

When I see the second orange buoy, signaling the turnoff back to shore, I've been going hard enough for long enough to have forgotten the fact that I went out slow. It's time for the sprint to shore. I'm almost done.

The course turns in toward Kahanamoku Beach at Hilton Hawaiian Village. You'd have to see a map to fully understand, but it's a tricky area for currents because you have a long break that essentially runs the length of Waikīkī, a man-made harbor, and a small peninsula of land called Magic Island all playing "Ring Around the Rosie." In this case, they're spinning around this swim course, funneling a huge surge of water in toward the beach and then ripping it back out toward the break and along the harbor walls. By the time I realize it, it's too late, and I'm caught in shallow water. The waves come up behind me and push me forward toward shore, only to stop me dead in my tracks and drag me backward, like I have a string tied to my toe. The process repeats as the next wave crashes on top of me. I'm watching the bottom of the ocean as I stop and get pulled backward faster than I was going forward. It's scary. This is how people drown. Now I get it. Now I see how you can be pulled under and tossed around, how you can be feeling great one stroke and then be thrown into a helpless state the next. I'm just waiting out my time in this funnel, trying to swim to the side of it but not getting very far. I remind myself to stay calm and breathe when I can. I'm not the only one caught in it. I can see two other guys. We all came around the buoy together. I try to keep an eye on them, in case they can't get out. When I see another pack come around the buoy, I mentally release myself from the responsibility of looking out for them. I muster up everything I have left and power toward the beach, breaking through the imaginary bubble and catching the current in to the shore.

I swim until my hand hits the sand on the downward pull of my stroke, then stand up. I'm in less than a foot of water. If there's a better feeling than seeing that final orange buoy, it's feeling my toes dig into the sand. I can see the crowd lined up along the chute, a large funnel gradually getting smaller. I run out of the water and across the wet sand, which then turns to dry sand. I hear a man yell out, reading the number drawn on my arm, "Nice work, 219!" It makes me smile and gives me a boost as I slog through the deep sand toward the finish line. As the chute narrows, the crowd noise intensifies. I can see the big clock next to the finish line. It reads 1:29 and change. I contemplate this time for a second before remembering that I have to subtract ten minutes from the total time, since there were five minutes between groups at the start. That means my real time is 1:19. Something about that time jumps out at me, but I can't place it. I cross the finish line as I clap my hands. I'm pumped. And relieved. It's over.

I thought something might happen when I crossed the finish line. Not sure why, just assumed. But all that's there is a person who collects your timing chip from your ankle. Otherwise, welcome to the Hilton Hawaiian Village, thanks for coming, we'll see ya later. The beach is filled with tourists, who look on at the race and the swimmers coming in. I see the people lining the finish chute. I'm very happy with my performance. I'm a capable swimmer and, based on my energy output today, I will have no trouble finishing the swim portion of the Ironman. This gives me such a mental uplift—I cannot even tell you how much different, and how much harder, things would be for me if I had fared poorly. Overall, I finished 146th out of 625 swimmers. In my age group (men 30–34), I was eleventh out of twenty-eight. That's plenty good enough for me. I've got the confidence I came for.

When I get home, I put a splash of vodka in my Gatorade. It's 9:30 in the morning, but I think I've earned it. Besides, the swim is starting to take its toll. I'm feeling fatigued, as expected, and the salt water has made my throat scratchy. More concerning is my armpits—they are *en fuego*. I raise my arm in front of the bathroom mirror to see there's a huge raspberry under each of my arms, mostly along the edge of my chest muscles as they dip down into my armpit. They're burning and chafed. What's more concerning is that there seems to be some internal inflammation in addition to the topical damage. My shoulder sockets hurt, and they hurt a lot. They are sore to the point where it's uncomfortable to raise my arms above my head.

The logical thing to contemplate in this moment is how I'm feeling physically, and whether I could go on to bike 112 miles and run 26 right now. I try not to dwell on that looming question. I'm not supposed to be able to bike and run right now. There's still two and a half months before that question will have to be answered.

September 11, 2017
Waimānalo, O'ahu, Hawai'i
69 Days Until the Ironman

> *The man who had a matter of two minutes lead in the race had an attack of boils, which were very painful. He sat on the small of his back. His neck was very red and the blond hairs were sunburned. The other riders joked him about his boils. He tapped on the table with his fork. "Listen," he said, "tomorrow my nose is so tight on the handlebars that the only thing touches those boils is a lovely breeze."*
>
> —Ernest Hemingway, *The Sun Also Rises*

It takes two days for the soreness in my shoulders to dissipate. I ice them every night by squeezing packs of frozen peas under my armpits. It works well and as they begin to feel better, so too does my outlook on the swim segment. My time of 1:19 puts me in a position where I don't need to improve—I could swim ten, twenty, or even thirty minutes slower and still be in good position to finish the Ironman swim in a reasonable time.

From here on out, I can remove swim training from my weekly concerns. I will let my shoulders heal up this week and then keep them loose by surfing and swimming recreationally as a by-product of living in Hawai'i. I will do no training. I am not going to get in the water and do laps or long distance until the second half of October or the beginning of November. I don't think it will take me more than a couple swims to get in a position to repeat my Waikīkī Roughwater performance in Arizona.

One of my friends asked me yesterday if I enjoyed the race. It made me think for a moment. I did, in the same way I enjoy going to the gym—happy that I went, glad that it's over. I did not overly fall in love with the race itself. I'm not chomping at the bit to race again, if that tells you anything. But I did enjoy it more than, say, a practice swim. Even though the night before a race is not fun—the feeling of something looming—there is an adrenaline high that comes along with the competition. In the running world, this is known as "runner's high." It happens across all disciplines—the strange feeling of euphoria that comes over an athlete—a pill to ease the punishment, if you will.

That all said, it does feel cool to know I was able to do the Ironman-length swim without much of an issue, without much training. It makes me wonder how my time compares to what I'll be up against in Arizona. I find an article* that calculates the average Ironman swim time to be 1:16. It's an imperfect comparison, because it averages the times from many different courses, and not all courses are created equal. The average swim time for Arizona, as reported by that same article, is 1:20. That makes me feel even better. I beat the average time for Arizona—a freshwater swim—on the open-water Roughwater course. I smile as I read. Then it comes to my attention that these calculations have been made across all age groups. It doesn't list the specific averages for the different age groups. Well, whatever. I'm in the ballpark.

Then I wonder: The Waikīkī Roughwater was the swim course for the first-ever Ironman. How does my time compare to those fifteen competitors in 1978? How do I stack up to historical figures, to the fathers of Ironman? The fastest time forty years ago was 57:35 by Archie Hapai. There were a couple others right around the hour mark. But get this: Eight of the fifteen times were slower than mine, including the

* Runtri.com: "How Much Time Does it Take to Finish an Ironman Triathlon?"

swim time of the eventual champion, Gordon Haller. He did the swim in 1:20.

Holy shit, I would have been beating the first-ever Ironman champion at the end of the swim! I realize in this moment that I have to talk to him. I'm assuming he's still alive? It was only forty years ago. I bet he could provide some wonderful perspective on the growth of Ironman. And who better to take training advice from than the very first Ironman? Searching for his name online, he's easy to find. *Sports Illustrated*. *ESPN*. Heck—even Walmart's blog did something on him. I request a connection on LinkedIn and send him a message. Who knows, maybe he'll respond?

I'm hunching over my computer when I hear a knock at the door. When I open the door and pop my head out, the delivery driver waves his hand as he hops back in his truck. I look down at the big box next to the small coconut tree on my front stoop. It is about four feet in length and three feet tall. It's my bike! I take care not to rip the box when I drag it inside. I want to save it for when I transport the bike to Arizona. I carefully cut the tape and unfold the flaps. I look down into the box and see pieces of the bike stashed in different corners. The two tires, pedals, water bottle cages. The main frame and the handlebars are attached by the brake lines. The brakes themselves hang free and dangle.

I hold the pedals and bottle cages in my hands. I have no idea how to put this thing together. None whatsoever. I mean, I can obviously see where the tires should be, and I know the handlebars go in the front. But as far as putting it together with any sort of precision, consider me clueless. I don't know how to align and adjust the brakes, and I don't know how the bike should fit. The sizing session I did at the tri shop determined my size, but it did not give me the specs on the height and angle of my handlebars, nor did it tell me exactly how high my seat should be. Those are important things.

I go see my friend Danny. He's a woodworker in Waimānalo, and used to be a bike mechanic. The bike box just barely fits in the backseat of my Corolla. Lying across the backseat, it touches the doors on both sides of the car. There is no way it would fit in the trunk. I drag the box into Danny's woodshop. As I pull the box, it carves a path in the sawdust on the floor, like a skier's tracks in snow. He walks me through the basic concepts of bike ownership. He teaches me how to put on and grease the chain. He measures out my seat height, shows me how to adjust the brakes, and helps me figure out the best angle for the handlebars. We install the aero bars together, measuring out the proper distance so my forearms land on them comfortably. He says I'll probably have to adjust them once I see how it feels. He instructs me very seriously that the plastic reflector—which came pre-installed on the back of the bike frame—should be removed immediately. He said if I ride this bike with that reflector, I'll be the joke of the Ironman. I tell him I'm going to keep it on there, like a rebel. He tells me I should really take it off. I unscrew the bracket and take it off. We lean the bike against the workbench and stand back to look at it. It looks sharp. The frame is solid white with red lettering. The handlebars and the long, narrow arms that go on either side of the front tire are black. The aero bars make the bike look like a buck with two big horns coming from its forehead.

"It looks good, doesn't it?" I say.

Danny looks at it and nods his head. "It looks good, man, glad I could help," he says. "Now, you know how to *ride* a bike, right?"

I tell Danny he's only getting five beers now instead of a six-pack. We try to put the bike in the car but it won't fit. We have to remove the front tire and twist the handlebars. The chain hits my seat and leaves a streak of grease. I tell Danny I'll come back for the box later. On the way home, I dwell on my lack of bike knowledge. It's something I'm going to have to work on. Here in Hawai'i, I have Danny and the tri shops to fall back on. But what about on the course in Arizona? What if I get a flat tire? What if my chain pops off? Better yet, how am I going to put this thing together once I land in Arizona? I need to know this thing inside and out. Can you imagine going through all this training, spending all this time and money, and then getting a flat tire that you can't fix on race day? That'd be a tough pill to swallow.

When I get home, I jump online. I find out that Ironman races have "roaming mechanics" that ride around the bike course and respond to problems. This makes me feel better, knowing there is assistance to be had. Reading on, though, I learn that relying on the mechanics is a bad idea. The number of competitors who ultimately need assistance, and the sheer size of the course, mean that you could wait a while for help to arrive. I can't think of a worse position to be in, pulled over on the side of the road with a flat tire, with no clue how to fix it, with no help in sight. I'll have to practice as I go along. I am sure I will get a flat tire at some point in the next two months, and I'll be able to practice changing it.

I don't have much room in my apartment to store the bike. For now, it's leaned up against the wall. A bike like this is too nice to keep outside in Hawai'i. Especially where I live, here in the rain forest. Too much water and mold and rust. Besides, I will use it enough to justify its presence in the middle of the apartment. In fact, I'm going to mostly ride it inside my apartment.

I can't remember if I told you already but I bought an indoor trainer for the bike last week. It cost seventy dollars. In a nutshell, it's a triangular, pyramid-like device that sits on the floor and turns a regular bike into a stationary bike. A bracket raises the back tire off the ground while stabilizing the bike, so you can ride in place without falling over. Bikers and triathletes love trainers because they allow you to ride your own bike inside, as opposed to having to go to the gym and ride a stationary when you can't, or don't want to, ride outside. Time on the trainer is also more intense because, unlike when riding outside, you don't have to ever slow down or stop. One guy at a tri shop told me that time on the trainer is worth time and a half on the bike outside. For me—someone who is looking to condense his workouts as much as possible—the trainer could turn out to be a useful tool.

I want to go on a ride right now. I clear off my coffee table and move my computer chair to make room. I set up the trainer and wheel the bike toward it. I put the bike on the trainer. I change into my bike leotard, put on my bike shoes, and get on the bike. It feels sturdy and balanced. I start pedaling.

Bmac said it's imperative I ride the bike I'm going to race on. He said I need to condition myself to the seat. You see, while the stationary bikes at gyms usually have plush, cushy seats, racing bike seats are rock-hard. Why? I have no idea. Wind resistance or something. He said the strength of my legs will mean nothing if my backside is weak. If I don't acclimate myself to the pressure the seat puts on my undercarriage, I'll have a myriad of problems to deal with on rides, including numbness and intense pain. I should build up a tolerance by way of time served, of callouses and the like. This can take weeks or months. I guess that means, with only two and a half months until the Ironman, my days riding the bike at the gym are over.

Which I'm OK with. It's certainly more convenient to ride my own bike. I don't have to waste time commuting to the gym. I can jump on the bike at a moment's notice, jump off to pee without worrying if someone will mistake me for being finished. Riding at my apartment is also more visually stimulating than the gym. One side of my apartment is floor-to-ceiling windows, and my position on top of a small hill allows me to look out into the rain forest. From where I ride, I see mango, banana, and papaya trees. I see the different colors of the plants, the green of the ferns and banana leaves, the dark wood of the mango tree, the burgundy leaves of the ti trees. Right now I even see a half-green, half-yellow papaya hanging from the tree. I can see the white tops of the tarps that hang over the workshop to protect it from the rain. Most of the tarps are, by now, stained by fallen leaves and branches. I cannot see the ocean but I know it's out there, two or three miles as the crow flies beyond the canopy. I feel the breeze come through the windows. The only real downfall is that I don't have a personal entertainment system attached to the bike, like I do at the gym. I don't even have a television. But I do have a desk and a laptop and I can set it up so that it is right in front of me as I ride. I can pedal and watch TV on the computer screen, and then, beyond that, I can look out the floor-to-ceiling windows that reveal the rain forest.

Riding at home is a great opportunity to experiment with food, too. I can incorporate new items each ride and see what treats me best, what digests most readily without gassy or bloating side effects. It's imperative that I practice eating on the bike, and it's easier to try out a variety of things here at home instead of looking like a complete weirdo at the gym. Plus, if I do run into digestive problems, I am safe here at home.

Today I set up a table next to my bike and fill it with different food and drink items—a tasting menu, if you will. Throughout the ride, I sample some of each, to see how my body reacts. I eat a peanut butter and jelly sandwich, a protein shake, some almonds, a GU packet, a Clif Bar, Gatorade, water, and water with an electrolyte tablet in it. Everything goes down fine, although eating that much while working out this hard leads to strong bouts of gas. Here at home, though, I can fart freely without worry.

So, you see, going to the gym is so yesterday. Instead, I can ride in my living room and watch TV on my computer in the comfort of my own home, eat as much as I want, and fill the room with methane gas. That's the reality of it. Bmac warned me about it.

"IM training is long, boring . . . Set the trainer up in a room where you can watch Netflix or whatever, you'll spend a lot of time on this."

There was so much wrong with this when I read it the first time a month ago. Yet looking back, I don't think I took it seriously enough. A part of me thought he was kidding. Like, ha ha, you can watch TV while you ride inside in your living room . . . syke! But you really can, and it's really accepted, and even encouraged in favor of riding outside.

It's hard to ignore the conflict in this behavior. Imagine basing your life around a hobby you need to distract yourself from. You've voluntarily taken up an activity—the Ironman—for which you need to practice. But practicing is something you deem boring, so you distract yourself—you watch TV—while you practice. You're trying to black out much of the journey—the practicing—to get to the endpoint of being in competitive shape. That's all I've been doing—trying to find something that will make me happy while I do something that makes me suffer. It turns the old adage on its head. In the case of the Ironman, it's the destination that matters, not the journey.

It's a big change in mentality for me. My last stint in competitive sports was college volleyball, and I loved the heck out of every practice. I loved playing the game—the more practices the better. It's strange to be involved in a sport where that's not the case. It reminds me of swimming when I was younger, that isolating feeling that comes along with training. Riding my bike in my living room in front of my laptop for the next couple months seems like a good qualifier for any future insanity pleas I might make. Don't mistake what I'm saying. I like riding bikes and going out for a ride is fun. But in the grind of Ironman training, it's not always convenient, or possible, to ride outside because it takes considerably more planning and requires a larger window of time. I have to map out the route. I have to bring food and water (or plan to stop and buy some). I have to make time for my workout during the daylight hours, which can be difficult if I have work meetings or deadlines. I have to deal with the weather, be it heat, rain, wind, or cold (the latter not so much here in Hawai'i, but a major hurdle for triathletes worldwide). I have to consider the possibility of mechanical issues, like flat tires on the sides of busy roads. I have to follow traffic laws. And finally, I have to avoid getting hit by a car. That's not a joke. I know several bikers, competitive and recreational alike, who have gotten into accidents of varying severity, some with long-term consequences. Bmac, for example. And my dad had a scare when I was in high school. He was riding his bike down a street when someone parked on the shoulder opened the car door. He smacked into it, flipped over the door, and landed on his head. Thankfully, he walked away with just a mild concussion. Scary stuff. A lot can happen out there.

Bike accidents don't just happen during training, but during the races, too, and they are not uncommon in triathlons. Perhaps even more dangerous than moving cars are your fellow competitors. Bike accidents happen frequently in bike-only events like the Tour de France, where everyone is an expert biker. So consider what can happen when you have a race with more than 2,000 people who are not necessarily bikers by trade. There's a reason they have medics and ambulances standing by. A simple Internet search reveals the extent of the threat. Several articles retell the stories of fallen athletes, including people who have crashed and woken up in the hospital, days later, with broken ribs and cracked vertebrae.

So, working out on a stationary bike has its perks.

Also, while the gym limited me to daytime TV eye-rollers like live news shows and reruns of *Jersey Shore*, and the occasionally well-timed live sporting event, having the Internet at my disposal makes things a lot more interesting. The possibilities of Netflix and other streaming services are endless. Scrolling through, I see some of my classic favorites—*Friends*, *The Office*, *Planet Earth*—and newer shows—*Breaking Bad*, *Walking Dead*, *Californication*—that I figure could pass some serious time. I also see another show that was once at the top of my list, *Lost*.

I queue up season one and complete my warm-up. I'm using clip-in pedals for the first time. They cost me forty dollars. It's not rocket science, but there is a small learning curve in terms of hooking and unhooking your feet from the pedals. Luckily the trainer acts like training wheels, keeping me upright and allowing me to practice clipping in and pulling out. The show starts and it's hard to hear. When I pedal, the wheel spins on the trainer and a low, bass-driven hum comes from the friction between the back tire and the trainer device. *VVVRRRRMMMM.* I have to turn the volume on my external speaker way up to hear the show. Have you ever gone over to your grandparents' house and been able to hear the television before you even enter the house? Yeah, that's me now, at age thirty-two.

It doesn't take long to realize that *Lost* is the perfect show . . . if I was still trying to bore myself with Celine Dion songs. The slow pace of the storytelling is great for building drama, slowly drawing you in over the course of the episode. But there's no immediate gratification. Time crawls along at a snail's pace. Sweat drips from my legs and pools on the floor below my pedals. I learned a big lesson: Shows that are good to watch when you're not exercising don't necessarily translate into good shows to watch while you are exercising. The melodramatic nature of *Lost* doesn't make time move faster—it makes it move slower. Instead of being a distraction from the workout, the dragging pace makes me more aware of time passing slowly, each minute longer than the previous. It does not make me ride harder. It does not make me want to ride more. It makes me want to kill myself. The 118-minute ride is excruciating.

After my workout, I go online to see if I can find workout-worthy show recommendations for next time. Turns out this topic has been covered extensively by lots of athlete-centered publications, like *Women's Health*, as well as mainstream news organizations like the *New York Times*. The common theme was that people were looking for shows that distract from the "inherent boredom" of working out. One writer was really into superhero movies and shows for their action-packed pace. Another suggested the light humor of sitcoms, or potentially motivating shows like *The Biggest Loser*. I'm not sure what will make the most sense for me. I'm going to have to keep experimenting as I move forward.

Perhaps, in general, I'm spending too much time thinking about what I'm going to watch while I ride. I have bigger problems to worry about. I'm still lacking basic necessities. I still haven't been able to run more than a couple miles without hurting. And, more importantly, I have general life issues to figure out. This past weekend, for example, revealed a new, bubbling problem: My love life and Ironman don't mix.

The problem is that, for all the exercise I'm doing—I worked out sixteen of the thirty-one days in August, and six of the first eleven days here in September—I've become a lazy person. You'll find me sitting on the couch most evenings, just like I have every night since the calendar turned to September. It's mental and physical exhaustion. I'm tired when I wake up, I'm tired when I'm working, I'm tired during my workouts, and I'm dead tired at night. It seems like forever since my last true form of socialization. No happy hours with colleagues. No surf sessions with friends. Not even sex with my girlfriend. Nothing but getting up, eating, working, eating, working out, eating, and sleeping. I don't want to do anything when I get home after workouts. I don't want to do anything, anytime. Nothing. Nada. Prop me up on the couch, and feed me until I fall asleep. The last time my girlfriend and I had sex was five days ago. As I recall, it was because she was overly aggressive about it. I pretty much just let it happen and put in about 7 percent effort. It's sad to say that's the way it's been.

Obviously, the workouts are getting to me. My body is giving all it's got. But there's another side of it, something deeper. It's not only physical. It's mental. A big part of the reason I don't feel the need to do anything at night is because I'm mentally satisfied by my day, and I feel very content about what I've accomplished. All I want to do is pour a beer, make a drink, sit down on the couch, and read or watch something while I consume as many calories as I can. Being social or having sex seems like a lot of work, and my day doesn't hinge on it, thanks to the fact that I worked out for three hours. Maybe this is part of the deal, a little honey in the pot, a beneficial by-product of the extreme training that triathletes value. Maybe if you work out hard enough, alongside the physical complacency comes a mental complacency, gifting you a state of mind into which no other part of your life factors.

An article from Out There Outdoors entitled "Training for a Triathlon: Living With (or Putting Up With!) an Ironman-In-Training" discussed the concept of Ironman training and its toll on relationships at length, quoting many triathletes who say that, after Ironman training and races, they need to do "serious recovery work" on their relationships.

"Nobody is going to understand or sympathize when you don't show up to an event because you had to ride your bike for five hours," one person said.

In this case, I don't want to become one-dimensional by letting the self-induced fatigue send me to the couch each night. But I suppose I can enjoy it for now, at least for a little while. To be perfectly honest, physically speaking, I'm happy to spend my nights free of obligation. I don't think it's fair for me to sit here and pretend like it's a big surprise that I'm tired. Originally, I didn't want this to hijack my life. But maybe it's inevitable with this kind of feat. Of course I'm tired. Triathletes call it "cumulative fatigue," where over time the workouts add up and slowly attach themselves to your body. You're breaking down your body faster than it can recover, and you reach a point where you feel a drag on your energy levels. The answer to this is obvious: more rest. It's the reason most people spread their training out over long periods of time. I can afford to take an extra rest day or two, but that's about it. My training intensity has to go up from here. Nowhere but up, if I want to stay alive on November 19. If I can't rest during the day, then it only makes sense to add more rest at night.

Unfortunately, my girlfriend doesn't agree that sitting on my butt is a good thing. In fact, she was very upset with me yesterday when I had no ambitions for us on a sunny, clear Sunday. I told her I wanted to rest all day. It was a rest day in my workout schedule, and I wanted to actually use it to rest. My body needed it. Real, good, old-fashioned, do-nothing-at-all rest. Plus, there was a Sunday night baseball game on at 2:00 p.m. Maybe we should all kick back and watch it.

Well, you can imagine how she felt about that idea. She said she felt like she was missing out on the weekend, and that I was being lame, not spending quality time with her. I told her to feel free to call some friends and do her own thing, but she said that's not the point, that she wanted to hang with me, since it's some of the only free time we get together. I wasn't particularly a fan of the guilt trip she was putting on me, so I stood my ground. She ended up going to the beach by herself. I sat there all day and watched baseball. I stretched off and on. I ate and ate and ate—cooked fish and sandwiches and protein shakes. I probably consumed somewhere between 3,000 and 4,000 calories by the end of the day.

I did not like the fact that she made me feel guilty for wanting to veg all day. But I can't blame her. After all, I am the one who is working out to death. I am the one who is spending all my free time on this. I was once an active guy who liked to fill himself up with a little bit of everything. Now all the energy I spend is on myself. She didn't sign up for that. I guess while I was developing cumulative fatigue, she was becoming cumulatively annoyed.

I did my fair share of thinking during the game, and I realized that if I'm going to keep my relationship healthy, I need to suck it up, and I need to be proactive about it. Instead of sinking into the couch, I've got to come up with some low-impact activities for her and I to do together on my down days. I don't want to make a habit out of not resting on rest days, but perhaps I can occasionally do a short hike or casual swim. Otherwise, I think being proactive about simple things, like a sunset walk on the beach or a meal in town, would be a good step in the right direction for me.

I think, in retrospect, the confrontation yesterday was a good thing, a chance for a course correction. The training is only going to get more demanding, more time-consuming. I have to actively think about how I'm going to keep other parts of my life afloat, how I'm going to continue to exceed, or at least meet, expectations for each of them. I still have to work. I still have to foster a relationship with my girlfriend. The alternative is that I become a freak who works out all the time, a loner who doesn't have friends and doesn't get laid.

Let's take today for example, when I spent 118 minutes riding my bike in my living room like a fucking idiot. Who does that? Ironmen, I guess. If you didn't before, perhaps now you can see why my girlfriend looks at me curiously nowadays, and why it must be a confusing time for her. Her boyfriend is now riding his bike in the living room while he watches television. That's his hobby now, his zen for the next couple months. Yes, her boyfriend is in great physical shape, and is, in fact, getting sexier by the day, probably not mentally but certainly physically. But, as a result of that sexification process, her boyfriend is one-dimensional, boring, severely fatigued, and consequently less interested in sex than ever. Talk about irony that isn't funny. I am sure significant others develop various amounts of support for triathletes. I think it would be easy to tolerate in the beginning, with resentment slowly building over time. As with anything else, I guess it depends on when you come into the game. It's one thing if you meet someone and it's already a part of their life, and that's what you sign up for. It's another if someone you are with discovers it after you get together. All of a sudden, their life becomes centered around something that wasn't there before. This is what I've done to my girlfriend.

So tonight, I'm focused on making it up to her. I can't do much in the way of cutting out exercise, or thinking less about the upcoming Ironman. But I can try to make our time together more engaging. I'm tired, but I have to suck it up. I'm going to have to put in more effort.

I think a great place to start is in the bedroom. I figure I've been pretty lame of late given my fatigue, and the least I can do is try to spice things up. You know, put some actual effort into turning on my girlfriend, stop being the guy who passes out like a drunk college student the minute his head hits the pillow. The most effort I've put in of late is my nightly request for a full body massage, which prompts her to roll her eyes. I then get in bed and start massaging myself, which prompts her to roll her eyes even more. That's when I usually pass out.

At the risk of sounding prudish, I'm not that good at manufacturing sex situations. I don't consider myself an overly sexual person. Everyone preheats the oven at different speeds and temperatures. Some guys deliver that emotional, pre-physical foreplay in a very physical way, using their body language as kindling, advertising their intentions—and warming up the woman—by sitting close, placing a hand on her thigh, twirling her hair, and other things like that. Many women love that kind of attention. That's never been my style. I like the buildup of real life, of real conversations and interactions, of shared experiences. A slow burn, some might call it. It's very rare that I go to the full-court press.

But in this case, I'm going to give it a shot. If not now, when? I don't think I've ever had more confidence in my body, and a well-oiled romp will do us both good. I need to let her know I'm still thinking of her in that way, and I need to do it sooner rather than later. I need to put myself out there. I need to be . . . sexy.

The foot of my bed faces the door to the bathroom. If you are sitting in bed propped up, you would look straight into the bathroom and see the sink. If you are standing at that sink and looking into the mirror, you see the person in bed in the reflection. I can't tell you how many times I have laid in that bed and watched my girlfriend stand in front of that mirror, pushing one hip out to the side, feeling sexy when she sees me staring, crawling toward me from the foot of the bed, her hair down and her clothes off. I want to turn the tables on this, let her be the one to relax and see the show.

As the night winds down, I fiddle around in the kitchen while she gets ready for bed. I want her to brush her teeth and all that before me, so I can be in the bathroom once she's in bed. As I push dirty plates around the kitchen sink, waiting for her to vacate the bathroom, I feel like an actor waiting to go onstage. I'm nervous. Which is a weird feeling, because I can't tell you the last time I was nervous to have sex with her.

I hear her come out and get into bed. That's my cue. I shut the lights off in the kitchen and walk by the bed, slowly. I'm still fully clothed in board shorts and a T-shirt, but I want to catch her eye, smile a bit, let her know I'm up to something. Instead, I see she's nose deep in a book. She doesn't look up as I pass through into the bathroom. Not a problem, I tell myself. Her eyes are going to be popping out of her head in a few minutes.

I close the bathroom door behind me so I can prep. I brush my teeth with more intent than usual. I scrub my tongue for at least fifteen seconds and swish the water around when I'm rinsing. I cup my hand in front of my mouth and breathe into it to make sure my breath doesn't stink. I'm all good, minty fresh. It's time for the curtain to come up. I open the bathroom door and stand facing the mirror, my back to the bed. I look over my shoulder and she's still reading her book. I put some water in my hands and rub them through my hair. I bend a knee slightly so that my hip comes forward and pushes my butt out, bringing some shape to my board shorts. I can feel my butt cheek pushing against my bathing suit, pulling the material taunt. It's a good feeling. In the mirror, I see her eyes glance up from the book. I have her attention now. She sees I'm doing something. Using both my arms, I grab the bottom of my T-shirt and perform a double-arm, cross-wrist dramatic lift of it, coming up and over my head. In a twist of flair, I twirl the shirt in one of my hands before dropping it on the floor. I look back at her. She's looking up from her book now.

"What are you *doing*?" she says.

I smile but stay quiet. The show is just beginning. I do a series of stereotypical sexual poses, running my hands through my hair, putting my elbows out so my shoulders are broad, turning around to face her and rubbing my chest. To my surprise, I don't feel awkward. Certainly not as much as I do now, writing about it. She's looking at me and the entire thing seems to be working. Now it's time to take my pants off.

I turn and face the mirror. I pull the strings in the front of the shorts and move my hips side to side. It's been a while since I've seen the movie *Striptease*, but I try to channel my inner Demi Moore. I put a thumb inside the waistband on either side, extending my fingers out as I bend forward, pushing my butt out. I wiggle my hips side to side, bringing my shorts down an inch at a time. Before they come off, I look back over my shoulder and smile at her. I want to see her reaction when they slip off.

When my board shorts hit the floor, she brings her hand up to her mouth. "Oh my god, Will, your butt!"

I look at her and she's looking at my butt. The way she says it comes as a surprise. It's not exactly a kitten's purr or a catcall. It's matter-of-fact and filled with concern. Less "oh my god" in the sense of being turned on, more "oh my god" in the sense she's seen something horrific. Huh. Maybe it came out wrong.

"Hunny," I say, turning my upper half around to see her, looking back like I'm on a runway. I shake my myself side to side. I look at her and smile, raise my eyebrows. "You like that?"

"Oh . . . hunny . . .," she laughs a nervous laugh, sitting up straight now, moving her book to the side, leaning against the wall. "Your butt is really red! Come here, let me see it."

I lean back over my shoulder so I can see it. I feel the blood rush from my head. My butt is completely red, big pimples scattered all over its surface. It is a disgusting sight. The tips of the pimples are white and stand out against the red, inflamed skin. I am instantly mortified. I feel like I am going to faint. I check my penis to make sure it's OK. It looks OK. My girlfriend is laughing now.

She tries to cover up her laugh by pretending to cough. "Will," . . . cough cough . . . "what's wrong with your butt?!"

I'll tell you what's wrong—that goddamn bike seat! All that sweat . . . that thing has apparently been making cottage cheese out of my ass for the past two weeks! I'm demoralized, a dancing boy laughed off stage. I don't know what to say to my girlfriend. I pull up my pants and walk over to the bed, my head hanging low.

"Oh my god," I mutter, sitting down on the bed. It's all I can say. There's nothing left to say. The mood is done, dead, without a pulse. I feel like I've seen a ghost. I'm shell-shocked. Worse, I'm hideous.

I fall back onto my pillow. My girlfriend is still sitting up, smiling hard to keep herself from laughing. I get under the covers and curl up tight, my back to her, the side of my face planted firmly in the pillow, my eyes pinched shut. She puts her hand on my hip and goes on reading. I can sense she still has the smirk on her face.

"It's OK, hunny," she says, patting my hip. "It will clear up soon."

That's all I remember before I fall asleep. When I wake up the next morning, my girlfriend is gone. I put the coffee on and head into the bathroom. I take off all my clothes, turn around, and look back over my shoulder into the mirror. My butt is a minefield, a mountainous, crater-filled terrain that looks like it would be fun to trek through. It's very obviously the beginning stages of what the bike community refers to as saddle soreness.

There's a photo on the *Cycling Weekly* site of a bike seat with nails coming out of it. It's a representation of saddle soreness and how painful it can be. Researching this condition online, I notice that publications have a hard time defining it because they don't want to say the words butt, balls, or vagina. For example, *Cycling Weekly* has this to say:

Saddle sores vary between individuals. However, a general description would be a sore, often raised area of skin in the region that makes regular contact with the saddle. Some saddle sores look a lot like spots and these are often caused by an infected hair follicle. Sores that look more like boils are usually larger and can be more painful. For some people, the main cause of pain is more likely to be abrasion caused by chafing.

Bicycling.com takes another shot:

The term "saddle sore" can refer to several different specific conditions, but generally it means problems occurring in the area where your cycling shorts' chamois contacts your body due to ongoing pressure or chafing from your saddle. "You know you have a saddle sore when you have a tender spot that is usually raised, pink or red and in an area that rubs your saddle," explains Chattanooga-based gynecologist Kristi Angevine. For most people, a saddle sore looks like a pimple or an ingrown hair, and essentially, it is the same thing: a bacteria-filled pore. In sensitive areas like in or on the back of your thighs or in your crotch, saddle sores can really hurt, making riding downright unpleasant.

A bacteria-filled pore. Awesome. I'm sure my girlfriend and I will be having lots of great sex in the near future. Within these articles I discover there's a product designed to combat it: Chamois Butt'r.

It's a white, creamy paste that you spread over your butt and surrounding areas. It's supposed to keep everything lubricated so your shorts don't stick to your skin and you don't chafe. At this point, I'll try anything. Maybe some extra grease down there will ease the tension.

I go, pick some up, and return to my apartment. I set up the bike on the trainer in front of my desk, where the computer is set up to watch. I tear open the package and squeeze a glob into my hand. It looks and feels like thick hand cream. I pull my shorts away from my waist with my left hand and go to town with my right, spreading the paste over both cheeks, my grundle, and my penis. I feel the cool temperature of the cream against my warm skin. I walk toward my bike. I can feel the cream between my butt cheeks when I walk. It feels like I've pooped my pants. I sit down on the bike and feel my pants slide on the cream. The seat slips in between my cheeks. I feel like a baby with a full diaper. I shake my head as I begin pedaling. Is this really my life?

September 15, 2017
Waimānalo, O'ahu, Hawai'i
65 Days Until the Ironman

It's better to be absolutely ridiculous than to be absolutely boring.

—Marilyn Monroe

I wake up and check my e-mail. I'm surprised—and stoked—that Gordon Haller wrote me back. He agrees to talk with me and gives me his number! I can't believe it. This guy has been profiled in *Sports Illustrated* and *ESPN*, and here he is answering my query. That's pretty cool of him. He might be famous—even infamous—but he's no stuck-up rock star.

I pour my coffee and read everything I can find about him online.

Remember that sports banquet in 1977, where the idea for the Ironman was originally tossed around? Gordon Haller was not at that banquet. He was at his home in Long Beach. He previously lived in Hawai'i from 1972–74 with the navy, but had since been transferred to Long Beach. He knew many of the athletes that were at the sports banquet, though, and when he coincidentally returned to Hawai'i in late 1977 for the Honolulu Marathon, he was tipped off about the upcoming "competition."

Haller, twenty-seven at the time, remembers the 1977 Honolulu Marathon very well, as he does many of his athletic endeavors. In this case, it wasn't a good day for him. He had to drop out of the race after six miles because of his sciatica. Off the course, he ran into a buddy, who told him about the new race that had been invented—the Ironman. He and fourteen others became part of the organizing committee. Two months later, in February of 1978, those same fifteen people—all men—became the race's first participants.

Twelve of them finished. Haller was not in the lead after the swim. Not even close. His time of one hour and twenty minutes (1:20) left him eighth out of fifteen, and an intimidating twenty minutes behind the leader—and one minute behind me.

Unfortunately for all the other competitors, with the swim out of the way, Gordon was ready to fly. Biking and running were his strong suits, especially the latter. He was named Hawai'i runner of the year three times by the Mid-Pacific Road Runners Club in the 1970s, and won the Maui Marathon twice, setting a course record in each victory. He crushed the competition after the swim, recording the fastest bike time (6:56) and the fastest run (3:27), catapulting him to a first-place finish (total time: 11:46:58). He is heralded, enshrined, and even revered for his victory at the first Ironman. To read the CliffsNotes of Haller's accomplishments paints a very clear picture—the guy is a beast, a fierce competitor who is no stranger to a race. But it's not until I talk to him that I realize the full extent of his . . . commitment. On the phone he speaks with a soft voice, very flat and matter of fact.

"When I first got to Hawai'i in 1972, I didn't know anyone, so I just worked out a lot," he tells me. "I ran a hundred miles a week. I didn't have a car, so I rode 200 miles a week getting around. I swam three days a week. Often what I would do is run ten to fifteen miles in the morning, ride a hundred miles, nap, swim a couple-thousand feet, then maybe run another ten miles.

"Looking back, I was doing about two Ironmans a week, five or six years before the Ironman was invented," he says.

We're on the phone, so he can't see the size of my eyes. I expected the man who won the first Ironman to be an athlete, but never in a million years did I think he'd be this intense. It's confusing, because despite his extreme lifestyle, he's not an abrasive person. He's so soft-spoken about such hard-core exercise that it's difficult to believe he's not messing with me. It is exactly the kind of exaggeration I would use if I was telling a joke, if I was messing with someone. The fact that this guy is serious when he says that he used to run ten miles, ride one hundred, take a nap, swim a couple-thousand feet, and then "maybe" run another ten miles if he felt like it is a little overwhelming for me.

I stay quiet and keep listening, and it only gets better. He tells me he can remember the volume of his training from more than forty years ago because he has kept detailed logs of his workouts in hand-written notebooks that go all the way back to 1969.

For example, he tells me that in the final seventeen days leading up to the first Ironman in February 1978, he ran 187 miles—an average of eleven per day—but rode only a total of twelve miles. He goes on to recall that it was because he had "done a lot of riding previously"—a modest understatement given his 200-mile-per-week history—and that he was still recovering from setting a personal best in the Marine Corps Marathon (2:27, sixth place) and getting past his six-mile sciatica debacle at the Honolulu Marathon.

I don't know what to say. All I can say is "Wow." I say wow after every single thing he says because I don't know what else to say.

"I rode 200 miles per week."

"Wow."

"I was cutting back so I only did eleven miles per day."

"Wow."

"Some days I do all three sports in a row just for fun."

"Wow."

"In January of 1973, I ran a total of 500 miles."

"WOW! Man, that's . . . oh man . . . that's . . . a lot."

"Yeah, I've been called obsessive and what not about that sort of thing, and there may be some truth to it."

I exhale a sigh of relief into the phone so he can hear. "I'm so glad you said that," I say.

He laughs and asks me what I'm up to. It's very clear that whatever training regime Gordon might suggest, it's going to be super insane. I don't bother asking him for a course of action. Instead, I ask him if he'll tell me more about the growth of the Ironman. "Someone told me you and a couple of the original founders filed a lawsuit against Ironman at one point?"

He says yes, and yes—he'll tell me. But he can't right now, because he's at work. I tell him I'll give him a shout in a few weeks, when I'm back from my next string of trips. OK, he says. Until then, happy training.

September 29, 2017
Mata'utu, Western Samoa
51 Days Until the Ironman

What you get by achieving your goals is not as important as what you become by achieving your goals.

—Henry David Thoreau

I must have been put on some kind of mailing list for Ironman, or multiple lists, because all of a sudden, I've started to receive a lot of e-mails from the organization. By a lot, I mean a few per week. All of them are marketing e-mails and they vary in what they're selling. Some are promoting and encouraging sign-ups for specific races next year: Hawai'i, Texas, and Colorado. Most, though, are advertisements that offer special deals and discounts on gear from the official Ironman online store. They seem to have a lot of deals. On September 5, there was a 50% off sale. On September 12, there was an e-mail advertising the final hours of a 50% off sale. It was not clear whether this was the same sale from the fifth or a different one. On September 19, I received an e-mail about a 40% off sale. On September 26, I received a promo code for $10 off a $100 order. On September 28, there was an e-mail promoting the fall collection.

Interestingly, the gear e-mails do not include basic gear, like bikes or running shoes. Ironman does not sell them. Instead, it's a myriad of accessories. Some are related to triathlons: bike jerseys; running shirts; GPS watches; goggles; and the like. Others are pure trinkets, like key chains, backpacks, coffee mugs, jewelry, and pet products. You can also get most of the accessories personalized to any particular race. There's a list of more than fifty past events online and you can get T-shirts, tri shirts, tri pants, swim caps, hats, swim caps, and even pint glasses that bear the logo for that particular race.

I'm going to keep track going forward to see how many e-mails I get from them as Arizona approaches. So far, my favorite is from August 29. The subject line is "*Dress Shirts Designed for Ironman Athletes Are Here.*" The marketing inside insists the dress shirts—which have the Ironman logo on the left breast—are designed for athletes. "The Fit & Feel You

Deserve in a Dress Shirt, You Sexy Ironman You," the ad says. OK, I added that last part, but the first part—The Fit and Feel You Deserve in a Dress Shirt—that part is real. They're made of "athletic performance fabric" with "temperature regulating cooling technology." They cost $120. Give me a break. Who buys this stuff?

In other news, things are better with my girlfriend. I put the humiliating striptease behind me and went for it again. This time, I brought home a bottle of wine and let it all take care of itself. No striptease. No dancing. Just seven hundred fifty milliliters of wine and a wonderful evening together. I turned the lights off so she couldn't see my butt. It all went really well and aside from wondering how long it might take for my cheeks to clear up, I feel pretty good about the whole thing now. She knows this training is temporary, and so long as I make an effort now and again, we will cruise through these next two months, sexually speaking.

Phew. The last thing I need is to take up an Ironman and become asexual in the process. It's a big sigh of relief, considering how impactful the training has been on other areas of my life. With every day that passes, the pressure builds. Am I doing enough? Am I on the right track? Have I put myself in a position to live through this event in fifty-one days? All these questions come up and hints of doubts are what keep me motivated. If you think I wake up in the morning craving a two-hour bike ride and a couple-mile run, you're kidding yourself. While the overall process of getting in shape has its perks, the individual workouts are far from fun.

And though one can anticipate the time commitment that will be involved in the training, I wasn't able to fully understand its impacts until now. On average, I've been working out every other day, both at home and on the road. I cannot overstate what a tremendous amount of physical and mental energy this demands. The physical part is obvious; the mental poison runs much deeper.

Social events? Late nights with friends? Saturdays spent relaxing on the beach? The things I once enjoyed have become distractions, something that stands in the way of my training. Now, these engagements are judged by the impact they will have on my ability to train and ready myself for judgment day. Let's take these last couple weeks for example. My mom was on island, hence why I haven't written. She rented a condo in Waikīkī.

I went and stayed with her for a few days. Sounds dreamy, right? A condo on the beach, within spitting distance of surf breaks and tiki bars. Not so much. Imagine the look on the valet's face when I unloaded the pieces of my bike into the lobby.

"Is there a big race this week?"

"No, I'm just an *idiot*!"

Throughout the week, I had to meticulously schedule my workouts in between work and my free time with her. Because she's in town—because it's a special occasion—I was typically able to convince myself to do "shorter" rides of only an hour. We did a side trip to the Big Island, on which I could not bring my bike. Seeing the volcanoes and stargazing from the top of Mauna Kea served as only small respites from the otherwise nagging, overwhelming pressure to keep the pedal down on my training.

It's no wonder triathletes submit to the lifestyle and go all in. If you are not going to schedule your life around the workouts, and you are determined to schedule the workouts around your life, then you better be ready to take advantage of absolutely every gap in your schedule. All of a sudden, as race day looms, it feels like you have a burden to bear, and any activity that doesn't make you break a sweat is a waste of time.

I've certainly stacked the deck against myself by starting late. Further complicating the idea of "sneaking" in workouts is the fact that I still can't run all that well. If there's a workout to "sneak" in, it would be a run. But thanks to the pesky IT band, I've done only seven runs in September so far (September 1, 5, 8, 14, 18, 24, 27). The longest of those—thirty-three minutes—happened two days ago on the Big Island. I felt good for most of the run, with only slight discomfort toward the end. I've been doing tons of leg lifts and using a foam roller whenever I can. It's getting better. Still, I'm not even close. I need to be able to run 26.2 miles in less than two months.

Another thing complicating my life is my job. I flew right from the Big Island to Samoa, where I am now, for a week-long work assignment. They never end, the distractions, the conflicts. Somehow over the course of the next week, in a foreign land where I'm busy ten hours a day with work, where I don't have access to a gym or a bike, in a world where a nagging injury allows me to run in only small doses, I'm supposed to find a way to further my physical progress. Yeah right, good luck!

For me, this is a crystal-clear window into what life must be like for people who do these races on the regular. The training is so demanding and time-consuming that life must be laid out around it.

I found an article on Active.com entitled "How to Train for an Ironman and Still Have a Life," which I thought might offer hope and promise. Instead, it deflated me further. There are three points made by an expert on how to incorporate training into your routine and still live a "normal" life:

1. The Early Bird Keeps His or Her Job and Spouse—*Get up early and get your workout out of the way.*
2. Share Your Passion—*"If you're lucky enough to have a spouse who also likes the sport of triathlon, you're set for life. Chances are he or she will understand your constant smelly clothes and constant hours away from the house."*
3. You Can Stop at Just One—*Full-length Ironmans take up a lot of time . . . duh . . . consider doing shorter distance triathlons instead.*

In other words, shack up with another psycho-athlete and be sure to quit while you're ahead.

My one saving grace is that I don't have a traditional nine-to-five job. That gives me more opportunities to mix in workouts throughout my day, because I don't have to be glued to my desk between certain hours. I can take a break from writing and go out for a jog. I have flexibility in that way. Though things are a little more complicated here in Samoa, where I have appointments set up and quite a bit of research to do, I can still find a way to mix and match. Today, for example, my plan calls for me to walk through a local village to take in the sights and sounds, to gather visual details for a piece I'm working on. But instead of walking through the village, why not run through it?

I step out of my hotel and jog down the long, stone driveway to the coastal road. It's beautiful here. The sun is shining off the ocean, and it looks teal. There are big, sharp, black rocks poking out of the water. On the left are open-air *fales** and banana trees. I'm in a small village called Mata'utu on the south side of the island. It's midday, hardly an ideal time to run. But I don't have a choice. I had morning appointments and I have afternoon appointments. So it goes. I look at it this way: The more suffering I take on now, the more I'll be able to handle later.

It's blazing hot and humid. The villagers have paused their yard work and refuse to move from the shade. I see many of them sitting under their *fales*, and they wave at me as I pass. I am hardly the first foreigner to come here, although tourism in Samoa is very mellow, and it is low season. I'm certainly the only person here training for an Ironman. Certainly, I stick out. The locals point and laugh as I run by. I can see their wheels turning. Why would anyone be running right now? Why would anyone run at all? Energy here is not spent on the superficial—it's spent in the fields, in the village, and in the household.

Kids wave and say hi as I run past. Everyone waves, even if they laugh at me. It's a sweet gesture, and I appreciate it. It's something you wish and hope for as a traveler, to be welcomed in such a way. However, as far as focusing on a workout goes, it's very distracting. I'm constantly having to smile and wave back at them, and it's difficult to get into a rhythm. If the kids see me far enough in advance—the tall white guy running through their village—they bolt down to the end of the driveway and wait for me. When I get close, they hold up their hands to give me high fives, screaming with delight when we slap palm to palm. It feels like they're cheering me on, and though it's distracting, it's actually invigorating at the same time. It feels like they're spectators and I'm running a race, way out in the lead, in front of everyone else. My triathlete brain says, this is cool! My traveler brain says, you have all these locals being so friendly and opening their world to you, and you're running right by them?

The good thing is that I'm seeing a lot. I notice that every family has a metal rack built on top of a pole at the end of their dirt driveway. This is where they put their trash and recyclables. They have to raise the racks off the ground so the dogs don't get into the trash. I see that almost every

* Hut-like, open-air dwellings of various sizes, similar to the "hale" of Hawai'i.

family lives in an open-air *fale* to take advantage of the sea breezes that flow through. I can see the long, floor-to-ceiling curtains blowing in the wind. I see that everyone has gardens in their yards: Banana, breadfruit, and coconut trees are the three staples. Samoans call the coconut tree the "tree of life." The coconut itself provides food and water, and the leaves of the tree are used to build houses. I see that every household has an outdoor kitchen where they cook over an open fire. There is usually a small, wooden *fale* built over the fire to provide shade. A lot of chickens and pigs mill about. I come upon one little piglet on the side of the road. He's digging around the tall grass and doesn't see me until the last minute. He squeals and runs off into the brush.

Who knows, maybe I'm on to something. Triathletes sure seem to have a lot of money. Maybe I can start running tours around the world.*

I loop through the village and arrive back at the hotel. I ran for fifty-one minutes and, once again, only at the very end, when I had conceded mentally, did my IT band make a fuss. It's a miracle—the leg lifts are working. I've got to stay on them. I hop in the shower and rinse the sweat from my body. I lay on the bed and look out the sliding glass doors at the ocean. I turn on my side and lift my leg, focusing on using my gluteus medius to raise the leg. Then I switch sides. The fan above my head is spinning fast. I keep a close eye on my toes as I lift my leg. I look up at the clock. If I don't hurry, I'm going to be late for my next meeting.

October 6, 2017
Waimānalo, O'ahu, Hawai'i
44 Days Until the Ironman

> *When setting out on a journey, do not seek advice from those who have never left home.*
>
> —Rumi, Persian poet

I'm back from Samoa, ready to kick off what will have to be a big month of training. I'm feeling positive and optimistic about my IT band after

* Turns out, someone beat me to it.

what I was able to do in Samoa. The fifty-one minutes I ran a few days ago marks the longest run of my training. Some of you are probably rolling your eyes, given that I'm a mere forty-four days out from the Ironman in Arizona. Seeing it here on paper, it sure does look bad. How long will the marathon part of the triathlon take me on race day? Four hours? Five? Six? Seven? Yet I haven't broken an hour of continuous running in my training. I know it doesn't directly translate—you don't need to run twenty-six miles in training to be able to run twenty-six miles in the race—but damn. On race day, I will have to more than quadruple my efforts thus far.

It's a similar story for the bike. Though I hopefully and optimistically project I can finish the 112 miles in seven or eight hours, so far, my longest continuous ride has been two hours. What's worse is that I haven't ridden my bike outside yet. I have forty-something days until the race, and those tires have never hit pavement. That is so ridiculous I can't even believe it.

Needless to say, I have a lot of ground to gain, and this month of October—my last full month of training—is going to make or break me.

The thought of how close I am to race day gives me the chills. The only thing I can do is stay positive. I'm banking on the fact that those massive gaps do not reflect my maximum abilities; rather, they reflect how much the IT band has held me back, and how long it realistically takes to build a triathlon-worthy base. With my injury on the mend, and my travel schedule relatively relaxed in the coming weeks, this is the month I can make big strides.

I eat three eggs, rice, and a protein shake for breakfast. I throw on my gym clothes and look in the mirror. Looking over my training log and thinking about how far I have to go does not instill confidence, but looking in the mirror gives me a ray of hope. The past two months of training have left me, all of a sudden, totally ripped. Looking at myself in the mirror, I can't believe it. I'm still just a skinny dude, but now I'm a skinny dude who looks like he works for it. My body, at age thirty-two, looks as good as it ever has. My abs are visible (at least five of them!), my thighs and glutes are rock-hard. People in line at the grocery store tell me I have nice calves. My shoulder muscles puff out like a peacock's feathers, rivaling the aura of my ego. To a regular person, I'm in tremendous shape—athletic and cut and, as my girlfriend told me the other night, "sexier than ever."

Of course, to the triathlete community, I'm still nothing. A nuisance. Another wannabe who is going to crash and burn on race day, if not before. Every time I go to the tri store, they make me feel like I'm doing something wrong. I get the sense some of them are hoping I fail. We shall see. The only thing to do is channel it all—the positive alongside the negative—into fuel for my workouts. Both emotions serve a purpose in motivation, and there's no reason to suppress either. Especially now, as I embark on a week of long workouts, starting today with three hours on the bike and a seven-mile run.

I hop on the bike, crank up the volume on a baseball game, and lean over the aero bars, bringing my face a couple of feet in front of the computer screen. Next to me on the coffee table, which I have moved adjacent to my right pedal, is my feast for the three-hour ride: a GU pack, a Muscle Milk protein shake, and a big piece of naan bread. It's garlic flavored,

Riding a bike is straightforward, but learning to eat and drink while racing is a refined skill. Though it seems trivial from the outside, eating, drinking, and digesting on a long ride is something that must be practiced with regularity.
JACKIE ROBBINS

Narrow shoulders and steady traffic make outdoor training dangerous and hairy. It's one reason why most triathletes prefer to train indoors on a trainer.
JACKIE ROBBINS

Looking back on this moment, it feels symbolic to me, turning my back to the ocean and the offshore island. Despite all the beauty, in the hard moments of training, none of it has any life. Training at these distances is not enjoyment; it's survival. JACKIE ROBBINS

and thus not ideal. But it will do the trick. I also have a bottle of water and a bottle of Gatorade (Fierce Grape) in the cages on my bike. My goal is to consume all of it. Food-wise, it's a reasonable estimation of what I will want to consume over the same distance on race day, and about half of what I should be drinking.

Oh man. I am sure you have been through many boring things in your life, but I guarantee you have never done anything more boring than ride your bike for three hours in your apartment. Holy shit. It takes the old adage of being a hamster on the wheel to a whole new level. I have to get creative to keep my mind active. I watch the baseball playoffs for a little bit, and I FaceTime with my sister and brother-in-law. I thought my sister would be really impressed to see me working out and sweating so much, embarking on this three-hour ride and seven-mile run.

"Hi!" I say. I rest the phone on the handlebars.

"Hi! What are you doing?"

"I'm training!"

"If you can FaceTime while you're training, then you're obviously not training that hard."

My brother-in-law laughs in the background. I hang up on them and go back to the baseball game. I look out the window for a while. The ride is dreadfully boring. I can feel myself growing weak mentally. Physically, I'm having trouble with the seat again.

Since I have left the comfortable, cushy seats of the stationary bikes, riding the bike has been extremely uncomfortable. I no longer care how my underside looks—I've come to terms with it—but I am getting tired of how it feels. The past thirty minutes have been a literal pain in the ass. And the penis. At first it was a small nuisance, a point of pressure that

Symptoms of "the bonk," which include extreme fatigue and sudden lack of energy, can come on fast and hit hard—seemingly out of nowhere—if your nutrition plan is even slightly off. JACKIE ROBBINS

was relieved by shifting my weight around on the seat. Then it was "just a little bit" of numbness. Now, I routinely experience what I can only describe as "Dead Dick," a condition in which my penis goes numb for the entire ride. There are no pins and needles—just complete numbness. The Chamois butt paste helps cool down my butt, but nothing short of getting off the bike can bring my penis back to life. Not the butt paste. Not my girlfriend. Not a bases-loaded, two-out double.

I finish the three-hour bike and then run the seven miles in 52:52 (7:33 minutes per mile). Two days later I do a two-hour ride followed by a five-mile run in 38:04 (7:36 minutes per mile). During both runs, I had to stop at least once to stretch out my IT band.

Neither workout was very much fun, but I'm not going to complain *too much*—my fellow competitors are doing enough of that for all of us.

There has been a lot of chatter on the forums lately about how hard training has become. With just over five weeks until the Ironman, people are in the midst of their peak training period, and I read comments from many athletes regarding how fatigued they feel, how the training is starting to wear them down. I consider responding to these posts by writing the word DUH in capital letters. But I restrain myself and read on.

Apparently, to train for the Ironman is to suffer. If you're not suffering, you're not training hard enough. The craziest thing is to see that many triathletes will admit this without hesitation. They willingly sign up, and willingly partake in the training, all the while complaining about how much they are suffering, how much they can't wait for it to be over. *Remember that the suffering and urge to give up are signs that your training is working*, one person wrote.

As someone who has yet to experience the aftermath of it all, I have a hard time understanding this. Something really cool must happen at the end of it for all these people to openly suffer. At this point, I cannot fathom what it might be, beyond a gigantic sigh of relief. But the forums seem to have an idea. One woman put out a post to her fellow competitors, reminding them that all the training and all the suffering will be worth it when they hear Mike Reilly say, "You are an Ironman!"

Picture yourself crossing the finish line and hearing from Mike Reilly, "You are an Ironman!!" Think about that your whole race and you will get it done.

The board rejoices in this notion. Seemingly, it's the advice they need to hear. For me, a question comes to mind: Who the hell is Mike Reilly? And why are these people obsessed with him? I go to Google to find out.

If you do a search for Mike Reilly, the guy that comes up is a hockey player for the Minnesota Wild. You have to put in "Mike Reilly Ironman" to find out that Mike Reilly is the official announcer of Ironman, the one who screams out "You are an Ironman" after each person finishes. If you didn't know that happened, now you know—it does. On his website, he describes himself as the "Voice of Ironman" and bills his "You are an Ironman" phrase as world famous.

I keep researching and apparently it's true—he is a huge deal in Ironman circles because competitors see that finish-line call (You are an Ironman!) as the seal of their accomplishment. The anticipation of hearing their name called out motivates them to push toward the finish. How famous is he? Consider this: To decide which races he would emcee in 2018, he put up a poll on his website and allowed athletes to vote. More than 10,000 people voted, presumably in an attempt to coax him to whatever event they were racing. I'll say that again: Ten thousand people voted . . . on the race announcer. I'm pretty sure less people vote in local elections.

So, I guess it's safe to say his presence at the finish line definitely has a pull for some people. Whereas I will be picturing a post-race beer the size of a trash can, many triathletes fantasize about Mike Reilly calling their name. To each their own. I try to find out how much he makes for emceeing an Ironman event, but there's no public record and he does not post a rate card on his website. I suppose sending him an e-mail asking him how much he makes would be a little distasteful.

Isn't that crazy though? The fact that this announcer has become a celebrity in that way? I guess I shouldn't be surprised, all things considered. Now that I'm in this la-la land of triathletes, nothing surprises me anymore—there are so many more crazy people in this world than I could have ever imagined. Every time I turn around I learn about a new group of people who are doing something athletically idiotic. In almost every case, processing and accepting that what I'm learning is true and not a joke comes with the same sense of fascination and wonder of the world's most nonsensical realities: religious cults that sweep the floor in front of them so they don't step on microorganisms,* for example, or people who don't have sex before marriage.

I have discovered some of these psychotic endeavors while doing research on the Ironman. Others have been sent to me by friends and family. Apparently I've been at this long enough that my closest confidants now think of me when they come across nonsensical athletic competitions. I don't know whether they think I'd actually be interested in doing the event or not, but they definitely have placed me in the same realm of sanity. They usually send the information over to me with a little fuck-you-type note; something like, "This seems right up your alley!"

For example, one I was sent recently is called the Kona Five. It's an event that takes place every year in Hawai'i in which people do the Ironman World Championship course on the Big Island five times in five days, without any organized support (i.e., aid stations). On its website, it lists five goals of the event. The first is "to give athletes (with the dream of completing the Kona Ironman) not only the opportunity to complete the Kona Ironman World Championship Course one time . . . but five times in five days!"

Another is "to give athletes the opportunity to see the beauty of Kona, Hawai'i (volcanoes, lava fields, beaches, sunrises, sunsets, stars, and moon) . . . all from a unique and unforgettable perspective."

Unique indeed.

In 2017, the Kona Five took place in November and cost $2,950 per athlete, which included eight nights of lodging in the "Kona Five House." Sounds like a reality show on par with *Jersey Shore*. Prospective participants need to apply to take part in the event and also submit to an interview with the event's organizers. There was no mention about whether they needed to undergo a psychological evaluation as part of it.

* If you don't believe me, look up Jainism.

Anyone joining this race with the hopes of being declared world's best triathlete should heed the warning of goal number four: The purpose is "to develop a spirit of comradery and mutual support among all the athletes . . . with the goal to see how many athletes we can get to the finish . . . NOT who finishes first." This is the part that blows my mind, and makes me laugh, because it attempts to draw a line of sanity, to insert a voice of reason. It's saying that doing five Ironmans in five days is totally reasonable—it's wanting to win that makes you crazy.

Spend thousands of dollars and five days of your life destroying your body, proving you have a lot to prove? *Totally!* Show up with the dream of crossing the finish line first? *Don't be ridiculous . . . This is just for fun, brah!*

There are other events of this caliber, including another nearly identical one here in Hawai'i called the Epic5. It's five Ironman-length triathlons in five days on five different islands. After all, anyone can do the same old course over and over.

In May 2017, ten people did the Epic5. They started out with an Ironman on Kaua'i, then flew over to O'ahu and did another the next day, then flew over to Moloka'i and did another one the next day, and so on. It has taken place every year since 2010, and in October 2017, Epic5 announced it was expanding with two more races in 2018. The Epic5 Canada will take place in August 2018 in Nova Scotia (swim in Atlantic Ocean), Quebec, Ontario, Alberta, and Vancouver (swim in Pacific Ocean); in October 2018, Epic5 Mexico will invade Cabo San Lucas, Puerta Vallarta, Acapulco, Cancun, and Cozumel.

At the end of the entry forms for the Epic5, there's a disclaimer you have to agree to before you can submit the application: "By submission of this form, I am expressing interest to be contacted for an interview for a 2018 event. I understand this is not an entry level event, and the team experience can cost $8,000-10,000 USD + travel & other expenses, depending on location."

Never in a million years would I have ever predicted that Hawai'i, a place where you have to weave in and out of people driving ten miles an hour under the speed limit, would be a hotbed for this type of madness. But I guess it makes sense, in some alternative-reality sort of way, considering the modern-day obsession with extreme endurance events started out here forty years ago when the Ironman was invented. And now that I'm two-plus months into my training, I do feel I'm starting to get a glimpse of why events like the Epic5 and Kona Five exist, and why they will most likely continue to grow.

It used to be that I could satisfy myself very easily. Before all this—before I started training like a madman—a couple of workouts a week was all I needed to feel in shape. They didn't even have to be official workouts, where I timed myself, or lifted something a certain amount of times. Practical, fun activities, like hiking and snorkeling and playing basketball, were perfectly reasonable workouts, where having fun was the main ingredient, and the main goal.

But now one thing I can already foresee about "life after Ironman" pertains to the definition of a "perfectly reasonable workout." You begin to develop a new definition of normal. What you once considered satisfactory, or even exemplary, can, seemingly overnight, become unfulfilling.

Consider this mental trap: My three-hour ride and seven-mile run, and then my two-hour ride and five-mile run a few days later. Both were *huge* workouts. From the outside, you might say, "Damn Will, you are a *beast*! In a span of a few days, you exercised, with high intensity, for almost seven hours. That's more than I've done this whole month!" And if you said that, you would be absolutely correct. What's the average recommended workout regime? Thirty minutes of cardio a couple times a week? And here I am, not halfway through the week, with seven hours under my belt, with two huge brick workouts to my credit. One would think, after all those IT band issues and a slow first month getting up to speed, these two sessions would rain confidence.

Yet, I can tell you very honestly I did not feel satisfied. When I arrived back home at the end of the second workout, and came inside to stretch and hydrate, the first thing that crossed my mind was that I had done less than I did two days before. I'm supposed to be building on my workouts, I thought, not scaling them back. I still feel weird about it, struggling with this new vision, and new definition, of accomplishment. There are certainly positives to pushing your limits, but this is perhaps the most dangerous drawback. This is what drives people to the extreme. I've only been doing this a few months, and I'm already feeling the pressure to do more. The desire to do more. The *need* to do more. It's like I've done drugs during a sunrise session at Burning Man and now I can't fathom the idea of going to a nightclub sober. This is the cycle that turns first-time triathletes into lifelong endurance fiends. How can you ever go back to a thirty-minute run before dinner? Once you've grown accustomed to working out ten hours a week (or more), how could a measly trip to the gym on Sunday morning satisfy this mental craving for physical activity? Unless you are very careful, and very disciplined, it's likely that you will slide down this slippery slope, this rabbit hole of constantly comparing what you did before to what you are doing now. The only solution is more workouts, longer mileage, more suffering. That's why the Kona Five is expanding next year. That's why you have ultramarathons and Spartan races. This is the dark hole from which some athletes never return.

Conversely, as grand and boisterous as these events are, the competitors themselves blend into daily life. They're not overly obvious, like a tall basketball player, body builder, or beefy lineman might be. Really, other than small smoke signals, like having defined calves or sporting a watch tan, there's not much to let you know someone on the street is a triathlete. The majority of them look like regular people, mostly skinny and lean but not necessarily, not overly jacked or anything. They walk among us undetected, undercover, until someone in the know reveals their identity to you, or you happen to see them when they're wearing an event T-shirt.

There's a joke that triathletes are the worst people to come across at a cocktail party. While everyone else drinks and dances, a sober triathlete will want to tell you about the 100-mile ride they're doing first thing in the morning. This is, of course, a stereotype, and I can't make a clear judge of it yet. For me, meeting any triathlete is a good thing still, because it's a chance to pick their brain. But, I can say for sure that some interactions have gone better than others. What I'm finding is it's not the accomplished triathletes who pose the problem; it's the wannabe triathletes who talk too much.

Since I began my Ironman pursuit, it seems like I can't go a week without someone introducing me to a triathlete—I had no idea there were so many. This is especially true at work functions, where a talking point like "Will is doing the Ironman next month" serves as a golden icebreaker for otherwise dull conversation. At one such mixer, my colleague introduces me to a friend of his. He breaks the ice and leads the conversation by saying that I'm training for the Ironman. Immediately, the friend begins asking me detailed questions about my training, specifically how long I've been doing it and what other races I've done. He wants to know about my training plan, he says, because he has done a few triathlons. He's vague about which ones and how he fared.

At first, I figure he is expressing honest interest as a genuine way to connect, two new buddies having a beer, chatting. But then I realize what he's doing—ferociously doubting me. He tries to make me feel unprepared by saying that it's "suicide" not to have a marathon under my belt before attempting the Ironman. He tells me "I'm a dead man" if I don't "get serious" about my bike training.

I tell him that I'm not worried about the swim, because I swam competitively for many years and recently completed the Waikīkī Roughwater in an hour and nineteen minutes—one minute faster than Gordon Haller. I throw in that last part to see if it will quiet him down. But he doesn't know who Gordon Haller is. He squints his eyes and nods his head.

"Right, but after the swim did you ride 112 miles and run a marathon?"

"You sound like my sister," I say.

"Yeah," he says, "big difference right there."

I ask him if he has ever done an Ironman. He says he has done a half Ironman—70.3 miles instead of 140.6.

"So how do you know it's a big difference," I ask, "if you've never done one?"

This shuts him up for a second. I tell him about my three-hour ride and my seven-mile run, and my two-hour ride and five-mile run. To me, both are serious declarations of intent—and prowess.

"It's a good start," he says. "After that, you'll just have another five hours on the bike and the marathon to deal with."

I lie and tell him it was nice to meet him. As I walk toward the bar he makes some comment about how I should "keep a close eye" on my drinking.

I bite my tongue. In a few days, I'll travel over to the Big Island to witness Ironman's World Championship Race, where the world's top triathletes will compete. I never thought I'd say this, but I can't wait to get there. Maybe those top-notch athletes will all tell me the same thing, but at least it will be easier to stomach, coming from someone who actually knows something.

Part Three

Behind the Iron Curtain

October 13, 2017
Kailua–Kona, Big Island, Hawai'i
37 Days Until the Ironman

> *It made no sense to me why anyone would care if a small contingent of men wanted to abuse themselves . . .*
>
> —Valerie Silk, Ironman race director, 1980–1988

I arrived last night, a quick flight from Honolulu to Kona. My buddy, who lives in Palisades above Kailua Town, is off island and letting me crash at his place. He's got a view overlooking the coast and the ocean, and a bonsai banyan tree on his lanai, which I really enjoy. Staying here is a huge help for me financially and logistically, especially this particular weekend. The sheer volume of people coming to the Big Island for this event means most of the hotels in Kailua are sold out, and the prices of apartments for rent have been set to cash in on the high demand. Not that Hawai'i is cheap in the first place—a couple of ten-minute cab rides between the race and the house will cost me close to a hundred dollars over the next two days. But at least I can stay for free, and cook reasonable, affordable meals at home instead of eating out.

I'm here to gain a better understanding of the Ironman by attending its flagship event, the Ironman World Championship, held every year in Kailua–Kona on the hot, dry, west side of the Big Island. Referred to simply as "Kona," the race is considered the Super Bowl of triathlons, the biggest stage in the sport. This place and this event are put on such a pedestal that the mere mention of the word "Kona" makes an Ironman stop in place and shiver, like a wind came through and they're not wearing underwear. It's the religious equivalent of heaven to these athletes, a place they are working toward, pining for—a place they will pay dearly to get to, both physically and fiscally.

"That's the aura of Kona: we know in our hearts it holds all of us hostage, now and forever, in a good way," Ironman explains on its website. "For 40 years it has pulled people from all walks of life to its black lava hearth, and after entering its front door we are never the same again."

For Pro racers there are two practical aspects of this reverence: glory and money. Win on the biggest stage, and you solidify your place in Ironman history. Most Ironman events throughout the year have a prize purse of $25,000 to $50,000. This year's World Championship offers $650,000. It will be awarded and distributed to the top ten finishers in both the men's and women's divisions. This event has the most street cred on the line, and it's also the race that can sort you out financially if you place well.

For these reasons, the top triathletes (Pros) spend all year qualifying and preparing for Kona. Athletes competing in the Pro division of races throughout the year are awarded points based on where they place. Each race awards a different amount of points, presumably based on that race's prestige (a regional championship awards more points than the Ironman Arizona, for example). A racer's best three finishes count toward their point total.

Ironman has the framework for the Pro process laid out on its website. In what I consider to be a good glimpse of Ironman's organizational culture, it reads more like a legal document than it does an event description, with a list of defined terms and qualifying explanations that start off with lines like "Subject to the requirements set forth herein . . ." I guess Ironman is striving to make a name for itself—as the only athletic event in the world that gives you the urge to hire a lawyer before you sign up.

Despite the terse language, the process is pretty simple, because, you know, it's a basic process used by athletic circuits all over the world, and even made-up circuits, like Mario Kart. The Pros compete in races throughout the year, earn points based on where they finish, and the people with the most points at the end of the year get to compete at Kona. There are separate standings for men and women. Fifty male and thirty-five female athletes earn spots to compete at Kona.*

Kona's qualifying process is different for Age Group (amateur) competitors. For one, there are far more spots and far more people vying for them—less than one hundred Pros compete at Kona compared to two thousand Age Group racers.

But at its core it is still very simple. The biggest procedural difference is that, as an age grouper, it only takes one strong performance at one race to qualify for Kona (whereas Pros need to be successful in several races). There are no standings or scoreboard. Each individual Ironman event has an allotted number of qualifying slots for each age group. The number of slots allocated is based on, and proportional to, the number of competitors in that age group. In theory, you have the same chance of qualifying regardless of how many people are in your age group. If there are 100 people in the men's 30–34 and 10 in the men's 60–64, there would be 30 and 3 qualifying slots, respectively (I made up these numbers). Plain and simple: Crush the course at your local Ironman and qualify for Kona.

Except, there is one other thing you must do, and you must do it immediately: Pay up. All age groupers who qualify for Kona must seal their commitment to attend the race by paying more than $925 in entry fees . . . within twenty-four hours of qualifying.

Check out this hypothetical: After the Ironman in Arizona this November, Bob is notified that he ran a time that qualifies him for next year's 2018 Kona World Championship in October. Cool! Bob's pumped. He's also probably pretty tired, since he just completed an Ironman. Still, Bob's juiced up. He's qualified for Kona! But, just because Bob has a qualifying time doesn't mean he has actually received the spot. There are still a few hoops to jump through before he's confirmed. Bob must do two big things: 1) The day after the race, Bob must be present at an award ceremony to formally accept the spot at Kona; and 2) Bob must confirm

* These numbers are the standard but not always exact. For example, in 2017, there were forty female and fifty-eight male Pros at Kona. We'll discuss this inequality soon, and use the standards of fifty male and thirty-five female competitors for the sake of the discussion.

his commitment by paying the nonrefundable* $925 entry fee for Kona by the end of the day. That means Bob has less than twenty-four hours from the moment he crosses the finish line to decide whether he is going to commit to going to Kona. Which, to reiterate, is in Hawai'i, and will cost, on top of the $925 entry fee, a couple grand for flights, hotels, and logistics. That's if he goes alone. If he decides to bring his family to Kona, so there's someone to peel him off the road if need be, Bob will have even more logistics on his hands.

When I read about this last week, I asked around to see if the pushy process bothers anyone. It doesn't. This is *Kona*, they said. You shouldn't even have to think about it—of course you will go. Whatever the cost, you *have* to be there. You're so *lucky* to have the opportunity to go. Think of how many others would *bleed* to be in your spot.

All right, fair enough. I get it—demand's high. But how high?

The Internet clues us in to the answer. In 2015, demand for the Kona World Championship was so high that more than 14,000 triathletes who failed to qualify on their athletic merit each paid $50 to enter a supplemental lottery held by Ironman. From this pool, one hundred names were drawn and given a spot at Kona, regardless of athletic ability. Lottery winners still had to pay for the spot—an $850 entry fee** and thousands more in travel expenses—but they were in, without qualifying.

Consider the reverence on display there. The fact that they didn't earn a spot didn't matter to these athletes. The fact that it's going to cost thousands of dollars doesn't matter. You *have* to be there—it's *Kona*.

Unfortunately for many hopefuls, the lottery has been shut down. Turns out it was illegal, and Ironman paid $2.7 million in penalties to the US Department of Justice for hosting it. Florida newspapers covered the story significantly because the World Triathlon Corporation (WTC), Ironman's parent company, is based in Tampa. The *Tampa Bay Times* reported that "because the practice involved an entry fee, chance and a prize, it violated Florida's anti-lottery law and other considerations

* A partial refund of $175 can be obtained if a participant withdraws by a predetermined deadline, usually the end of August, before the October race. Ironman also sells an insurance plan called the Full Refund Plan that covers injury and other life occurrences, like pregnancy.

** At that time, the entry fee was $850 and has since been increased to $925.

made it a violation of a gambling provision of federal racketeering code." In other words, they were running an illegal lottery.

In an author-less company statement posted on its website, Ironman said it was proud of its lottery system because it "has changed lives." The statement said the company had done nothing wrong and was only settling so it could get back to business as usual.

> *We are proud of the longstanding tradition of the IRONMAN Kona Lottery. Thanks to the vision of IRONMAN Co-founders, John and Judy Collins, the IRONMAN Lottery has changed lives and provided athletes of all abilities the opportunity to participate in the world's most challenging and iconic one day endurance event, the IRONMAN World Championship in Kailua–Kona, Hawai'i.*
>
> *The IRONMAN Kona Lottery has operated in a substantially similar manner since 1983. Several months ago, the Tampa office of the U.S. Department of Justice contacted IRONMAN to claim that the IRONMAN Kona Lottery is not compliant with existing lottery and gambling laws. Since that time, we have fully cooperated with the Department of Justice through a series of meetings and correspondences. As a result of our cooperation, the Department of Justice and IRONMAN have come to an agreement to no longer operate the Kona Lottery in its current form. While we do not agree with U.S. Department of Justice's interpretation of the relevant statutes or that there has been anything untoward or inappropriate in our operation of the IRONMAN Kona Lottery, IRONMAN chose to settle so that we can focus on our priorities—our athletes and our events.*

The *Tampa Bay Times* provided details on the financials for the 2015 lottery:

> *The complaint states that WTC represented to athletes that it was "unable to release exact numbers" with regard to the number of people who register for the lottery or the chances of being selected; however, the complaint concluded that WTC received 14,254 entries for the 100*

slots in the 2015 lottery. The complaint says WTC earned more than $10,000 per open slot it awarded via lottery.

You can go online and find a million different opinions about what Ironman did with the lottery. Interestingly, a lot of the debate is not about whether or not Ironman broke the law. Triathletes seem less concerned with whether a law was broken and more curious about what the information released during that lawsuit—i.e., the financial stuff—says about Ironman and the way it operates. Some were turned off by the lottery for its very nature; some saw it as a reasonable business decision.

For example, here are a few of the voices from the comment section of Ironman's statement on the lawsuit:

HOORAY FOR THE US JUSTICE DEPT!!! IRONMAN was charging big money for a slim chance to purchase a Kona slot at full price, which I always found distasteful and inappropriate, and which I am now happy to find out was also ILLEGAL.

As much as I admire the Ironman athletes, I despise the organization. I am happy to hear that the DOJ is cracking down on this lottery scam. . . . Shame on Ironman for screwing the nonprofessional athletes.

Others said, hey, no one forced anyone to enter the lottery. Why blame Ironman?

Wow, so many people with such sad remarks. First, anyone who enters the lottery isn't forced to do so. They do so by choice, knowing well in advance the odds of getting a slot. That's called making an informed, responsible decision. People should be allowed to spend their own money however they see fit. Whether it be on a $10,000 bike like some of you haters or on a Kona lottery slot.

The only outrage in this decision should be the fact that the DOJ is now involved in my triathlons! . . . Everyone who entered made that *decision because they wanted to go to Kona and were willing to part with $50 for that opportunity.*

Ironman paid the $2.7 million fine and has moved on. Since paying the fine, there has been little talk of the historic lottery. But, another controversy from that fateful 2015 season still forms a cloud over the brand today. This one is a little heavier, because it has many opining that Ironman has been unfair to women.

You may have taken notice earlier that there are fifty male slots but only thirty-five female slots for the Pro division at Kona. This difference was brought to the forefront in 2015. At the center of the push was an organization known as TriEqual. Aside from the obvious gender equality issue, TriEqual claimed the fifteen fewer spots for women had drastic implications:

Professional athletes need support from sponsors in order to have the time and financial stability to train and race. This financial stability often comes from sponsors, and sponsors want results—specifically seeing their athletes racing on the big stage at Kona. As there are more opportunities for professional male triathletes to race in Kona, there are also more opportunities for greater exposure. Less opportunity for professional women to race in Kona means less of that exposure necessary to secure and maintain vital sponsorships. Providing equal slots for male and female professional triathletes puts male and female triathletes on a level playing field.

Through social media and organizations like TriEqual, attention to the disparity spread throughout the triathlete community and into the mainstream media. The discussion and call for equality became such a hot button issue that Ironman put out another of its author-less statements on April 1, 2015,* entitled "The reasoning behind the allocation of Kona qualifying slots." Here's part of what it said:

* Ironically, this was a month after Ironman settled with the DOJ on the lottery case. In fact, the lottery is mentioned in Ironman's response to its gender-equality accusations.

Qualifying for the IRONMAN World Championship is extraordinarily difficult. Just completing one of the 40 full-distance races around the world requires courage, perseverance and dedication. Earning a Kona qualifying spot puts you among the world's endurance elite; only three percent of age group athletes qualify for Kona. As the sport of triathlon has surged in popularity over the last 15 years, managing the immense global demand for the most popular and iconic triathlon in the world—the IRONMAN World Championship—takes a principled approach as there is a finite number of spots the race can accommodate.

. . . The system isn't perfect. Since IRONMAN commits that each and every age group has at least one qualifying spot and that slots not taken in an age category roll down within their gender, women receive, proportionally, more slots for Kona. In 2014, 19 percent of IRONMAN athletes competing in full-distance qualifying races around the world were female while 28 percent of those who competed in Kona were female. The same holds true in the professional ranks due to the Kona Points Ranking system qualifying process: 34 percent of pro athletes competing at qualifying races last year were female, yet 42 percent of the professionals who raced on the Big Island were female.

The goal of the Kona qualifying system is to ensure that age groupers, regardless of gender or age, have a roughly equivalent path to Kona. In this spirit, arbitrarily increasing Kona representation of females or specific age groups would be unfair since the additional slots would come at others expense. It would also create a separate, lower standard of performance for the arbitrarily advantaged group, which is antithetical to the spirit of IRONMAN.

IRONMAN is committed to growing female participation in triathlon. Ultimately IRONMAN would like to see a balanced number of men's and women's slots thanks to the overall growth of female participation in the sport. The Women For Tri initiative with Life Time Fitness is designed to identify ways to increase female participation in the sport of triathlon, which, in turn, should increase both the relative and absolute number of female athletes racing in world championship events. We look forward to playing a leadership role in growing female participation in the sport of triathlon.

It is for these reasons that there will be no changes to the current qualifying procedures in 2015.

Why Ironman's public relations department chose to operate like a doctor who slept through the class on bedside manner, I'll never understand. Fuel had been thrown on the fire. As you might imagine, that explanation did not sit well with many—not only the explanation and refusal, but the touch of arrogance in the opening paragraph ("... *managing the immense global demand for the most popular and iconic triathlon in the world . . .*").

The comments on the statement were interesting to read. Some vented and called for a boycott, like one woman who said, "It seems the 'power house' brand feels it can do whatever it wants, because their confident that they'll bank on events anyway. Well, being so blatant about your discrimination without wanting to change, will eventually lead to your own demise. There are so many non-Ironman events out there that people will realize they would rather participate in events away from Ironman in order to make you realize you need to change."

Others pointed out hypocrisy and contradictions in the explanation. "So you can magically create more slots for 'charity' and publicity stunts, but not for more women pros? Bullshit," one woman wrote.

Another woman wrote about one such publicity stunt, when Ironman allowed celebrity Gordon Ramsay, who had never done an Ironman before, to participate at Kona in 2013: "So many things wrong about this pronouncement. No mention of the actual issue of pro equality. Instead we get misdirection and faux analysis. Are you stupid? Or do you think we're stupid?! And if toeing the start line at Kona 'puts you among the world's endurance elite,' why was Gordon Ramsay racing his first Ironman there? I would take an extra female pro over that man every time. You are on the wrong side of history. You just don't know it yet."

Still another wrote, "Extremely disappointed in you IRONMAN. As an age group athlete I look up to the pro women. You have disregarded the female pros on so many levels. It is funny that you try to say this is unfair for age groupers yet you allow celebrities entry to these championship races without them having to ever enter another race!?"

The common theme was that people could not get behind, or really even comprehend, Ironman's reasoning. As an outsider reading back through it all, I can't help but wonder why Ironman put itself through all this negative exposure for fifteen spots. There has to be something more to it.

Commentary was not limited to individuals in the comment section or on social media. Major media outlets also picked up the story. Right after Ironman released that statement, *Outside* ran an article on April 6, 2015, entitled "The Fight for Gender Equality in Ironman." In it, the (female) author praises Ironman for its mostly fair gender policies—equally split prize pools, for example—but argues that the unequal representation in Kona is a problem that should be fixed. CEO Andrew Messick's quotes in the article offering extended reasoning for the company's decision only further aggravated onlookers. He said, in so many words, that giving more women more slots could water down the competition and lead to a reduction of the World Championship's prestige. He also was on record saying that adding fifteen spots to a race of this size (at the time, the race had 2,301 competitors) was difficult due to capacity issues.

Most people didn't buy the capacity argument, considering Ironman had, in the past, made room for celebrities and had, in fact, added 145 age-group slots to Kona the year before (before its 2014 race). The latter is unsettling in that it reveals an interesting side note: Age groupers pay $900-plus to compete at Kona; Pro racers pay $900 per year to be a part of the circuit, and do not pay an additional entry fee if they make Kona. In other words, adding 145 age groupers brings in $130,500. Adding fifteen Pro racers is not the same.

The watered-down competition argument is more complex, but is disputed by TriEqual. TriEqual says it subscribes to the idea that "participation follows opportunity." It opines: "Prior to the passage of Title Nine in 1972, only 29,977 women participated in college sports. Over the next 35 years, women's participation in college sports increased by 456%. Today, over forty years later, 45% of college athletes are women.

Greater opportunities for collegiate athletes encouraged greater participation at all levels and particularly increased participation by girls in youth sports. Increased professional opportunities for women in Kona will increase participation for women at all levels in triathlon. Conversely Ironman's current regressive policy serves as a deterrent to women interested in long course triathlon."

A few months later, in October 2015, Vice Sports took a look at the issue in a piece entitled "The Push for Equality at the Ironman World Championship," as did *Sports Illustrated* in its story "Making a Case for More Women in the Ironman World Championship." Another interesting read came via ESPN in October 2015. The headline was "Ironman Power Couple Sees Kona World Championships Gender Gap First Hand." It relayed the story of Beth Gerdes and Luke McKenzie, two consummating triathletes who put in thirty hours of training per week each. The article takes a deep dive into the debate over the unequal representation, specifically showcasing how Luke, a man, had already qualified for the 2015 World Championship with 4,450 points, but Beth, a woman, still had not with 4,515 points. Again, the main point was the principle of the matter—it's not fair that women with more points could be excluded on the grounds that men have fifty slots and women have thirty-five. Ironman was involved in the article, and once again stood its ground.

> *[CEO Andrew Messick] explains that because there are more male professional Ironman competitors than female—about 650 vs. 350 (not all of whom are eligible for Kona qualifying)—it would give women an unfair advantage if they had 15 more slots.*
>
> *"We just philosophically don't agree that having the same nominal set of slots is a fair outcome because you are making it dramatically easier for female pros to get to Kona than male pros," he says. "And we don't think that's right."*

While I was hard-pressed to find a media outlet or article that defended Ironman's stance on the gender issue, I did come across individuals on social media and in article comments that expressed support.

"I actually think the number of slots available should be based on the number of pros competing on the Ironman circuit for each gender," one man wrote. "I am not sure but I believe there are less women competing so there should be less slots. That's the way it works for age group slots. Otherwise it would be easier for women pros to qualify if a greater percentage make it."

After that bubble of media coverage in 2015, the debate sat like an elephant in the room until recently. This year, Ironman announced it was changing the qualification process for Kona. The changes, according to TriEqual, come with pluses and minuses. On one hand, the new qualification specs make it possible that the same number of women line up alongside the men at Kona. On the other, it doesn't guarantee it, TriEqual said.

TriRating.com projects that the new process, which goes into effect for Kona 2019, will mean a total of forty-one female slots and fifty-nine male slots. TriEqual comes to a similar conclusion, estimating that there will be somewhere between forty-three and forty-seven women and somewhere between fifty-three and fifty-seven men at Kona in 2019.

That's where we stand today, waiting to see how the actual numbers play out in the years to come.*

The race is tomorrow, first thing in the morning. Today, I'm going to head down into town, to see if there are any triathletes hanging around, see if anyone's doing anything weird. From where I'm staying, it's eleven miles to the event center in Kailua–Kona. I figure, why not run down there? I can plan my route so that a lot of the run takes place on the actual World Championship course. I think that will be a cool experience, to actually run it and see what it's all about. I am sure there will be other athletes doing the same.

The thing to know about the World Championship course is that, while it does not contain the extreme hills of some other courses, it boasts

* I encourage you to follow up on the issue. Due to the lengthy publishing process of books, we are not able to update or include the numbers for the 2019 World Championship.

one of the most torturous stretches of terrain on the circuit. The bike and run course are centered around Queen Ka'ahumanu Highway, which cuts through the hot, dry, barren lava fields of the Big Island's west coast. It is subject to extreme heat and high winds and I don't think there's a single shade-providing tree, building, or structure on any stretch of the highway. The sun beats down on the black tar of the road and the gray and brown hardened lava, and reflects right back into your face.

When I make a left-hand turn onto Queen Ka'ahumanu from Kaiminani Drive—more or less across from the airport—I'm already four miles into the run. From here to the finish area in Kailua–Kona, it's seven miles. Up until this point, my track had been downhill coming from Palisades. There had been trees lining the sidewalks and I had been able to find shade. That luxury now comes to an end on the World Championship course. The projected high today is 88 degrees, and it feels every bit of that here in the eleven o'clock hour. The small, rolling hills seem longer because of the heat, and the road plays tricks on my mind. There's a mirage at the bottom of every hill, a twinkle of light off the blacktop that looks like water. There is certainly no water. Kailua–Kona is one of the driest places in the Hawaiian Islands, receiving only eighteen inches of rain per year.* A couple of bikers and runners are out on the road. They seem very serious. Most of them are coming from Kailua–Kona, probably headed up toward the airport. I smile and wave at them when I pass. Most of them ignore me. I don't take it personally—it's likely they are realizing the extent of the misery they will suffer tomorrow on this same road.

I start to hit a wall around the nine-mile mark. It's so hot. My shirt is drenched, the tips of my hair wet. My arms are starting to sunburn. Really, the only thing I have going for me is that my IT band isn't bothering me. Every once in a while, I sense that it's one wrong step away from aggravation, but I try to stay mentally strong and avoid thinking about it. Luckily, there are other miseries to focus on.

I've got a GU packet and a credit card in my pocket. I'm an hour and twenty minutes into the run, and I'm overdue for nutrition. I also haven't

* Compare that with Hilo on the other side of the Big Island, which receives close to 130 inches per year.

drunk anything since I started. I see a gas station across the street and decide to run in. I buy a twenty-ounce Gatorade and find a slice of shade under the overhang on the outside of the building. I open the GU packet and suck it down, running my fingers from the bottom to the top to squeeze it all out. Then I follow it up with the Gatorade. I consume both in less than forty-five seconds. I'm out of breath when I finish drinking it. I feel like I could drink six more Gatorades.

This terrain is the opposite of what you picture when you think of Hawai'i. There is beauty to it, when you're admiring it from a geological perspective. That appreciation is hard to summon when you're left exposed to its elements. Though you can see the ocean at certain points from Queen Ka'ahumanu Highway, you are by no means cruising oceanside. The wind for which Kona is known is not your average ocean breeze. You are basically in the desert. You are on a pitch-black asphalt road in the middle of a lava field.

Once again, the beloved nature of the course confuses me. Quite frankly, from what I've seen, this course is for masochists. It's torture. Its beauty is—let's call it understated—in the face of the heat and the sun beating down and the black asphalt and the fact that you have to bike and run on it for the better part of a day.

To be fair, the location was not selected for its beauty. If you remember, the Ironman started on O'ahu in 1978 with the original fifteen. That inaugural race, the one following in 1979, and the one in 1980 were all on O'ahu and combined the three existing races we talked about, the Waikīkī Roughwater, the Around-O'ahu Bike Race, and the Honolulu Marathon. In 1980, a woman named Valerie Silk, who co-owned some local fitness centers, became the race director.* She served in that position or as chairman until 1988, meaning she presided over, and was responsible for, the race's drastic transition. The first two Ironman races in 1978 and 1979 both had fifteen competitors. After the 1979 race, *Sports Illustrated* released an article about the Ironman. After sponsoring the 1979 race, Silk agreed to take over the planning for the 1980 race, but instead of a small, fifteen-person affair, participation jumped more than 700% to 108,

* In 1979, her company, Nautilus Fitness Centers of Honolulu, sponsored the second Ironman.

thanks in part to the *Sports Illustrated* article. The 1980 event was televised by ABC, and participation exploded again for 1981, from 108 to 326. In 1982, a competitor named Julie Moss helped Ironman make world news when she, collapsing every other step, eventually crawled across the finish line.* At the end of Silk's tenure in 1988, the number of participants had surpassed 1,000.

Funny thing is, she apparently didn't even want to run the race, nor did she think it would become a big thing. An Ironman.com article** reveals that when she was first asked to take over the race, she said no.

"Frankly, I hated the event," Silk told Ironman.com. "My number one priority was running the [fitness centers]. And the race was a horrendous drain on the business, both in terms of personnel and funds. It made no sense to me why anyone would care if a small contingent of men wanted to abuse themselves in that way. It just made no sense to me."

Luckily for everyone involved, Silk stuck with it and found success. In 1981, she moved the race to Kona. She felt O'ahu posed too many problems with congestion and logistics. She told Ironman.com back in 2003—before the twenty-fifth anniversary—that she made the decision because she felt the Big Island was "the safest" for an event of this kind. The event was growing, and long stretches of country road were just what the doctor ordered.

Interestingly, after calling the course a "sauna" and pondering the appeal of its desolate lava fields and howling winds, that same article asked Silk to comment on the reverence for Kona. Why do people worship it so?

"Once you've biked the Queen K you've been to hell and back," Silk said. "That became part of the mystique."

In other words, it's the torture they love. The suffering becomes part of the allure, because the more suffering you overcome, the greater the sense of accomplishment in triathlete circles. I've already identified this path to addiction in my own training, in the definition of a "perfectly

* Google "Julie Moss Ironman crawl."

** The article is worth a read. It's a tribute to her, but its odd title makes it seem like there is bad blood: "If Valerie Silk Had Gotten Her Way, There May Never Have Been An Ironman."

reasonable workout." It seems a tougher challenge is always needed to obtain the same amount of satisfaction and accomplishment. It's about proving you can do more and go farther and it's about taking pleasure in the suffering it brings.

I am not taking much pleasure in it at the moment. I'm slogging up the last hill and getting ready to turn off down the main drag of Kailua-Kona. The lava fields are gone, replaced by concrete sidewalks and shopping centers. I make the right turn down Palani Road. It's a downhill slope, and I decide to stride out for the final quarter mile. It feels good to be off the highway from hell and closing in on the waterfront. I let my legs loose and swing my hips farther than normal, almost twisting to allow my legs to reach farther and my trot to lengthen. I can feel the breeze and the temperature dropping as I close in on the ocean. But the incredible feeling of being almost done is suddenly interrupted. I feel a pinch in my left leg, below the knee. It's my IT band. It's had enough. Maybe striding out aggressively eleven miles into a run—my longest distance of training to date—was not such a great idea. My jog slows to a power walk and finally to a frustrated walk. My hands are on my hips. I can see the ocean now from Ali'i Drive and I don't care. This sucks.

I buy a water from the ABC Store and sit down on the curb. I begin to cool down with the help of the breeze. In front of me I can see the main entrance to the harbor. I drink the water and look at the ocean. Five minutes later I feel better. My IT band has relaxed and calmed down, and so have I. OK, I think, remember what you've told yourself all along. It's the big picture. I had a good day on the course. I ran eleven miles in 91:37, an average of 8:11 per mile. That's pretty damn good. It was the longest run of my training, and the longest of my life! Three weeks ago, I couldn't get past two miles without my IT band flaring up. Today, I went eleven. That's improvement. That's something to be happy about, even if I would still have fifteen miles to go.

I stand up and walk down Ali'i Drive. It's waterfront, and quite nice. This is where the finish line will be tomorrow. I'm done pouting, and I've got more exploring to do. Just down the road is the Ironman Village. It's full of tented booths, bought and paid for by sponsors and partners who want to sell their gear to participants. I'm interested to see what's there, for curiosity's sake. I also still need to get a wet suit, so maybe I can find one there. I walk onto the field-like lot with its tents, back-to-back-to-back. Clif Bar has a stand, and I grab a sample bar from them. Chocolate something or other. I eat it in four bites. There are other tents from a variety of companies I've never heard of, all selling high-end gear of some sort, everything from tires to T-shirts. There's a booth for this workout powder that you make into a shake. They have one for energy, one for recovery, one for pre-workout, and one for bedtime. I contemplate this—is there really such a difference that you need four different formulas for four different times of day?

At the far end, I see a sign for Roka. I recognize the name. Drew told me they were a popular wet suit maker. I have also seen a lot of ads for them in various places over the last couple months.* They are a regular sponsor of Ironman. I start looking at the wet suits. A representative comes over and launches into an explanation about the different types of wet suits they offer. I can see obvious differences—some are sleeveless for example—but he's diving deep into the cuts of neoprene, or some number of the neoprene. When I ask him about the different sizes, he says most people wear a wet suit that's too big. I should buy the smallest size I can squeeze into, he says, adding that a wet suit should be tight enough that it takes ten minutes to put on. Ten minutes? Sure, he says. Covering your skin with a wet suit makes you swim "ten seconds faster per hundred meters," and the technology of the suit makes it easier to swim because the whole suit is not the same thickness. The thickness is different on your chest and under your arms and shoulders—maybe three millimeters in one place and two in another—so as to reduce the resistance of your stroke as much as possible. All I can focus on are the price tags. Nine hundred dollars. Seven hundred dollars. Do you have anything cheaper? Here's one for $400. Yeah, OK. Four hundred dollars. Sure.

The wet suit will have to wait a little bit longer. My legs are starting to feel sore from the run. I decide to walk back to the center of town. As I'm making my way back through the village to the exit, I see a tent I

* Because I had been doing so much research on Ironman and triathletes, the targeted Google ads displayed a lot of Roka ads to me.

missed before. It catches my attention because a guy is seemingly drilling into an athlete's back out in front of it. I don't know how else to describe it. Picture a huge power tool, with a thick plastic handle, a big on-off button near where your thumb would rest, and a huge, mechanical piston on the end that pounds back and forth when you turn it on. I approach for a closer look. It's a massage gun called the Theragun. I *love* massages. I have to try this thing. I approach the table and ask about it. The Theragun G2PRO, as it is fully named, is a massage "gun" that uses vibration therapy. At the end of the piston is a large round ball that springs back and forth very quickly and punches your skin. The handheld nature of it allows you to massage most of your body by yourself. The guy hands me the gun to try it out. When I turn it on, it buzzes like a piece of heavy machinery. It makes me think twice. Is this thing safe? When I touch it to my thigh, I can feel my muscles vibrating, and I can see the ripples flow through the muscles in my leg, like the way the grass is blown by a helicopter overhead. It sounds like I'm boring a hole through my leg, but damn does it feel good. I ask him if it will help my IT band and he assures me it will. I look at the price tag: $599. I tell the attendant I could never afford it. He offers to let me try it out at home for a couple days, on a loan, no questions asked. OK, I say, let's do it! I fill out some paperwork and he packs it up in a padded briefcase and hands it to me.

I shake hands and make my way to the exit and turn back toward the center of town on Ali'i Drive. Not bad. Walk in to the Ironman Village empty-handed, come out with a six-hundred-dollar massager packed tight in a cool, sleek briefcase. I'm done with the official Ironman stuff—I'll see plenty of that tomorrow—but I still have one mission I want to carry out before heading back: I want to see if, on the eve of the big race, I can find any athletes destressing. There are a bunch of bars in this area. Might I find someone erasing a few pre-race jitters?

The first bar I go into is absolutely empty. I mean no one is in there at all. I go next door and it's a different story there. The restaurant is packed, and so is the bar. Many athletes are eating at the tables with their families. But no one is drinking. I see a lot of water cups. At the bar, it's mostly older men and couples who are obviously not participating in the race tomorrow. Hmm . . .

I check farther down Ali'i Drive. A few bars sit right on the road next to the finish line. I feel like James Bond carrying the briefcase as I pop my head in and scope out the bar. I don't see any athletes. It's a small place, and the barmaid sees me. She tells me to come sit down.

"That's OK," I tell her, and I hold up my hand and wave.

"You looking to come back tomorrow?" she asks.

I tell her that I don't know, should I? She points to a flyer pinned up behind the bar. The patio overlooks Ali'i Drive, she tells me, and you can reserve a table for tomorrow to watch the racers sprint toward the finish line. Two hundred bucks per seat to reserve it, she tells me, and they only have two left. I tell her thanks, but no thanks.

The last place I want to check is Kona Brewing. In hindsight, I should have just gone there first. It's Hawai'i's most popular craft brewery. It's busy but not packed. Athletes or no athletes, I need a beer. I find a seat at the bar and set the briefcase down under my feet. I order one of the fancy IPAs. The guy next to me is also alone. We have a short back-and-forth but he is more interested in his phone than in the human race. The bartender brings the beer over and I pay for it. It feels good to be in out of the sun. The first sip of beer reminds me that I went on an eleven-mile run earlier. It triggers something in my brain and I take another big gulp. I look around and identify athletes sitting at the tables, eating food. Some of the people they are with are drinking beers, but I can't find an actual athlete with one.

Then, the good grace of Kona—the town, the course, and the brewery—shines upon me. The phone addict next to me pays his bill and gets up. As soon as he vacates his seat, another guy steps right up to take it. He's a tall, lean man with a face so skinny that only one of two things could be true: He's a triathlete, or he's been held captive in a basement for the last six months. He's wearing warm-up gear, running shoes, and a hat, which he takes off and sets on the bar. He picks up the menu and looks at it. Holy shit, I think. This could be *one of them*.

He sees me blatantly staring at him. In fact, I think I freak him out a little bit. He looks up from his menu at me, sees me staring, looks back at his menu, then looks up again to see I'm still staring. He says hello. His accent reveals he's not from here. I say hello. Are you in the race?, he asks.

I tell him I'm not. Are you? Yes, he says. He's come all the way from Italy. His name is Mimmo, and he is in his fifties.

"Are you a real Ironman?" I ask.

"Yes," he says. "Fifteen times in the last twenty years."

"Are you going to order a beer?" I ask.

"Yes, of course," he says.

I watch him order the beer. He looks at me funny.

"This is so cool," I tell him. "You're drinking a beer."

He looks at me. He's perplexed. "Why not?"

"I don't know," I say. "You just . . . have a lot of shit to do tomorrow."

This makes him laugh. He holds up his glass and clinks it against mine. He tells me he's done Ironmans all over the world. He tells me again that he's done fifteen in the last twenty years. He tells me he always has a beer the day before the race. I ask him what his expectations are, and he says just to finish.

"Fourteen, fifteen hours, whatever it takes."

Clearly, he's in good shape to qualify for Kona. But he doesn't take himself, or the race, too seriously, he tells me. He said his message to himself is to "have fun, be happy."

My kind of dude. I begin to trust him—even if his idea of having fun and being happy includes a 140-mile triathlon. I decide to run my story by him. I tell him that I'm doing Ironman Arizona in thirty-some days, and that I've only been training since August. I admit to him that the eleven miles I ran today were the most I'd run in my life. I go on about all the doubt I've received regarding my lack of experience.

"Man, don't worry," he says. He raises his hand and taps his finger on my chest. "You are in good shape, you have the right attitude. Just keep training and you will have no problem."

The combination of his confidence and the 7-percent beer after an eleven-mile run turn the conversation pleasant. Finally, a down-to-earth dude. I ask him about other things, like what he will do tonight, the night before the race.

"Does it feel like Christmas Eve?" I ask.

He tells me he will go to bed at "twenty" tonight—better known to us Americans as 8:00 p.m. He'll wake up at four, have breakfast in the room—some oats or yogurt or whatever he picks up at the store later. Then he'll hang out with his wife and two kids—who also made the journey from Italy—before heading out to the race. His hotel is just a block or two from the starting line, he says. I ask him what he will eat during the race and he says, "Nothing. I drink all my carbs during the race."

I've heard of people doing this. Drew, if you remember, drank only Gatorade and he finished in just over ten hours. It seems to be a viable option. It's probably too late in the game for me to try to switch to it, however. Mimmo and I carry on for a while longer. When he decides not to get a second beer, I bid him goodbye. I have one more beer by myself. I pay for it. I pick up the briefcase and step back out into the heat of the afternoon. My sunglasses hide my crooked eyes. I feel very fine about everything again. Everything is going to be fine.

I stop in to the grocery store to pick up a piece of chicken for dinner and some items for breakfast, then call an Uber. Back at the house, I cook an early dinner. I feel very hungry. I cook the chicken, along with a bag of rice and a potato I brought with me from home.

After dinner, I open the briefcase and take a look at the massager. It comes with a variety of "drill bits"—one is big and round, one is narrow and pointed. Both are very firm. I choose the round one, because it seems less terrifying. When I turn on the gun, it vibrates and rattles like a power tool. I do as the guy showed me earlier. I run it over my thighs, inside and out. It feels really good. I push it harder against my skin. I watch as the ripples run down my leg, pulsing my muscles. It feels *really* good. I slide the legs of my shorts up as high as they can go to expose my upper thigh. I lift up the back of my shirt to do my lower back. I pull up the sleeves of my shirt to do my triceps.

Before I know it, I'm naked in my friend's living room, using the massager on every inch of my body that's not my penis, then starting over and going back over every inch once more. I push even harder the second time around, feeling the deep tissue massage as my tight muscles open up to breathe. When it's all done I lay on the floor of the living room, the gun next to me, staring up at the ceiling. My entire body is buzzing with delight. I doze off in the afterglow. I wake up several hours later. I look up at the ceiling at the smoke detector. I really hope it isn't one of those hidden surveillance cameras. I would need to leave my friend much more than a bottle of whiskey.

October 14, 2017
Kailua–Kona, Big Island, Hawai'i
36 Days Until the Ironman

> *Anyone can run six to seven miles after the bike. After that . . . there will be some epic meltdowns. There always are.*
>
> —Ironman announcer

When I wake up, I am so sore that I can barely stand up out of bed. As I wobble into the bathroom to brush my teeth, I chalk it up to yesterday's run. I went eleven miles, the farthest I've ever run in my life. I guess this is what accomplishment feels like. Sore quads. Sore hamstrings. Sore calves. At least my feet don't hurt. Apparently, I bought decent enough shoes after all. As I slug around the kitchen putting some butter on a bagel, I notice that my arms are sore, both my biceps and triceps. Come to think of it, my shoulders are also sore. I move them around a little bit. My neck, too. Hmm . . . that's weird.

I have a funny time of it putting on my socks. Seriously, my whole body is sore! The run would explain my lower half, but why would my arms and shoulders be sore? I literally did nothing with my arms yesterday. The toughest thing I did was lift a beer to my face.

I get my stuff together and prepare to head out the door. It's 5:00 a.m. It's still dark when the Uber arrives. It's a Prius. I open the door and get in the backseat. Sometimes I sit up front with Uber drivers but it's too early for that. I do circles with my shoulders and lean my head back against the headrest. Then it dawns on me. I might have overdone it with the massager. The scene from last night plays back through my head. The massaging. The intensity with which I used that thing. I really hope my friend doesn't have one of those cameras.

The driver takes me as close as he can to the starting line. There's not much traffic. It looks like I'm late in that regard—roads have been blocked off and there are already hundreds of cars parked along the roads and in shopping center lots. I get out and walk the remaining few blocks down toward the waterfront. I can feel the soreness in my calves and legs and the straps of my backpack on my tender shoulders.

I have fifteen minutes to spare until the start. I decide to get a cup of coffee. I see a place called Kona Coffee Café. It's just a block from the water on Ali'i Drive, where I want to be. There's a long line. I wait in it for, I don't know, five minutes or so. Twice now, a woman—seemingly the head honcho behind the counter—has made a public announcement about tips. She keeps yelling out that her team has been up since 4:00 a.m. to make this coffee thing happen. She says that we are encouraged to show our appreciation. I wait patiently until I am next.

"Yes?" the cashier says.

"Morning," I say to her. "How are you?"

She stares at me. I tell her I'd like black coffee. She asks me if I want medium or dark roast. I tell her dark. She takes a cup from beside the register and walks over to a row of stainless steel, portable coffee dispensers. She puts the cup under the spigot of the one that says dark. She pushes down the button on the top and the coffee spurts out. She pushes it a few more times before it becomes clear the canister is empty—only air is coming out. She looks down into the cup. She steps to the side and slides the cup under the spigot for the medium roast coffee. She pushes down the button on the top and fills the rest of the cup with it. She puts a plastic lid on top of the cup, walks back over, and puts the cup on the counter. She looks up from the register.

"Four ninety-five."

I am shocked by what I have seen. I am shocked by the price I have heard. I hand her my credit card in disbelief. She rings up the card and says, "Sign this." There's a space for a tip. I put a line through it and hand it back to her. I follow a walkway past the coffee shop down toward the water. Overhead, a helicopter zooms past. The sounds of its engines are especially loud here in the early morning.

There's a small crowd lined up along the water, but it's not packed or dense by any stretch of the imagination. Some sitting here and others standing there, like the lawn of a concert venue during the opening act. I'm able to find a vantage point standing between a couple groups.

There are a few distinct types of people here. There are two friends who are operating a drone. Their plan is to fly it out over the pack during the swim. I am positive this is illegal and dangerous, considering there is a helicopter in the air. But, I'm curious to see what happens. On the other side is a family. It's a woman and two teenagers. Presumably, the father figure is in the race. Later, from their conversations, I gather that the two teenagers are not sisters. They're friends.

"Your dad is crazy," one says to the other. "I honestly can't think of anything I'd rather do less than an Ironman. But at least we got to come to Hawai'i."

I sip the coffee. It's terrible. The start should happen any minute. There are many safety boats floating off the harbor. I can see the line of yellow buoys going off down the coast. Some of the athletes are in the water, swimming around and getting warmed up. I scan the crowd again. I notice an abundance of wardrobe similarities. Half the people here are wearing a racing shirt of some kind, either a T-shirt or workout shirt that corresponds to a past race, probably one they've done. A lot of them are marathons, but I see some for other Ironmans or half Ironmans. I guess it's no different than wearing your sports jersey to a game. I see the boys warming up their drone. It's hovering ten feet above us. It sounds like the biggest bug I've ever heard. It doesn't seem to bother anyone else.

Minutes later, the buzzing of the drone is replaced by the boom of a cannon. The first heat—the Pro men—take off and thrash out of the harbor. I'm not sure who is supposed to win. To be honest, I can't name a single competitor. The only thing I know is that one guy who was supposed to be a favorite is not racing today because he got into a bike accident a few days ago and is now in a neck brace. The online report said:

> *Tim Don, Ironman world record holder, will not be competing at this year's premier event in Kona, HI, due to injuries sustained from a Wednesday, October 11 car collision while cycling. Described as one of the favorites in the race, Don fractured his C2 vertebrae and though surgery is not needed, he will be out of training for five to six weeks in a brace.*

Every five minutes, a new heat enters the water and takes off. Soon the water is a stream of competitors, carving through like a current. When a wave comes in, you can see the athletes rise and fall with the pulse as it passes, each individual lifting their head to readjust their path afterward. The boys send off their drone and I look over their shoulders. They fly it to within ten or twenty feet of the water. The footage is incredible.* The pods of swimmers look like giant schools of fish, bubbling up at the surface. They kick and thrash and seem to bite the air when they breathe. For me, standing here in a soreness that comes and goes with every move, it all seems a little intense. I'm thankful to be standing here on shore, drinking my half-dark, half-medium coffee.

There's not much to see after the first ten minutes of the swim. The swimmers head off out of sight and only come back to this point as they finish. I have about an hour to kill. I decide to check out the Ironman Official Shop. This is different from the Ironman Village I visited yesterday. That was more vendor, industry, and product oriented. The Official Shop is where Ironman sells all its branded merchandise. They have many racks of clothing, men's and women's sections, all sorts of outfits and accessory items. But much of the store is flair. Branded T-shirts are a big thing, including targeted designs, like the "Irondad" shirt. I see some more $700 wet suits. Then they have all the trinkets: shot glasses ($8); koozies ($6); dish towels ($9.95); cake pans ($29.95); and ice cube trays ($19.95). The cake pans and ice cubes are in the shape of the Ironman logo. I can't believe it but, yup—just googled it—people celebrate their finishes by making Ironman cakes. Some of them are actually pretty impressive.**

I don't buy anything and head toward the start of the bike leg. By now, the best racers are out of the water. The general public is not allowed in the transition area. In fact, it's entirely out of sight. I find a spot along Palani Drive, right where the bikers come out of the transition area. When they emerge, the announcer calls out their names. Many of them that come out of the gate are lathering themselves with sunscreen as they pedal. Some of them have so much on they look like ghosts.

* You can see similar videos on YouTube if you're interested.

** Search for "Ironman tri cakes." "Ironman cakes" gets you Ironman, the superhero.

One thing I notice right away is that everyone has a really nice bike. Aside from having two tires and handlebars, they look nothing like my bike. In some cases, the frame is built in a way that makes the seat look like it is floating, held up from the front instead of underneath. I see several with odd-shaped water bottles that rest between the two aero bars in front of the handlebars, making it unnecessary to reach down and grab a bottle, and possible to drink without getting out of the crouch position. Or the "pain cave," as triathletes call it. I think that's how Mimmo rolls, with his liquid-only race diet. Oh, Mimmo! I pull my phone from my backpack. Ironman has an app you can download that allows you to track the progress of athletes. You can put in to receive pop-up notifications. I find Mimmo and sign up for alerts on his progress.

Another thing I see is that many racers are still trying to get their feet into their shoes as they pedal out onto the course. You can save time by attaching your shoes to your pedals ahead of time, and then putting your feet into the shoes; this is apparently faster than putting on your shoes, getting on your bike, and clipping the shoes into the pedals. So they say. It's not five minutes after I make that first observation that I see a man, who is reaching down to try to fix his feet in the shoes, swerve into the man next to him. The first guy's pedal gets caught in the second guy's wheel. I can hear the spokes crack and break. The first guy continues to ride off and the second guy comes to a stop. He's looking down at his bike and seems demoralized. He pulls off the course and finds some space in the grass where the crowd is thin. Race officials head his way. I follow them. I hear the race officials say that they will call for a mechanic. The racer and the officials go back and forth about the specs of the bike and the type of wheel he needs. It's all Greek to me, but from what I gather, the guy has a specialty wheel on his bike, and it might be complicated to find a replacement. Yikes. Travel all this way to Kona, pay all that money, and then get run into by a guy who is playing footsie. And then realize that your specialty gear is hindering your progress when they can't find a replacement. Maybe it's a good thing I bought a basic bike after all.*

* I took down the man's race number and looked him up later. Turns out he finished the race in 12:53:20. From what I could gather from the splits, the wheel took about an hour to fix and/or replace. Then he crushed it. Good for him!

I feel bad for the dude, but what can I do? Aside from that drama, the race is b-o-r-i-n-g. Competitors keep coming out of the transition area, hopping on bikes and riding off. The announcer calls out their names. It's . . . riveting. I have to find ways to distract myself. Walking around, I keep an eye out for product samples and such, but there doesn't seem to be much outside of the Ironman Village. I pass one pop-up shoe store. Some company from Switzerland. They are not giving away free shoes. They are selling them, and they are very busy. Part of that, I think, is because they've set up a projector in the middle of the pop-up area and surrounded it with seats. People are coming in for a break from the heat to watch the bikers on the TV and all of a sudden their shoes are off and they're trying stuff on. I stand off to the side for a while to watch. Half the TV is showing the race, and the other half is displaying ads—training regimes, programs, products . . . you name it. I walk back into the Ironman Village to grab another of those free shakes I got yesterday, but unfortunately the tent is closed. In fact, most of the vendors have already packed up, or are in the process of packing up.

I find my way back to Ali'i Drive and the harbor, near where that restaurant was selling its patio for $200 a seat. Those same bars that were empty yesterday are now packed to the gills, some of them providing views of the finish line from their second-level balconies. It's a narrow street, just a two-lane road between a line of shops and the water. At the junction of the finish chute and the transition area is a little square with a tall tower, television screen, and live broadcast. Raised high above the square, it's showing live footage and updates from the race, as well as event commercials and sponsor messages. Again, sometimes, these ads are shown on split screen, with the race on one side and the ad for a product on the other. I have a very quick gag reflex for commercialization, but no one else seems to mind. A couple hundred people have spread out and found places to sit in view of the big screen, a few lucky ones under the shade of the palm trunks, some standing hunched under the small store awnings, others bearing the heat and sitting with their backs to the guardrails, pouring sweat.

Overall, it's a colorful scene. You have the water right there shining a deep blue under the full sun, the activity of the shops and bars and restaurants that line the finish chute, the palm trees waving in the slight breeze, the tall tower and the finish chute itself, lined with red carpet. In a few hours, people will pack this area like sardines as the Pro racers come in for the finish. But for now, everyone's eyes are glued to the television as the leaders pass mile thirty-something on the bike.

Unlike my upcoming race in Arizona, which is a three-loop bike course, Kona is an out-and-back bike route. It limits the opportunities to see the racers. Obviously, any course that is out and back (as opposed to multiple loops) reduces the spectator-friendliness of the course and reduces the number of times you can see racers go by. Most people stay put here at the harbor, where the start, both transitions, and finish all take place. In theory, you could drive out somewhere along the course, but with race-day street closures and traffic, you would probably return with a headache. It's easier to stay here, where it's convenient, and there are bars that serve booze. But, that also means you have a lot of downtime.

Consider you are here to watch a friend or family member of above-average ability: eighty-minute swim, 6.5-hour bike, four-hour marathon. You would catch a glance of this person from afar at the start of the swim if 1) you have binoculars, 2) aggressively search the crowd as the swimmers waddle down the chute at the far end of the harbor, and 3) secure a place to stand among the crowd on Ali'i Drive with a sight line to the starting area, a quarter mile or so across the harbor. Most likely, you will join the thousands of other spectators who line the coast farther down and watch the pack swim by without a clue of who is who—once they are in the water swimmers all look the same; the only distinguishing mark is whether they are wearing a green cap (men) or pink cap (women). Identifying your participant is impossible. You can forget about any meaningful interaction or observance.

So you show up and wait—in this case, eighty minutes—until they are out of the water and into the bike transition. This is your first opportunity to get a good look. When they come out of transition on the bike, they ride up a spectator-lined chute on their way out of town toward the main road. It's a narrow chute and there's only one way to go, so if you position yourself there, you will catch a glimpse of them. Make sure you take a good look, because that's the last time you'll see them until they finish the bike—in this case, six and a half hours later.

The run at Kona is the most spectator-friendly part of the race. You'll get to see your racer finish on the bike at the transition area, then again see them as they run out of transition to start the marathon. Because they are now running and not biking, your glimpse of them will be a little longer, but still brief. The course eventually takes runners out of Kailua–Kona and down to the airport, but it weaves through the town on the way in and out. The average spectator with average mobility should be able to see their participant pass two or three times during the first part of the run, before they head out of town to the airport. Then there's a gap of a couple hours until, finally, it's time to cross the finish line.

There's a lot of time to kill as a spectator on this course. You will literally have an entire day—six, seven, eight hours—to kill while your participant is doing the bike course alone. What do people do all that time?

Well, a lot of people are here now watching the live feed on the television. It follows only the top Pro racers, so you won't see your participant unless they are in the top ten. But it's a way to pass time, I guess, and some people are really into it. For me, because I've been spending so much time researching, training, and interacting with age-group participants, the idea that the Ironman is actually a race gets lost. Age groupers, by definition, cannot win the race—only Pros can "win." An age grouper can finish first in his or her age group, but they cannot win the race. To stand here and see that people are actually interested in the outcome comes as a shock to me. I'm even more surprised when Gordon Haller, the winner of the first Ironman, texts me from Paris to say that he's watching the race. I calculate the time and realize it's the middle of the night in the City of Lights. When someone tells me they're in Paris, I imagine them sitting on the side of the Seine with a bottle of champagne and a blanket, the cathedral of Notre Dame lit up on the far side of the water, couples slowly walking the banks, and teenagers drinking bottles of beer with their feet hanging over the side. That's what I'd be doing.

But not Gordon. He's in his hotel room, watching the race on his computer.

Oh well. I suppose Kona is just like any other major sporting event, the same as an American waking up in the middle of the night to watch a soccer game happening in Europe. People put on their race day shirts, just like a sports fan would a jersey. I guess I just didn't understand that people follow Ironman as a circuit and competition, like one would follow NASCAR. But I guess it makes sense, since the Pros have standings and everything.

I make a series of phone calls to friends to pass the time. Simple, catch-up sorts of calls that tend to get put off. Then I walk along the water for a while. I'm officially bored when it's announced that the front of the bike pack has reached the turnaround point out at Hawi and is on the way back to Kailua–Kona.

The announcers, who are sitting behind a news desk under the television tower, look up at the television and provide live narration and analysis. The cameras are focused on the pack leaders as they make their way back toward us. The sun is scorching the black tar of the road and you can almost see the heat coming off the lava fields. Close-up footage shows one athlete gritting his teeth.

"He's using a lot of power," one announcer says as the camera zooms in on his face while he churns up a hill. "A lot of wattage."

The announcer welcomes a female athlete behind the desk with him—it seems like she is famous, a former racer. He asks her about the upcoming, all-important bike-to-run transition. What's in store for these athletes?

"Anyone can run six to seven miles after the bike," she says. "After that . . . there will be some epic meltdowns. There always are."

Two hours later, when the bikers are approximately forty-five minutes out, the announcers begin discussing how they believe the transition really starts right now, and that the athletes should start preparing.

"This is the time to be getting the last of your nutrition," one announcer says. The camera zooms in and we all watch as an athlete unwraps an energy bar and eats it. Before taking a short break, the announcers work in a few ads from sponsors, like Gatorade Endurance, just like you would hear on the radio.

The announcers are a big hit with the crowd gathered under the television tower. It gives them something to do over the course of the long day. I have to be more creative. I check in on Mimmo. He's somewhere near Hawi, at least three or four hours before he gets back here. What am I going to do with myself? I stand up and head toward the row of restaurants. On my way, I notice a woman in a purple shirt lingering by herself on the metal gate near the finish line. She's a volunteer.

It seems like it's less boring to be a volunteer. They have a task, a purpose. Unlike family and friends that have come to see one athlete—their athlete—every athlete is a volunteer's athlete. The most visible form of volunteer is the one you find at the aid stations. These people line up along the road and hand out food and water to racers while they are on the bike and the run. The transition area is chockful of them, too, guiding athletes to where they need to be at the changing tents and bike corrals.

I've been reading online that volunteers are the lifeblood of Ironman. Without them, there would be no race. The triathlete community holds volunteers in high reverence, and Ironman makes an effort to encourage athletes to thank volunteers, suggesting it in much of the race literature and briefings. I've noticed that a lot of advice columns and "how-to" articles also recommended thanking a volunteer.

I decide I should thank her, then. It's an easy icebreaker as I approach her and thank her for helping out today. I ask her where she's from, and she tells me Minnesota. Her face lights up. Her voice is full of excitement and pride. She's very proud. She tells me that she's also a triathlete, but admittedly operates at a lower level of competitiveness. She appreciates all the volunteers who have worked her races throughout the years, and the triathlete community as a whole, and she wants to give back. She has hopes of doing a full Ironman one of these years, and to experience the World Championship here in Kona, even as a volunteer, is a dream come true.

"Wow," I say. "Do they set you up with your flight and hotel and everything?"

She starts to smile before I can finish the sentence. "No," she says. "You have to pay your own way."

I inquire further, and she tells me that every Ironman race around the world—there were close to seventy in 2017—is essentially run by volunteers. At each race, she estimates, the number of volunteers to the number of paid employees is approximately 400 to one.* She says she is volunteering because she wants to—out of the goodness of her Midwestern heart—and because she liked the idea of coming to Hawai'i. Other volunteers, she said, have different motivations. Some volunteers come from a local charity or club associated with the race. Still others have more personal reasons. For example, she says, the way it works at most Ironman events is that if you volunteer, you get preferential registration for the following year. With the way Ironman has grown in popularity, she explains, this is a very strategic move—some of the most popular races, like the one I will do in Arizona, sell out in minutes, so having preferential registration is almost essential.

This intrigues me greatly and brings up a lot of questions. But I don't get the chance to ask them. While we're talking, we see on the big screen that the pro bikers have come in and are transitioning to the run. She has to go, she says; duty calls. I thank her and say goodbye. Just adjacent to the square, Paradise Brewing has a second-floor patio that hovers above the finish area. Unlike yesterday, the place is busy today, but not so packed that I can't get in and find a table. I order a beer and pull my laptop from my backpack. I do a search and spend the next two hours reading articles about volunteering for Ironman.

I learn that Ironman is not the only race-organizing company to rely on volunteers. In fact, it seems almost industry standard, with many companies using thousands of volunteers to run their events. In the case of Ironman and others, volunteers work in almost every phase of the event, including registration, aid stations, medical stations, and transition areas.

The concept of volunteer labor has become controversial in recent years. In 2014, for example, the then-parent group of the Rock 'n' Roll Marathon Series, Competitor Group Inc., was sued by a volunteer.

* Fact-checking what she told me was difficult because there are no official public reports about the number of volunteers or the number of employees working on each race.

Runner's World reported that "the lawsuit . . . alleges that the company uses its partnerships with charities that provide volunteers as 'a veneer for recruiting free labor' to operate water stops, escort runners, direct traffic, and do other jobs, in violation of the Fair Labor Standards Act, and contends that these thousands of workers must be paid at least minimum wage—$7.50 an hour in Missouri." In addition, it argued that the volunteers were misled into thinking they were contributing to a good cause when in reality they were being used as unpaid labor.

The lawsuit was allowed to move forward by a judge in 2015 and in January 2016 the court granted Competitor Group Inc.'s request for summary judgment, ruling that there were not enough facts to prove the lawsuit. From what I have seen, there have been no fallouts or policy changes that have resulted from the failed lawsuit. A year and a half later, in June 2017, the World Triathlon Corporation (Ironman's parent company) bought Competitor Group Inc. and the Rock 'n' Roll Marathon Series, and operates it today.

Over the years, there have been mixed reactions to Ironman's (and other races') use of volunteers. Some people see the volunteer thing as an ingenious business plan, free of any bad motives. Others think Ironman is pulling a fast one. In an opinion piece for the *Times Free Press* in Chattanooga, Tennessee, entitled "Ironman Should Pay Its Volunteers," a former volunteer walks us through his experience at the 2014 Ironman Chattanooga, where the number of volunteers was 4,000. He estimates that Ironman received $300,000 in free labor while simultaneously receiving nearly $1.5 million in entry fees alone, concluding that Ironman is making its fortune off volunteers they should be paying.

The sentence makes me stop in my tracks. *Ironman is making its fortune*. Wait . . . What fortune?

My research comes to a screeching halt when an announcer—I think it's Mike Reilly but I'm not sure—comes on the mic at the finish line. He announces that the leader is closing in on the finish. I get up from my table and walk to the edge of the patio. I lean out over the railing. I stick my head over to see the finish line and the big-screen television. I watch the leaders on the screen as the camera follows them along Queen

Ka'ahumanu Highway. It looks unbearably hot, and you can see the heat coming off the blacktop. I stand with my beer, my backpack over both shoulders, looking out over the water and the finish line below. Someone turns the volume up on the television in the square, and I can hear the two announcers restart their play-by-play. They hone in on each guy, one after another, and talk about how they look—do they look strong? Are they going to make a push in the last few miles?

"Just because he looks good doesn't mean he isn't pushing through something," the announcer says about one guy, who looks fine. "He's hurting for sure."

With the hoopla building, I ask the guy next to me, who is wearing a Lake Placid Ironman T-shirt, how much time we have until they finish. He says he thinks they still have about thirty minutes to go. I go to the bar to order another beer. I sit down at the bar. A man in the adjacent stool asks me what I'm up to. I tell him I'm gaining inspiration from the big race in anticipation of mine next month in Arizona. He says he's here completely by coincidence. He's here in Kona for a couple of weeks for work. He offers to buy me a shot of whiskey and I accept. We watch the Astros beat the Yankees in Game Two of the American League Championship Series.

Before long, the announcer is back on the mic and getting ready to welcome home the winner. I make my way back to the railing and look down upon the crowd in the grandstand and under the big television in the square. The camera is fixated on the leader, a German dude named Patrick Lange. He's less than a mile from the finish line, and he has unofficially been declared the winner—he's that far in front. The announcer starts talking about his backstory, that he's from Germany. He looks like he's going faster than a speeding bullet as he cruises around the final turns. There's a motorcycle riding a few feet in front of him, the cameraman on the back of the bike. I check out the back of his pants and they look clean. He hasn't pooped himself. You can see the colored chalk on the road beneath his feet, messages and words of encouragement from onlookers to competitors. He looks strong, as if it was his first mile and he hadn't swam or biked. You can tell he's all juiced up. He knows he's going to win.

At one point, the camera catches Lange fixing himself—he wiped his face or something.

"Oh, he's getting himself all pretty!" the announcer calls out. The people in the grandstand, their heads all turned to the television tower, clap their hands and cheer. "He's getting the sponges out!"

I did not see the sponge, but I remember hearing him say that. Hey, you've got to look good for the big finish. This is the world's stage as far as triathlons are concerned. I look down and see there are two men holding an Ironman banner across the finish line. When Lange finishes, he grabs this banner with both hands and holds it up over his head, as one might hold a wrestling belt in the middle of a ring. The crowd roars with delight. He barks back at the crowd and claps his hands. Mike Reilly calls out, "The 2017 Ironman World Champion Patrick Lange! And a new course record!" His time of 8:01:40 is two minutes and sixteen seconds faster than the old record.

The top competitors continue to make their way in over the next hour. Right now, it's a small trickle. Later, it will be a large leak as the rest of the 2,200-plus athletes make their way to the finish line. I won't be around to see them all, though, because I have a flight to catch. I enjoy another beer with my new friend. Now and then I get up to look at the finish line, but by now, I get it. It's time to go to the airport. With traffic and road closures, it will take extra time to get there.

I say goodbye to my friend and walk back up Palani Drive. One half of the street is closed for the runners. There's an aid station there on Palani, as the course climbs the hill up to Queen K Highway. Most of them look miserable. Many are walking, others are shuffling. One woman dumps water on her head. One guy is walking up the hill, using his hands to push on his thighs. I can tell a few of these racers are experiencing "the bonk," as they say. With every step, another drop of life falls from their eyes. It's hard to watch, like someone getting pummeled in a boxing match. I realize that by following the Pros the whole race, you get a very skewed perception of the average competitor's experience. The Pros make it look easy. The Pros give you the confidence to sit back, drink beers, and make sarcastic comments all day. They make you feel good like that. But the reality is things will not be that easy for me. Perhaps I should have spent more time here in the trenches to see the truth.

In this way, it's hard to say whether this weekend gave me more or less confidence. On one hand, I have looked into the belly of the beast. I'm more aware of what a race looks like as it plays out over the course of the day, and I picked up a few tips—stay away from everyone else in the bike transition, and the importance of nutrition in the final miles of the bike, to name two. Yet in reality nothing has changed. This is a long race and today I saw people struggle to complete it.

As we head for the airport, we pass some riders still coming down Queen K on their bikes. I look at my watch and it's close to 5:30 p.m., three hours since Lange finished. Many of the bikers look very tired, slow and sluggish, like they are pedaling through mud. It seems they may be in line to suffer the same fate as the runners I just saw on Palani.

Almost as unbelievable as Lange's eight-hour finish at 2:36 p.m. is the other side of the coin: The last people to finish will do so with times approaching seventeen hours, as the clock strikes midnight. Here, at 5:30 p.m., that's six and half hours from now. Even crazier is that the finish line will be just as—if not more—raucous as it was for Lange's first-place finish. Come to find out, Ironman has a very strong tradition of supporting its own. It is said that the top finishers always return to the finish line at midnight to cheer on the final finishers, as a way of recognizing the tremendous effort those final competitors have put in over the last seventeen hours.

I can't stay to cheer them on for two reasons: One, I have to catch my flight back to O'ahu; Two, I . . . am just not there yet with this Ironman thing. But I think it's a cool thing they do, and I look up videos of previous midnight finishes on YouTube as I wait for my flight to board. Pretty damn inspiring. One video follows a woman as she finishes just after midnight. The crowd is banging on the sides of the gates and they're blasting "Don't Stop Believing" over the PA. It's unbelievable and heartwarming, possibly all the more so because I'm still very buzzed from the beers and the whiskey.

I doze off for part of the short flight back to O'ahu. They offer me a choice of juice or water, and I choose water. When I step out in Honolulu, it's settling into darkness. I still have to do this thing, and it's only going to get worse from here. I saw it in person this weekend. Next month I have to do it in person.

October 15, 2017
Waimānalo, O'ahu, Hawai'i
35 Days Until the Ironman

> *Who would ever believe it? . . . None of us expected it would become this. If we did, I wouldn't be sitting here at my desk at Bank of Hawai'i.*
>
> —Ian Emberson, one of the original fifteen Ironman organizers and competitors

When I woke up this morning, the first thing I wanted to do was learn more about the volunteer situation with Ironman. The aforementioned article in the *Times Free Press* said that Ironman is using volunteers as employees and that's how the company "is making its fortune." What does that mean?

I have always been under the impression that Ironman is a modest company, financially speaking. A couple thousand people get together, torture themselves for a couple hours, buy a T-shirt, then go home, right? I assumed the $850 entry fee went toward a myriad of expenses, like event setup and hosting costs. There are mouths to feed, bills to pay, aid stations to set up. It can't be cheap to "rent out" a town for a day, with road closures, police, and medical support all costing their fair share.

Well, I followed up on some of that this morning, and you're not going to believe what I found out. None of my assumptions are true. In fact, it's just the opposite. Ironman (and its parent company, World Triathlon Corporation) is big, big business.

How big? Get this: In 2015, it was sold to a Chinese company for $650 million.

Six hundred and fifty million dollars! To put that amount of wealth in perspective, $650 million was the exact evaluation of the Pittsburgh Penguins in 2017, the professional hockey team that won back-to-back Stanley Cups in 2016 and 2017. In 2015, the year of the transaction, the Penguins were worth $560 million, almost $100 million less than the World Triathlon Corporation. Only after winning back-to-back championships was the organization worth as much (but not more!) than

Ironman's parent company. I tried to find out what the World Triathlon Corporation is worth today, a couple years later, but because it remains a private entity, no facts and figures about its value are publicly available.

I simply could not believe those numbers. It goes to show how under-the-radar Ironman* flies. Regardless of whether you like hockey, you know that it exists. You know that cities have professional sports teams. The awareness is there. And yet, even though most people have no idea what the Ironman is, it's a better bet than the Pittsburgh Penguins, the Philadelphia Flyers, the Colorado Avalanche, the New York Islanders, and about twenty other National Hockey League franchises as far as investments go.

Even at the previous evaluation of $650 million—it is, for sure, worth more than that now—Ironman is nearly *double* the value of a half-dozen NHL teams. Its worth is also on the heels of a half-dozen baseball teams—the Cincinnati Reds, Oakland Athletics, Tampa Bay Rays, Milwaukee Brewers, and Cleveland Indians, for example—which come in valued at somewhere between $800–$950 million.**

According to the *Wall Street Journal*, sources estimated that Ironman's value was closer to $900 million at the time of the 2015 acquisition but provided no reasoning for the sale price of $650 million. According to the *Guardian*, the Chinese group that purchased Ironman, the Dalian Wanda Group, is headed by Wang Jianlin, China's richest man, whose fortune was estimated by *Forbes* at the time to be somewhere around $26 billion. A 2015 article on Active.com gave a historical financial summary of Ironman and its parent company, the World Triathlon Corporation (WTC):

> *WTC is headquartered in Tampa, Florida. It is the world's largest operator of IRONMAN events and the most well-known full-distance brand; as the owner of the sporting brand and the operator of the competition, WTC accounts for a 91 percent global market share*

* I'm using "Ironman" going forward in this discussion in reference to the World Triathlon Corporation.

** According to *Forbes*, "Baseball's Most Valuable Teams," 2017.

of long-distance triathlon events. WTC has organized, promoted and licensed triathlon events for 37 years, and owns five exclusive triathlon brands, operating at least 250 events every year around the world. Its flagship brands are IRONMAN (2.4 mile swim, 112 mile bike, 26.2 mile run) and IRONMAN 70.3 (1.2 mile swim, 56 mile bike, 13.1 mile run) and are the world's largest competition participation platforms—holding more than 130 races with more than 230,000 competitors. WTC's gross revenue has risen at a CAGR [compound annual growth rate] of 40 percent for four consecutive years, while net profit has grown at 40 percent a year. Due to its strong brand and unique business model, the company is expected to maintain a high visibility and shows fast-growing future business prospects.

How can such a seemingly small (relatively speaking), streamlined business be worth so much? Where does all this money come from? What exactly is Ironman's "unique business model"?

Well, first things first: We've already seen the organization saves a lot of money on labor thanks to the thousands of volunteers that donate their time at each event. In the aforementioned case of Chattanooga, for example, if those 4,000 employees were each paid $10/hour, the cost to Ironman would be $40,000 per hour. Considering each event is seventeen hours long, plus the days before and after, the ability to reduce labor costs is essential to its success.

In terms of direct revenue coming into Ironman, there are several streams. The most lucrative are sponsorships, brand licensing, and entry fees.

Sponsorships come in various forms and again, because it's a private company, most facts and figures are not public. For example, it's hard to say what sponsors like Gatorade, Roka, and Clif Bar pay Ironman, not only because they keep these figures private but because these sponsors most likely have a multi-event or annual deal they work out internally, since they appear across events and products are actively promoted by Ironman across the board, including on its website and mailing lists, and on display boards at events. For example, Gatorade and Ironman announced a multiyear partnership in 2015. In the official announcement from Ironman on its website, neither the length or financials of the deal were revealed. In a separate article by *Bloomberg*, the length of the deal was reported as three years.

But I can provide you one example of a single-event sponsorship so you can get an idea of the size of the ballpark we're playing in. The upcoming Ironman Arizona is held in the city of Tempe, and a major sponsor of the event is Tempe Tourism. Because Tempe Tourism is funded by taxpayer dollars, all transactions and financial agreements it makes are public information. I was able to find out that Tempe Tourism pays an annual sponsorship fee of $50,000 to Ironman to host the event each year. In exchange for the $50,000, Ironman guarantees the following:

- All transitions will take place in Tempe.
- The race logo will include the name Tempe.
- Ironman is required to use Tempe hotels for its staff.
- Ironman is only allowed to promote Tempe-based hotels to its participants (although where participants ultimately stay is up to them).

That's not all. In addition to Tempe Tourism, the city of Tempe* itself also pays a $50,000 sponsorship fee to Ironman. Also a public entity, the city of Tempe's transaction is public record, too. Here's what I learned from reading the agreement:

- According to the agreement, the $50,000 from the city and the $50,000 from Tempe Tourism (TTO) will be "utilized in paying for the Race's marketing, television/internet production, and media activities."
- The city agrees to take care of "hard costs," including park staff, police and fire, solid waste expenses, traffic engineering expenses, and parks maintenance. For the 2016 race, those costs were

* Tempe Tourism and the city of Tempe are two separate entities.

estimated to be around $142,700. The city of Tempe estimated the costs for the 2017 race would be similar.

- There are other commitments in the agreement that may cost the city of Tempe additional money. For example, the city is required to undertake a certain amount of advertising and marketing of the race at their own expense. The city is also responsible for very specific tasks, including erecting the WTC race banner at its own expense.
- The sponsorship is for five years, for the 2014–2018 races. Each year a $50,000 payment is made by the city.
- WTC (Ironman) provides, at its own cost, management staff for the race, including a race director and media director, as well as other administration services.
- WTC has the exclusive right to sell sponsorships, merchandise, and licensing agreements in conjunction with the race, everything from advertisements and VIP ticket packages to beer concessions.
- WTC guarantees the city a certain degree of media exposure and commits to use its "best efforts" to attract the top athletes to the event.
- WTC will donate money from its community fund to Tempe. Exact amounts are not included in the agreement.
- WTC gets paid out on a portion of income from the hotel rooms occupied by participants of the race: "The TTO will require Host and Participating Hotels to pay a $12.00 per room night rebate (the 'Rebate') to the order of the TTO within sixty (60) days of the conclusion of the Race for each WTC athlete room night and each WTC guest room night booked at each Host or Participating Hotel. Out of each $12 Rebate, TTO will keep $2.00 to be used for the purpose of reinvesting in the Race and marketing the Race. The remaining $10 will be split equally between WTC and TTO ($5 per recorded room night to WTC and $5 per recorded room night to the TTO)."

The next revenue stream comes from the vendors at the Ironman Village, the open market I wandered through in Kona. They pay for booth space at each event, similar to the way a company would pay for a booth at any other meeting, event, or conference. What it costs to rent a booth is not publicly available—you must inquire directly with Ironman and figures vary based on the size of the event. One company I spoke to declined to comment on its agreement with Ironman.

Another big avenue of income is merchandise. Remember the Ironman ice cube tray, and all the other swag you can buy at the Official Ironman Store? That's all money in the bank, both in person at the events and every day online. Ironman earns money through direct sales as well as by licensing its brand to companies who create the merchandise. Exact figures about sales are not public.

Finally, don't forget entry fees. They aren't insignificant. For Ironman Arizona, the entry fee is $850, and there will be approximately 3,000 competitors (there will be more than 3,000, but let's keep the math simple). Three thousand competitors times $850 a person equals $2,550,000. That's one race. Now multiply that by twenty-some full-length events held per year around the globe.

Regardless of what the exact numbers are, and with the understanding that I'm leaving out other revenue streams, like television and broadcasting deals and race licensing—and operating in a little bit of darkness considering the company is private and does not release its exact figures—it's safe to say that Ironman's business model has been very successful.

Now, I have to be fair and tell you about the other side of the coin: Ironman might make a lot of money, but it also brings a lot of money to the destinations that host its races. In other words, it doesn't just take, take, take—it gives back, which is why cities are more than happy to pay to host its events. Ironman may not make direct contributions to its host cities (for example, it doesn't pay Tempe to hold the race there), but given the nature of what it has built, it offers a large and significant economic impact to destinations.

According to tourism officials I spoke with, the economic impact of Ironman (and any other major sporting event held in Tempe) is based on a standard formula that takes into account the number of participants, the size of their parties, how long they stay in town, and the estimated amount of money each spends on lodging, dining out, transportation, and other services during their trip. After the 2016 Ironman Arizona, Tempe Tourism reported an estimated economic impact of $3,642,187 for the city of Tempe.

It's an impressive number for a long-weekend event, especially considering it's one that a lot of everyday people are still clueless about. Let's take a look at an event everyone knows about: the Super Bowl.

After the 2017 Super Bowl in Houston, the greater Houston area issued a report* that estimated a total of 150,000 visitors brought $347 million in net contributions to the economy. Per person, that comes to $2,313 spent on the ground. How does that compare, per person, to Ironman's impact? For Arizona 2016, the $3,642,187 was brought by 2,419 participants, for an average of $1,505 per person. It's a sizeable gap between the two numbers, but considering the Ironman is a much more manageable event with a significantly smaller footprint—it doesn't take as many man-hours or as much of an investment to pull off, and price markups aren't as severe—I'm sure many destinations around the world would rather host an Ironman than deal with the logistics and headaches of a Super Bowl, all things considered, pound for pound.

For me, learning this is fascinating. It's hard to believe that forty years ago this race was nothing more than a novelty among friends and now it's a $650 million company. I wonder how Gordon Haller feels about this? I get in touch with him to find out. How was Paris? Good. Awesome. Hey, did you know Ironman is now worth $650 million? Yeah, thanks for rubbing it in. We sued them, you know. For real?

Haller tells me that in the nineties, some of the original fifteen athletes, including Haller, filed two separate lawsuits against Ironman, hoping to reclaim a piece of the pie. Both would be denied. In the years and decades that followed, the original fifteen watched as Ironman grew and grew and grew before their eyes in unthinkable fashion.

* Figures from Housuperbowl.com. Phoenix hosted the Super Bowl in 2015, but I thought it better to use the 2017 Super Bowl figures for two reasons: 1) Phoenix's economic estimates were for the entire state, not a single city; and 2) I wanted the figures to be as current as possible for comparison's sake. For those interested, the Super Bowl's economic impact in general was looked at in-depth by CNBC in an article entitled "Super Bowl benefits host city, but by how much?"

"Who would ever believe it?" said Ian Emberson, one of the fifteen competitors and one of the members of the lawsuit. "There were events going on all the time back then. Biathlons, swims, runs. We thought the Ironman was just another event."

To understand just how insignificant the Ironman was at its beginning, consider that the original fifteen literally gave the event away to the aforementioned Valerie Silk, the owner of a few local fitness centers. She became race director in 1980 and under her watch, Ironman grew from a fifteen-person race on O'ahu to an event with more than a thousand participants on the Big Island. In 1990, ten years after taking the reins, Silk sold Ironman to the World Triathlon Corporation for $3 million. Now, in conjunction with WTC's other races, it's worth at least $650 million.

In speaking with Emberson, it seems enough years have gone by to eliminate any and all bitterness toward Ironman. In fact, he gives credit to Silk for creating the Ironman we see today. Still, what could have been is hard to ignore.

"None of us expected it would become this," Emberson said in a phone interview. "If we did, I wouldn't be sitting here at my desk at Bank of Hawai'i."

October 20, 2017
Waimānalo, O'ahu, Hawai'i
30 Days Until the Ironman

Just go, man!

—from *Dumb and Dumber*

It took me a couple of days to get the bad taste out of my mouth. All along I thought I was participating in a grassroots event of sorts, maybe not an underground event but at least one where the participant experience was the driving force. Now I just feel dumb about it. It's the money, stupid! How could I have been so misguided? How could I have missed the signs? After all, what grassroots event costs $850 to enter? Ugh. I am the dumbest of the dumb.

Despite my regret, I am too far along to turn back. I have too much invested, having bought a bike and a plane ticket to Arizona. I have trained too much to get nothing out of it. The only thing to do is take it on the chin and continue. If that isn't the theme of the Ironman experience, I don't know what is. I'll no doubt channel these emotions into today's benchmark bike ride. Not just any bike ride—a long, remarkable one. And then, I'm going to go on a long run.

The plan is to ride from my place in Waimānalo through Kailua and Kāneʻohe, using the back roads that run alongside the ocean, to Lāʻie, which is way up on the northern end of the east side, before the road cuts west and takes you along the North Shore. It's thirty-five miles . . . one way. It will be the longest single-day ride of my life. I want to follow that up with an hour-long run.

I'm properly rested—it's been three full days since I biked last—and it's time to push myself. While all my friends have been hitting the beach or the trails or the breweries in their free time, I've spent a considerable portion of the week weighing the benefits of bike tires. My interest began when I walked into a tri store in Honolulu and saw a single tire—just one of the two you need—on sale for $400. I was shocked. A set of these tires costs more than my entire bike. Can a tire make that much of a difference?

For a professional triathlete, absolutely. I read on a forum that certain bike tires can save you considerable time over the course of a 112-mile ride—upward of fifteen minutes in some cases. The idea that I could go faster using the same amount of energy is intriguing, for obvious reasons, yet it also falls into the same category as aerodynamic bike helmets. Do I need to be spending hundreds of dollars to save fifteen minutes? Some people on the forums think I do. They tell me there's a big difference between tires in terms of speed and puncture resistance. Usually, the faster a tire rides, the less resistant it is, and vice versa. They propose two options as an upgrade from my stock tires: Gatorskins for their puncture resistance, or GP 4000s for their speed.

One man on the forum sent me a blog article comparing the two, which concluded that the GP 4000s were sixteen minutes faster than the Gatorskins over the course of an Ironman. "From a modeling standpoint, I've assumed 3w/kg FTP, IF's of 90% for Olympic and 70% for IM,

CdA's of approximately 0.31 (typical of non-optimized body position), 6' 175 lb male, and 5'-4" 125 lb female," the author writes of his calculations.

I crave the Gatorskins for their puncture resistance—my worst nightmare is a flat tire, and Arizona is known for goat's-head thorns—but I bite the bullet and buy a set of the GP 4000s for a hundred dollars. Why? I don't know. Because everyone on the Internet is telling me to?

"The GP 4000s have a much lower rolling resistance especially if you use latex inner tubes. You would save close to 20 watts which translates to a fair bit of speed," one person wrote.

"The 4000s are a much faster tire in terms of aerodynamics and especially rolling resistance. I forget the specific stat, but something like 10-12 minutes faster than Gatorskins over an Ironman. So, enough of a difference that if you [get a] flat on a 4000, you could stop, change it, and still end up with a faster split than if you had used Gatorskins," another said.

I ordered the GP 4000s last week and yesterday they were delivered.

I eat a big breakfast—eggs, oatmeal, a protein shake, and coffee. Then I turn the bike upside down so it's resting on the handlebars and the seat. I take off the two tires. They are easy to take off, though the back tire is more complicated because of the gears and chain. It takes a little extra patience than the front. In this way, just the experience of putting the new tires on is worth it. The more hands-on time I spend with the tires, the more confident I become that I can change a tire on the fly. I know how to adjust the brakes now. My knowledge is coming along. I clean and lube the chain, turning the pedals with my hand to ensure the lube coats the chain evenly. I pump the tires up to race pressure.

I've got a peanut butter and jelly sandwich, a Clif Bar, and a GU packet in my bike jersey, and two bottles of water on the bike. I drank a lot of water this morning—pre-hydrating as they call it—so I should be all set. I pedal off. The breeze blows through my helmet. I'm riding outside for the first time—which is hard to believe considering the race is a month away—free from the four walls of my apartment. Until this point, none of my bike training had involved actually riding a bike. I didn't have to steer. I didn't have to deal with the elements. I didn't have to watch where I was going. The only thing I watched was the television. Hell, I can't even tell you whether or not the new tires feel different, because I never rode the old ones out on the pavement.

It's embarrassing to tell you this, but the first couple of miles do not go so well. One thing I notice immediately is that riding on the aero bars is not as straightforward as I thought. It is certainly not something you should try for the first time in heavy traffic. As I lean over the handlebars and rest my forearms on the aero pads, I swerve into the middle of the road, trying to get a feel for how the balance of my weight affects my navigation. Luckily, I have a couple miles on the quiet back roads of Waimānalo to get the hang of it. I switch to the upright position whenever I hear a car coming. Oh man, I could have sworn I knew how to ride a bike.

I climb the hill out of Waimānalo into Kailua and head toward the beach roads. I zigzag through Kailua town before I reach Kailua Beach Park and turn left onto Kalaheo Road. I take this small, two-lane road all the way to the Marine Corps base and follow it around into Kāne'ohe. Once through Kāne'ohe, Kamehameha Highway hugs the coast and the scenery gets very interesting and beautiful. The ocean is in plain view on the right, and I can see the jagged ridgeline of the Ko'olau Range on the left, green and bright. I pass palm trees and beach parks and the small, rolling hills that offer perspective on the landscape.

I know it's pretty because I've been here before, but I'm barely noticing any of it now because I can't take my eyes off the road in front of me. For one, I'm still unstable going around turns in the aero position. This nervousness is compounded by the condition of the road. I'm riding on what I like to call Hawaiian cobblestone—bumpy asphalt that has been topped and finished with small rocks, creating a jarring, uneven surface. There are many potholes on the side of the road. Most are open, a few inches deep. Others have been poorly patched and now sit a half-inch higher than the original road surface. All I can think of are these brand-new tires and how they are less resistant than the Gatorskins. The crosswalks are outfitted with raised reflectors and rounded bumps that extend into the shoulder, which contains maybe a foot of space between the white line of the road and the grass. Each unavoidable thud leaves me gripping the handlebars tight and I struggle to keep myself in the aero position. By the time I get to Kualoa Ranch and Kahana Bay, one of the most scenic sections of the east side, my undercarriage is completely numb, and I'm in constant pain as I rattle down the road. The wind is blowing hard off the water and is trying to push me into the center of the road. At times, I consider letting it.

At mile twenty, I eat a Clif Bar. I take the water from the bottle cage and squirt some down my back. Even with the wind, it's hot in the sun and I can feel my arms burning. I pump up the hill that climbs out of Kahana Bay and close in on Lā'ie. The wind is strong as I pass through Punalu'u. I take a drink and then it hits me. I have to pee. All that water this morning and all that jostling on the way here have my teeth floating.

I look down at my bike computer and see that it reads twenty-nine miles—six more miles to my turnaround point, Kokololio Beach Park. Because of the wind, I'm only doing twelve to thirteen miles per hour, meaning I'm still a half hour away. The pressure in my bladder mounts as I bounce over the rough road. My tire thuds down into small divots and potholes. I don't know if I'm going to make it! But there's nowhere to pull over. The coast is open and treeless on the right. On the left are the front yards of the houses. What's a cyclist to do? Maybe this is an opportune time to try out one of the tricks of the trade. Maybe I can try to pee right here on the bike.

I was introduced to this concept by Drew. I then confirmed what he told me with many others, including Bmac, Tommy, and the Internet at large. I posted something in one of the forums about it, which drew funny responses. Some people reported being "splashed" by pee in previous races, and recommended that if I was going to pee, I should look behind me first. I thought it was a joke, then someone else said, "I remember reading a particular Pro used to pee on the bike and let it splash if she felt someone was hugging her wheel a little too close. Drafting deterrent!!"

This prompted a lot of other comments about pee.

"At [Ironman Arizona] I saw a guy standing at the aid station, with porta johns right next to him. He stood there and peed himself holding his bike. At IM Boulder, a guy had some sudden intestinal issues and crapped

himself right in front of me on the run. He shook it out of his shorts and kept on running. Needless to say me and the guy I was running next to let him get much further [sic] *ahead as he stunk to high heaven."*

"There are way more people that do it [pee on the bike] that may not want to admit it. Use the water to splash on yourself . . . it may be hot anyway!"

"Triathlete bikes are messy between pee and sticky nutrition #whymechanicsdontliketriathletes"

"I saw someone at Austin 70.3 last year who peed in his wet suit BEFORE the swim . . . which was then cancelled due to fog."

There were serious pieces of advice to go along with these tall tales. Drew admitted to me that he pees on the bike because if you're trying to win or qualify for Kona, every second counts.

"You won't see any Pro stopping to go to the bathroom, so just do the math," he said. "Most are probably peeing once or twice on the bike and then maybe again on the run."

Tommy told me I should pee while going downhill, since it's hard to let it fly when you're pedaling like a madman. He said to slide my penis to the side under my bike leotard—which is really tight—and point it down my thigh. The pee will run down my thigh and out the end of the pant leg, he said, or it might just rise up out of my pants. Either way, I should hold my leg out a little bit and it will drain down to the ground.

There's no downhill between here and Kokololio. I'm on relatively flat road now, minus the Hawaiian cobblestone, and I slow my cadence down to under ten miles an hour. I reach down into my pants and move my penis around. The seat has cut off a lot of my circulation, blurring the line between the sensation of having to pee and the sensation of pain that comes along with saddle soreness. I have to shake things loose with my hand for all the feeling to come back. I point my penis down my right leg, toward the shoulder of the road. I try to go as I pedal slowly. In spite of the pressure, nothing comes out.

This does not surprise me. Cars are passing with regular frequency and I keep making eye contact with the drivers. I'm convinced they know what I'm doing. How could they not? I'm standing up on my left pedal and extending my right leg like a dog on a fire hydrant.

I feel like I'm on the verge of peeing when the wind gusts and gives me a shove toward the middle of the road. I hear the roar of a horn behind me as I swerve out and then back into the shoulder. When the car passes, the driver shakes his head at me. OK. That's enough. I'm not going to die out here. What the hell am I doing? Do I really want to ride home with pee in my pants? I clip my right foot back into the pedal. It's only four more miles to the turnaround point.

When I arrive at Kokololio Beach Park, just south of Lā'ie town, I ride my bike through the door and directly into the public restroom. I lean it against the concrete wall and dash over to the urinal. My bike shoes make the sounds of high heels on the hard floor. I wheel the bike outside, stretch my legs, take a drink, and open my peanut butter and jelly sandwich. I mount my bike and ride off as I begin to eat the sandwich. The stop takes less than four minutes.

I try to eat the sandwich but can only get half of it down. I'm not hungry at all. I put the second half in my pocket and ride back toward Kahana Bay. I thought the wind would be at my back now, but I'm met with an unpleasant surprise: Somehow, the wind is still blowing in my face. I don't know how that works scientifically; how it can be blowing in my face in both directions. It brings new meaning to the idea of discouragement.

So much for an easy ride home. I come around the corner at Kahana Bay and, after battling and grinding up the hill in the face of the wind, I begin a downhill section. The sloping curve comes out of the valley and heads right toward the ocean. It's a pretty view . . . and a ferocious wind tunnel. As I crest the hill, thinking I can now coast downhill, I am met by a headwind that stops me in my tracks. The bike is pointed down the hill but still does not move. I sit in disbelief, slowing to a near complete stop before I resume pedaling. I have to pedal as hard as I can just to move the bike downhill.

I spit and curse and power my way through the wind, working myself into a mental frenzy about how the wind could possibly blow both directions. Fuck, shit, bitch, and cocksucker make up much of my vocabulary. It's draining and exhausting, mentally and physically. When I make the turn out of the valley and the road once again hugs the coast, there is little relief. The wind continues to blow across the road, diagonally from the left-front to the right-back. I still have to deal with the constant vibration of the Hawaiian cobblestone. Each thud sends a shockwave through my undercarriage.

I'm not sure when it happens, but by the time I pass Kualoa Ranch and approach the boundaries of Kāne'ohe town, I am in bad shape. My legs ache. My butt hurts. I have no energy and feel completely depleted. When I come to a red light, I stop and put my head down on the handlebars.

I'm fifty-some miles in, and still more than seventeen from home. I have to dig deep. I shift down a gear and try to find a cadence my legs can handle. Physically, down-shifting is a good idea, but mentally, it is torture. I am pedaling faster than I was before, yet going slower than ever. I can't get comfortable. My legs are screaming. I don't think they've ever been this tired. How I'm going to take a single step after this, let alone run, I couldn't tell you. If I don't act quick, this is going to turn into a full-on bonk.

I see a 7-Eleven at the corner of the intersection and I pull in. I immediately take down the rest of my Gatorade. I try eating the other half of my sandwich. It makes me want to throw up, so I throw it out. I bring my bike inside the store and buy another Gatorade. The woman looks at me like I'm an idiot as I try to balance the bike with one hand and fish the dollar bills out of my pocket with the other. I go back outside and chug the entire Gatorade. I find the GU in my pocket. I rip open the package and jerk it into my mouth. I take a deep breath. I lean my bike up against the side of the building and stretch. I touch my toes and then pull my heels back to my butt, one at a time.

The rest of the ride, I have to constantly switch positions to take the pressure off my undercarriage. I'm in the aero position for a few minutes, then sit up for a few minutes. I lean on my right butt check for a few minutes, then my left. I stand up and coast. I sit back down. I go back to the aero position but try to pedal with my butt completely off the seat. That does not work. I go back to sitting upright. Through it all I am very uncomfortable. But I am determined to keep going. Of course, I really have no choice—how else am I going to get home? The good news is that I have, in a sense, regained my vitality. The Gatorade and the GU gave me sugar to burn. Calories are good for you when you're exercising—imagine that! And I've started to draw inspiration from those who have doubted me. I picture Mr. I'm on Another Level at the tri shop. The thought drives energy into my legs.

The closer I get to home, the more I anticipate the glory of getting off this bike. Seeing the sign for my street is one of the greatest moments I can remember from all of my training. I rode thirty more miles and a hundred more minutes than I had to date. The seventy miles took me four hours and fifty-one minutes.

There's a mental difference between getting off the bike on a break and getting off the bike when the ride is over, and this mental difference impacts me physically. When the ride is over, my body lets go. My legs are wobbly. They want to rest. But it's not time to rest. It's time to run. I push my bike through my door and lean it up against the wall. I take off my bike shoes and change into my running shoes. I'm not looking forward to the run. However, I'm so happy to be off the bike. I jerk another GU into my mouth and head out the door.

The start of the run feels like I'm pulling a parachute. Everything is happening in slow motion, or so it seems. My thighs ache as they pound the pavement, and a rhythm is hard to come by. After the first mile, that changes. I feel like Forrest Gump breaking out of his leg braces. I look at my watch. The first two miles are a sub-nine-minute per mile pace. Wow. All along I had felt like I was barely moving, and yet, here I am, on a reasonable pace. I can feel the confidence building inside me as I realize my body knows the drill. I've practiced this bike-run transition more than a dozen times now, and it's paying off. It's hard to believe that two hours ago, I was resting my head on my handlebars at a stoplight. I could barely pedal. Now here I am, recharged, regrouped, running! It's an amazing feeling, when you prove something to yourself like that. I *can* keep going. I return home fifty-eight minutes later after completing just shy of seven miles.

Walking back inside, I feel like a king. There were times during the bike when I questioned how I was going to finish the ride. My legs ached, my butt screamed, my body was uncomfortable. I questioned how I was going to take a single step after the bike ride, and how I was going to do the run. But that's the funny thing. You can't think about that. Of course, you think about it. But you can't dwell on it, or convince yourself of it. When you're suffering in a specific moment, you're going to question everything. In the midst of the pain, you're only going to be able to imagine more of it in the future. You have to fight through those individual moments of struggle. You have to get through the rough patches. Because you can get through them. That's what training teaches you. When you hit a snag, you have to find a way around it, find a new position, choke down a GU, dig deep and get over that hump, physically and mentally. Even if it means dropping down a gear or six and getting your legs spinning again. Worry about the next thing when you get there. Don't get too far ahead of yourself. I have learned all of this today and I am glad for it.

I take it easy for the next thirty minutes. I'm physically shot. I feel very tired, and my legs ache. I lay on the couch and prop them up against the wall in an elevated position. After fifteen minutes, I get up and start walking around, slowly but surely. I shower. Looking at myself in the mirror, I see that I have a farmer's tan, red from the middle of my biceps down to my hands.

I take out a couple pieces of chicken for dinner, with rice, two baked potatoes, and broccoli. After I eat, I feel rejuvenated, still tired but no longer aching. I feel full of accomplishment. I had been through a battle. Today was a big test for me. I didn't quite go as fast as I wanted on the bike—I only averaged 14.4 miles per hour—but there were a lot of elements working against me. The wind, for one, and I didn't manage my nutrition well. It's a good lesson to learn. No matter how much you drink, you have to eat, dummy. That I was still able to run at a nice pace—seven miles in less than an hour—and that I had no IT band issues are reasons to celebrate. All things considered, I'm happy with it. Hell, I worked out for six hours today!

I lay in bed later that night and my legs are restless. So is my mind. I'm trying to be positive, but there's still that nagging voice. This is the cycle, I've come to learn. I'm happy and pumped up in moments of physical exhaustion, and when the dust settles, my mind takes over and reality tends to set in. Today was a great accomplishment. Still the obvious remains: The Ironman is less than a month away, and 70/7 falls well short of 112/26.

October 23, 2017
Waimānalo, O'ahu, Hawai'i
27 Days Until the Ironman

> *You have to learn the rules of the game. And then you have to play better than anyone else.*
>
> —Albert Einstein

I feel him bump into me. Fuck that. I throw an elbow into the side of his rib cage. *Get the hell out of my way!* I snarl as I blow my breath out my nose and plow forward. I pass him, kicking hard. When my feet align with his head, I strike with my best kick. I feel my heel crush his nose. I look back and see him grab his nose, the blood surging through his fingers.

I snap upright in my bed. The dawn is calm and all I can hear is the sound of crickets. I'm not sweating or breathing hard, but I feel like I should be, given the violent dream. Did someone slip something into my Muscle Milk? Where did that burst of testosterone come from? Maybe it's the competitive fallout from the pain-free, fourteen-mile run I did yesterday here in Waimānalo—my heart, mind, and lungs all felt great, and my IT band was 95 percent pain free. With a time of 1 hour, 47 minutes and a 7:44-minute-per-mile average, it was by far the most positive workout of the journey thus far, and it was a new record for me, the longest run of my life. So why the hostility?

I hear my phone vibrating on the bedside table. I have a bunch of social media notifications on my phone. The bib numbers came out today (it's already the middle of the day on the mainland), and they've been met with excitement by the forums. I look in the posted document and find that my number is 1970. It is the number I will use as my official form of identification throughout the race. I will write it on my clothes bags, for example, and it will be printed on a sticker that I'll slap on my bike. There will also be a small, rectangular piece of paper with the bib number on it that I will safety pin to my jersey during the run. While the Pro Division is a different story, bib numbers for age groupers are meaningless. It has been assigned to me at random,* and it has no practical impact on the race or my starting position.

But for many they are far from insignificant. Members of one forum have already changed their profile pictures to display their numbers. I'm confused by this reverence. No one makes any direct comments about what the number means to them, but obviously they hold water somewhere. Looking back through old posts, I discover that people began inquiring more than three weeks ago about the status of the bib numbers, wondering aloud when they would be released. I don't understand . . . what's the big deal?

I find an article on Triathlete.com entitled "Can Bib Number Affect Your Performance?"

"No, the number on your race belt shouldn't impact performance," the article begins. "But it can have unintended, sometimes amusing consequences." It goes on to provide anecdotes of people who have found meaning and been inspired by their race numbers. Someone once got their birthday as their bib number. I read half the article before closing the tab. I don't have time for this stuff.

Last night, I downloaded the Athlete Guide for the Ironman Arizona. It was released a few weeks ago—on October 13, when I was in Kona—but I forgot it existed until I saw someone post something about it last night. Its discovery comes at a good time. We're less than a month away from the race, and there are many questions about the logistics of the big day. I have been able to gain a little bit of insight by talking to people and reading other guides online, but each race has an "official" Athlete Guide that sets in stone the schedule of events, check-in times, cutoff times, practice times, where you need to be when, race start time—pretty much everything you need to know about race day and the days before it.

They might seem like trivial things, things you could figure out on the fly. I would be the first person to say this if I wasn't going through

* For the Pro Division, lower numbers are generally worn by the most accomplished athletes. If not randomly assigned, Age Group numbers can be loosely based on external factors like registration date, age, name, and others.

it myself. But you have to understand how much else you have to deal with, mentally and physically. You've been building up to this massive challenge, with all those workouts over the past couple of months (or in most people's case, the past year), and you have so much going on in your mind about the race itself, in mental preparation for the execution. You are thinking about the course, what the weather will be, what the water temperature will be, whether you'll need to wear a wet suit. You're thinking about what you should pack, whether you'll need long sleeves on the bike or the run. You're thinking about whether you should change after the swim. You're focused on how you have to pack your bike in a box, praying it doesn't get damaged in transit. You're thinking about your food and drink plan. You're thinking about how to fix a flat tire on the bike. You're thinking about the small, short workouts you will do the few days before to stay fresh, and what time you'll go to sleep each night, whether you'll go out to dinner or try to cook something in your hotel room. You're crossing your fingers your flight isn't delayed, that your hotel isn't too noisy.

You have all this going on in your mind already, and to wake up a month before race day and realize you still don't know something simple, like where to stash your clothes, how to drop off your bike, or where to park when you get there . . . well, all I can say is that for someone with all that going on, who is perhaps already mentally exhausted, those small little details can cause extreme anxiety. In this way, what they say about the Ironman is true—it is indeed as much a mental challenge as a physical one, juggling all these things in your head and keeping your sanity along the way.

So it is with open arms that I receive the Athlete Guide. I download the pdf and am shocked to see that it prints out to forty-four pages. Forty-four! Of course it does. This immediately increases my anxiety. My first instinct is to avoid it, to push it aside and think about it later, maybe tomorrow or next week. But if I've learned anything by now from this experience, it's that pushing things aside or avoiding tough situations gets you nowhere in the long run. I need to tackle this piece by piece, one page at a time. I need to start now.

The front cover is a full-page printout of the race logo.* I had not seen it before. It depicts an orange cactus front and center with a wheel underneath it—it looks like a cactus riding a unicycle. It looks strange, and there are a lot of bizarre things about it—the most immediate is that the position of the cactus's arms makes it look like it's a gigantic middle finger. I can't be the only one who sees that, can I?

I go online to see if there's been any discussion about it. There has been. One or two people think the logo looks cool. Everyone else is, like me, confused. Here are some of the reactions:

> *"My first thought was that the runner is headed from T1 to his cactus unicycle."*
>
> *"Looks like the cactus is giving the finger."*
>
> *"Seriously?"*
>
> *"Worst design ever."*
>
> *"Thank g-d I've been training on my cactus-cycle all season, lol."*
>
> *"How does this represent a triathlon let alone an IRONMAN which we have all worked so very hard for. It does look like the middle finger."*

One couple posted a photo of themselves standing in front of a real-life cactus, holding up their middle fingers. Others posted about other terrible shirts Ironman has made, specifically Ironman Florida, which is happening on November 4 and has a giant pineapple for a logo. Florida has a history of pineapple farming but it hasn't been a significant industry there since the 1930s, leaving people confused about the choice of design. At least here the cactus makes sense, someone said.

---

* Each Ironman has its own individual race logo. It's the logo on the finisher's T-shirt. It's extremely difficult to find a picture of it online—not sure why.

I breeze through the packet. I skim the titles and content. Many of the pages do not contain any information about the race. There are a lot of full-page ads. Some are from race sponsors, like Gatorade and Roka. Others are self-promotion from Ironman, reminding athletes to purchase their official picture packages or pick up their official Ironman race bags. There's a full-page advertisement for Nulo dog food, billed as the "official pet food" of Ironman and "pet nutrition inspired by world-class athletes." I can't roll my eyes hard enough. Next is a bunch of pages that fall under the category of sponsored content—advice or information designed to look official but actually promoting a product.

I take all the advertisements out of the guide. In total, of the original forty-four pages, the number that truly pertain to race day information is about half that, a simplified twenty-one pages,* broken into sections that include a welcome letter, event schedule, race day info, post-race info, and overviews of the swim, bike, and run courses. I spread it out on the coffee table, sit down on the sofa, put my feet up, and crack open a beer. Here and now, I can still afford the luxury of a cold beer, both mentally and physically. I know it will help with any creeping anxiety as I read through my journey to come.

At this point, the major thing for me, beyond reading the race-week logistics, is learning the rules of the race. There is information on the location of the aid stations along the course—one every fifteen miles on the bike and one every mile on the run course. I learn that each racer is allowed two "special needs bags," one for the bike course and one for the run course. In these bags, I can put anything extra I might need on the course but don't want to carry. Things like extra bike tubes, or food. The bags will be staged at an aid station and I can stop if I need something.

This intel is invaluable in terms of formulating a plan of attack on race day. Most important are the cutoff times for each stage:

Swim: 2 hours and 20 minutes; rolling cutoff. Regardless of when you start, you have 2:20 to finish the swim. If you start at 7:00 a.m., you have to be out of the water by 9:20 a.m. If you start with the last groups at 7:20 a.m., you have to be out by 9:40 a.m.

* Not including the cover page, table of contents, etc.

Bike: 5:30 p.m.; hard cutoff, regardless of start time.

Run: Course will close 17 hours after the last athlete enters the water (between midnight and 1:00 a.m., approximately). Athletes must be out of transition and starting the run course by 5:40 p.m.

The big takeaway is the hard bike cutoff of 5:30 p.m. This means that every extra minute I spend in the water is one less I have to complete the bike. So much for this Athlete Guide reducing my stress level. Now I'm worried about the bike cutoff time. If I'm in the water with one of the first groups a little after 7:00 a.m. and swim my projected time of 1 hour and 15 minutes, that will put me on the bike around 8:30 a.m., factoring in ten minutes for transition. That leaves only nine hours to complete the 112 miles. And what if the swim takes longer than expected? That's a tight time frame, one in which any number of mechanical or physical setbacks could spell disaster. There's not much room for error of any variety, be it self-induced or circumstantial.

Here's an excerpt of other bike rules:

> *Absolutely NO DRAFTING of another bike or any other vehicle is allowed. • Athletes must keep six bike lengths of clear space between bikes except when passing. Failure to do so will result in a drafting violation. • A pass occurs when the overtaking athlete's front wheel passes the leading edge of the athlete being overtaken. • Overtaking athletes may pass on the left for up to 25 seconds, but must move back to the right side of the road after passing. Failure to complete a pass within 25 seconds will result in a drafting violation. Athletes may not back out of the draft zone once it is entered (drafting violation). • Overtaken athletes must immediately fall back six bike lengths before attempting to regain the lead from a front running bike. Immediately re-passing prior to falling back six bike lengths will result in an overtaken violation. • Overtaken athletes who remain in the draft zone (6 bike lengths of clear space between bikes) for more than 25 seconds, or who do not make constant rear progress out of the drafting zone, will be given a drafting violation. • Athletes must ride single file on the far right side of the road except when passing another rider, or for reasons of safety. Side-by-side riding is not allowed and will result in*

a position violation. • Athletes who impede the forward progress of other athletes will be given a blocking violation.

For me, an inexperienced biker, this is barely English. I'm interested to see how the idea of drafting plays out on a three-loop course. It stands to reason that, with 3,000 people going around the same loop three times, it could get quite congested. The thought of staying six bike lengths back when there are bikers everywhere seems like a tall order. It would be like trying to stay six car lengths back in rush hour traffic. Funny enough, if you do get caught drafting or blocking, you are charged with a five-minute penalty, and you physically serve it out in a "penalty box"—a small backyard tent with a sign hung on it that says Penalty Box. I looked it up and it's not just a figure of speech. There actually is a penalty tent.

I've decided that the fourteen-mile run I did yesterday will be the longest of my training. It's not worth pushing mileage and risking injury this close to the race, and besides, I really do feel great about it. It seems like forever since I've been able to run without IT band issues. There's always been that pain at the end of the day. Here and now, this feels different. It feels truly behind me. It's an important step, physically and mentally. There was a voice in the back of my head that wondered if it would ever heal. With less than a month to go until the Ironman, that voice has now finally gone quiet.

From here on out, it will be short runs after bike rides, and maybe one or two stand-alone efforts of six to eight miles. I will continue to do my leg lift exercises and to stretch out my hips. But believe it or not, after the seventy-mile ride and now the fourteen-mile run, my training has peaked. For better (injury prevention) or worse (not enough training), these will be as far as I go before I attempt 112 and 26.2 in Arizona. I also won't do much the next couple days. Maybe a light bike ride or jog. I need to let my legs recover from the big ride and runs. The break comes at a good time. I'm off to Kaua'i on a work trip for what should be a very fun story about the Nā Pali Coast.

When I get back, it will be time to flip the calendar to November and do something I've been wanting to do since day one: stop training.

November 2, 2017
Ala Moana Beach Park, Honolulu, Hawai'i
17 Days Until the Ironman

This is not the end. It is not even the beginning of the end. But it is, perhaps, the end of the beginning.

—Winston Churchill

Kaua'i was great. It's always a good time over there. I checked out a few hotels, did some hikes I had been wanting to do, and researched a couple of stories for down the road. I also did some light running, stretching, and ordered a wet suit. On the last day, I had beers on the beach. It was a wonderful time. I returned home to find the wet suit waiting on my doorstep. I went cheap, at least in comparison to what the Roka suits cost. The wet suit has all the same bells and whistles, including different cuts of thickness for the shoulders. Only this one, because it's not a brand name, was less than $200.

I haven't done any official swim training since the Waikīkī Roughwater. I've been surfing and snorkeling, but I haven't put my head down in the water and swum hard. I've been spending all my time biking and running. With seventeen days to go, it's time to flip the switch on that. Going forward, I want to cut down on my biking and running and replace those workout sessions with a handful of swims. That doesn't mean I will fully stop biking or running, just that I will take it a little easier, and throw in more rest days this next week and a half.

In the triathlete community, cutting back your workouts as you approach an event is known as "the taper." The idea is to give your body a chance to rest and recover, so you can show up at the starting line at full strength. People get very excited about the taper and look forward to it very much. Part of it is because whatever event they are anticipating is approaching. Most of it is because they get to cut back on their workouts. Can you guess which camp I am in?

"Am I the only one already smelling the sweet scent of TAPERING almost here?" one person wrote in the forums.

My taper plan is a little different than most. I'll cut back on biking and running, but I need to catch up on swimming. In the next two weeks, I want to get in three or four swims of at least a mile—basically, more or less the same thing I did leading up to the Waikīkī Roughwater. Today, I'll start with an open-water swim down at Ala Moana Beach Park. It's usually very calm there, so I won't have to deal with any current or seasickness, and it should be a good simulation of the water conditions in Tempe. Minus, of course, the water temperature difference. It's a hot day, somewhere in the mid-80s, and the water temperature is in the high 70s—79 degrees, I think—but it's probably even warmer here at Ala Moana because the water doesn't circulate like it does at other beaches. There is a break a couple hundred yards offshore that does a good job of keeping the water calm and pool-like on most days.

A couple of people stare at me as I zip up the full-length, black wet suit on the beach. I feel elastic, like Stretch Armstrong, as I wade out into the calm ocean. It feels like bath water. From where I'm starting at the west end of the beach, it is a half-mile swim to the other end, where it dead-ends in a small lagoon. I begin the swim. The wet suit feels tight. I can feel it rubbing on the sides of my neck. I stop a few times to try to adjust it, with varying results. Overall, though, it feels OK. It adds an extra bit of buoyancy, making it easier to stay on top of the water. I swim the half mile down to the other end of the beach and look at my watch. Fourteen minutes and change. I haven't lost much since the last time I was in the water, and it makes me happy. I turn around to swim back. It's getting hot in the water with the wet suit. I can feel my head getting hot and turning red.

Halfway back, something doesn't feel right. Each time I bring my right arm over my head, I feel discomfort in my shoulder. It feels sore, a discomfort in the joint. I consider stopping. The last thing I want is to mess up my shoulder. I can feel the wet suit adding resistance on my strokes—something I'm not used to—and I think that's the culprit of the problem. All good. A few swims, and my muscles should get used to it. I push through the discomfort and finish the mile swim in 31:52.

I get out of the water and take off the wet suit. I rinse it under the beach shower, wring it out, and throw it into my trunk. I open the back door of my car, get in, and close the door. I take off my wet bathing suit and put on dry underwear and shorts. I get out of the backseat and sit down on the lip of my trunk and dry off my feet. I put on socks and shoes and take off running. There is a path along the beach here and out onto Magic Island, a small peninsula that has great views of Diamond Head. I run a couple loops and then back to my car for a total of 3.73 miles in twenty-eight minutes (7:30 minutes per mile).

Two days later I ride on the trainer for seventy minutes. I take it nice and easy. The day after that I complete a wonderful run through Waimānalo, eight miles in one hour, again for a 7:30-minute-per-mile pace. I'm feeling strong in the running department, and what was once a source of stress has become an area of confidence now that my IT band is healed completely.

The next day I ride outside through Kailua and Waimānalo, about twenty-one miles. The day after, I go back to Ala Moana for another swim. This time, the plan is to swim a mile and a half. Literally, the exact same thing happens. I swim down to the lagoon, and on the way back, my right shoulder starts to make noise. It's almost as if I have summoned it with how much I'm thinking about it. Instead of easing off, I decide to push it. I want to see how it holds up. With every stroke, I can feel the wet suit pulling on my shoulder, and I can feel my shoulder ache. Then something really bad happens: I feel a sharp pain. It starts in the socket and shoots down my arm, dropping my arm to the water mid-stroke. No! I stop and tread water and shake my shoulder around. I lift it above my head. It feels sore, but I don't feel the sharp pain anymore. I don't risk swimming freestyle any farther. Instead, I swim breaststroke back to shore and walk to my car. Mentally, this is a bad blow. I thought swimming was going to be my throw-away event, but perhaps I've gotten a little too complacent. Here we are less than two weeks out, and I'm having shoulder trouble. I blame the wet suit, and I blame myself for not buying it sooner.

I go to sleep in a bad mood but wake up optimistic about tackling my final bike-run brick workout. It's a huge success. I bike for two hours on the trainer and really work hard at it. I don't watch anything. I don't listen to anything. Mostly, I chew on the stress of having a sore shoulder, imagining that I have to make up time on the bike after the swim. I look out at the fruit trees and the rain forest canopy. I eat two peanut butter and jelly sandwiches, a protein shake, a Clif Bar and, right before I dismount, a GU gel. Then I run the three-mile loop in Waimānalo in 22:03. It's the last bike-run brick workout, and it's also the last time I'll ride my bike before the Ironman.

Both realities are simultaneously relieving and terrifying. The race is closing in so fast—it's already November 8, one week until I fly to Arizona. I'm happy to have a distraction the next couple days. Tomorrow I fly to Washington, D.C., for a long weekend. My sister is baptizing her second baby. It's a bold move, traveling this close to the race. But, I'll be able to jog while I'm there, and real life doesn't stop because you decide to sign up for the Ironman. I'll be back Sunday night, November 12, with plenty of time to pack, and even hit the YMCA for a few light workouts. Then, race week will begin.

November 15, 2017
Waimānalo, O'ahu, Hawai'i
4 Days Until the Ironman

I hate when I have to waste my sick days on being sick.

—Government employee

I collapse into my apartment sometime in the afternoon. I push open the door, throw my backpack on the floor, and fall face first onto the bed. I snort through my nose to stop the snot from reaching my upper lip. I close my eyes, then snap them open. I want to nap very badly, but there is no time. There is still a list of things to do that seems to get longer every time I turn around, and I've got to catch my flight to Phoenix later tonight. The fact that I'm feeling this way is something I'm just going to have to deal with. It's my own damn fault, anyway. I screwed up.

I was trying to be a good uncle. My nephew was being baptized in Washington, D.C., and I wanted to be there for it, to see the family and friends. I hadn't seen most of them in a couple months, and it was a good chance to catch them all in one place as a primer for the upcoming holiday season. This meant I had to travel from Hawai'i to D.C. and back in a span of a few days, brave the cold weather there, mix in a workout among the eating and drinking, and come out the other end healthy. Given the presence of all the kids, maybe it's no surprise what happened. I remember walking in the door and seeing my two nephews. One had snot coming out of his nose. When I picked up the other, he coughed in my face. That was last Friday.

Flash forward a few days and I was on a plane back to Hawai'i, throwing up in one toilet and then ten minutes later emptying it all out the back end into another. You don't want to reverse those processes and use the same toilet, I've learned. I sat on both planes—first from D.C. to Phoenix, then Phoenix to Honolulu—in full winter getup, a big puffy jacket and a warm winter hat. Still, I rocked back and forth, shivering, my legs aching and my stomach churning. Up and down, to and from the bathroom, sipping on Sprite or whatever the hell they gave me. When I arrived in Honolulu, I could take about ten steps before I started to get out of breath. It's a very, very bad feeling when you are a week away from a 140-mile race and you cannot walk through the airport without stopping to rest.

I felt weak and tired and vulnerable, like I better not do too much, or else risk not recovering in time. My grand plan to get a jump on things this week and take the bike apart, pack the suitcase, and get all the gear organized went by the wayside. I kicked off my final week of preparations, which was supposed to be largely mental and logistical, by lying in bed, physically defeated. In total, nine people got sick that weekend via my nephews, some nasty black-plague kind of bug. Of course, I'm the only one with an upcoming Ironman. For the past three days I have been missing in action. Friends ignored, text messages unanswered, e-mail unread.

Yesterday morning my appetite started to come back, along with my energy. I could let out a sigh of relief knowing that, physically, I would recover in time. But that also meant I needed to spend the next two days—every minute of each—making up for lost time. I needed to get my body moving again, on the bike, on a run, and in the pool. And I needed to fill my empty suitcase. Yesterday, I took care of the former. I rode the stationary bike at the gym for thirty minutes—a nice and easy 7.5 miles. I had to wipe my nose with the gym towel a couple of times, but that I was able to ride at that pace without feeling considerably taxed was a good sign. It gave me confidence. I *can* do this, I thought. That high was quickly erased when I got in the pool. My shoulder started to flare up after only a few laps.

I went to bed early again last night. When I woke up this morning, I felt better. Significantly better. My appetite came roaring back within an hour of being awake. I made up for lost time at breakfast and lunch: Gatorade, electrolyte tablets, a protein shake, oatmeal, a peanut butter and jelly sandwich, and a couple pieces of fruit. I shoveled it in with pleasure. I could feel my body rebooting itself. All that's left is a little snot and some fatigue. I'll continue to hydrate throughout the day, and sprinkle in some snacks. Tonight, I'll have a big piece of chicken, potatoes, and rice for dinner before my flight.

I called my sister this morning and she said her other friends were reporting the same thing, a twenty-four to forty-eight-hour bug. They all felt better, she said. I asked her if this was all part of her plan to see me die at the Ironman. She told me not to make excuses. Fair enough. I pulled myself out of bed this morning by my own hair. I went out and ran errands, crossing off a dozen items centered around getting to the starting line with all my ducks in a row. I hit the grocery store for some energy bars, the tri shop for some spare tubes and butt paste. When I came home I fell onto the bed and felt tired. But now I have to get up.

I fly out tonight on a red-eye flight to Phoenix. Overnighting on a plane is not the best way to kick off Ironman weekend, but there's little I can do about that coming from Hawai'i. That's just the way it is when you fly east. And, I don't know, it seems fitting, doesn't it? After all I've been through, why not throw another wrinkle into the fold? Why not sacrifice a night's sleep three days before the race? These are the obstacles that Ironmen dream to overcome, aren't they? Let's go ahead and see how ridiculous I can make this for myself. Maybe I can schedule a root canal for Saturday morning.

I'll arrive mid-morning tomorrow, Thursday, leaving me three nights to recover from the travel before the race on Sunday. I have already prepped my mom and aunt that I will be out of commission leading up to the race—in other words, don't count on me for anything. There will be many things to do. The most important one is to rest, but I already know that will be a challenge, given the lengthy list: My transition bags need to be planned; the food for the day needs to be purchased; the special needs bags need to be packed; transportation to and from the event needs to be arranged; I need to set up and tune the bike (or fix it if it is damaged during travel). Then there's the check-in and athletes' meeting on Thursday, and the practice swim and bike drop-off on Saturday—it goes on and on.

Today, now that the errands are done, the number one thing to do is to pack. I have to get all my clothes together, as well as take apart the bike and pack it into its box. But before it gets too late on the East Coast, I call Bmac to get his last-minute advice. I tell him I'm heading to the airport later tonight, that my journey is about to begin. He sounds excited for me until I tell him about what I have gone through the last few days, the throwing up and the weakness and the lack of appetite. That concerns him. Do you feel better now? he asks. I guess, I tell him. I'm eating more now. I'm feeling better by the hour.

"Man, what a shitty thing to happen right before the race," he says. "You're lucky . . . if it were a few days later, you'd have gone through all this for nothing."

I tell him not to remind me. Could you imagine? I understand now why triathletes are so careful with themselves the week of the race. Suddenly, it doesn't seem so psycho. Imagine training for six, eight, ten, twelve months for a race and then coming down with a cold a few days before. You've paid all that money to enter and to travel. That would be a very tough pill to swallow. As I talk to Bmac, my mentality changes. I no longer feel like the victim. Instead, I'm grateful I was able to get better in time. Three months ago, I would have been open to using this as an excuse to bail out. Today, after all the time I've put in, you better believe I want to toe the line this Sunday.

"I know, man, I know," I say. "I'm lucky."

"How are you feeling otherwise?" he asks. "Are you ready?"

"I think so. I'm in the process of getting packed. Any last-minute advice?"

Bmac tells me the reason people come back race after race is because it's a fun, great community. He says I will be tested like never before on

Sunday, but that I should embrace it and have fun, that I shouldn't stress too much. He says the hard work is already done, and all that's left to do is trust my training. I tell him it would be a lot easier to trust my training if people hadn't been telling me all along that I wasn't doing enough. He asks me how far along I got with the bike and the run.

"Seventy miles on the bike, once," I tell him. "The farthest I ran was fourteen miles."

"Oh," he says.

He tells me, in that case, there's going to be even more unknown for me on Sunday. He says not to go out too fast—it's a long day—and to try to get in the "sweet spot" as quickly as I can on the bike and run. Just get to a pace where you feel comfortable, he says, and work from there. Don't worry about what everyone else is doing. I'm going to have times when I'm down, he says. Just stay as positive as I can. I thank Bmac for all his help and guidance. I couldn't have done it without him. He says hold on, we're not done. The most important thing to remember on race day is to always be eating. Eat little bits at a time, on a reasonable schedule. He, for example, ate at least one GU an hour, plus other snacks. I tell him I'm all set, that I've picked up enough bars, GU, and other junk to last me through the first week of the apocalypse.

Good, he says. Make sure you do most of your carb loading two days before. Then, the day before, eat your biggest meal at lunch, and be reasonable from there. Don't overload, he says. I ask him what he ate the morning of his race. Did he get up early?

"A whole wheat bagel with banana and peanut butter," he says. He encourages me to get up at least a couple hours before the start of the race. "You'll want to get there early to double-check your bike, and you definitely want to take a shit before the race." He wishes me luck and tells me he'll be following along on Sunday. Goodbye, I say. See you on the other side.

The conversation doesn't make me feel better in any way. In fact, it only heightens my anticipation and anxiety. It's only four more days until the race and there is still so much to do. So many hurdles to jump through. So much to worry about. It all starts right now with packing.

I find the list I made of all the things I need to bring for the race: bike, bike shoes, bike clothes, bike helmet, bike tools, bike pumps, bike computer, wristwatch, bike water bottles, rain jacket, long-sleeve T-shirt, running shoes, running socks, swim goggles, wet suit, jammers, Clif Bars, Bonk Breaker bars, GU packets, electrolyte tabs, protein powder, rice, oatmeal, flip-flops, KT tape, rice cooker, foam roller, Imodium pills, ibuprofen, clothes for day-to-day life leading up to the race. There are a few more items, but you get the idea.

The rice cooker probably sticks out as being a weird thing to bring. I could find a restaurant to sell me some white rice. But it's a comfort thing. I've been eating rice as one of my staple food items since day one. To know that I have the cooker in my hotel room, and that I can make rice when I want it, puts me at ease. It's all part of a plan to control what I eat. I want to make sure I can keep my diet as similar to what I've been eating as possible despite the fact that I won't have a stove top or microwave in the hotel room. My goal is to eat out as little as possible this weekend. Every time I eat out, I put myself at risk of something not sitting well. I know it sounds a little crazy, but people do get sick when they eat out. It doesn't have to be full-on food poisoning—any small disagreement can turn into a big problem on the course. I want to minimize my risk. So I'm packing a rice cooker in my suitcase along with ziplock bags full of rice. When I arrive in Tempe, I'll hit the grocery store to pick up other things. The usual suspects—bananas, apples, whole wheat bread, peanut butter, Gatorade.

I start playing Tetris with all the gear. I want to fit it all in one big suitcase. Then I'll carry on a small backpack and check the bike box. The bag will cost $25; the bike will cost $150. What else? I jump online to the forums to see what people are talking about. People are posting a lot of photos of themselves packing. All the gear spread out on the bed, or all the bags piled up in the back of the car, with a caption like, "See you soon, Arizona!" I see one woman's post about how she got a hundred miles from home before realizing she forgot her bike! It's easy to laugh at something like that, but I will say, in her defense, the packing part can be overwhelming. It's easy to overlook something when there are a million things. That's why I made a list and I'm checking it twice.

I put the big suitcase in the trunk and the bike box in the back. Before I know it, my bags are checked, I've got my boarding pass, and I'm through security. I'm handing my ticket to the gate agent and ducking my head to step off the jet bridge and onto the plane. I'm finding my seat. The plane backs away from the jet bridge and taxis away from the gate. I look out the window as we pull away. I hope my bike got on board, and I hope it got on board in one piece.

Oh, hell, what's there to do about it now? That's all behind me. That's all accomplished. The bike is down below. Maybe it's not. Maybe the guys were rough with it when they loaded it. Maybe they broke a wheel. Maybe it's fine. I'll find out when I get to Arizona. Whatever it throws at me, I'll be ready. I've come too far to let something derail me now. Bring on the course, and the elements, and the physical challenge. For me, the Ironman has already begun. It began with those eleven hours of sickly flying, the following day in bed, and the two days of frantic, stressful packing that followed. It continues right now on the red-eye flight from Honolulu to Phoenix. I hope to get a few hours of sleep. Tomorrow will be a big day. The pilot comes on the intercom and tells the flight attendants to prepare for takeoff. I take an Ambien. I remember taking off but not much after.

Part Four

Swim Fast, Don't Breathe

November 16, 2017
Tempe, Arizona
3 Days Until the Ironman

> *You guys are lucky. You get to race, you get to have fun, you get to go 140.6 miles, and we cater it all for you!*
>
> —Ironman employee

I wake up when the wheels hit the runway with a thud. I've drooled down the front of my shirt a little bit. I zip up my hoodie to cover the wet spot. I collect my big suitcase from the luggage conveyor belt. I have to wait an extra fifteen minutes for the bike box to be brought down by hand. I lift up the bike box and set it on top of my big suitcase. Wearing my backpack, I push the four-wheeled suitcase with the big box on top through the airport and out the door to the shuttle stop. It's ten minutes before I'm in the van and on the way to the hotel. It's 8:45 a.m.

The descriptively named Sheraton Phoenix Airport Hotel Tempe is a ten-minute ride, though it's not at the airport like the name suggests—just close. I guess they wanted to get as many keywords into the name as they could. Welcome to 2017. It's a nice place, clean with a restaurant in the lobby and a very nice, oasis-like pool area in the center of the complex. It's a little more than four miles to Tempe Beach Park and downtown Tempe. I check in but my room is not ready. I store the bags and the bike and call an Uber. I'd like to get all the logistics out of the way as soon as possible. Athlete registration is open all day today and tomorrow. There are two athlete briefings per day, and it's mandatory I attend one of them, per the Athlete Guide. This works out well, actually. I can head over there now, check-in at registration, attend the mid-morning briefing, hit the grocery store, and then be back here by early afternoon. By then, the room should be ready, and I can assemble my bike. My mom and aunt arrive in the late afternoon.

The ride to the race's main hub at Tempe Beach Park takes ten minutes. Within the span of a few city blocks is the starting line for the swim, the finish line, the transition tent, the registration tents, the Ironman Village, and the main drag of downtown Tempe, Mill Avenue. It's all right there, which makes it easy on everyone. This is the reason Ironman Arizona is considered one of the most spectator-friendly events on the circuit. Everything happens in the same place, providing multiple opportunities to see the racers pass by. When there's downtime, the shops, bars, and restaurants of Mill Avenue are a short walk away.

The driver drops me off by the finish line. Or, rather, where the finish line will be. There's a bunch of metal gates set up and a couple of trucks parked in the street, but the finish chute hasn't been constructed yet. I walk through, across the open green spaces of Tempe Beach Park, to the registration tent. There's barely a line and I silently rejoice. I show my ID to one of the volunteers. I sign a form releasing Ironman from any liability should I die during the race. Then I'm whisked off to a series of tables under the large tent, where more volunteers slap a wristband on me and present my race packet. I am assigned my race number—1970—and given a bag of goodies. In it is my race bib (the piece of paper with my race number on it), stickers for my bike, product samples, and literature. I'm also given an Ironman-branded backpack, my bike and run clothes bags, and my bike and run special needs bags. There's a container of safety pins and I take four of them. I'll need to pin my race bib to my shirt. Before exiting the tent, volunteers at the last table give me my timing chip. This will be worn around my ankle during the race, like I'm a convict.

I look at my watch and it's 10:15 a.m. There is an Athlete Briefing at 11:00 a.m. I put all the stuff in the Ironman backpack, zip it shut, and walk up Mill Avenue. I find a small cafe called the Delicious Factory (how could one resist?) and get a breakfast bagel sandwich to go. I walk back toward Tempe Beach Park. It's relatively quiet, a couple dozen early-bird arrivals like me but no hustle or bustle to speak of.

The Ironman Village is open and I head for it. Similar to the World Championship at Kona, there is a section of small tents and booths from which vendors promote their products to athletes. I walk through, not because I'm overly interested but because they've set it up along the main pathway between Mill Avenue and Tempe Beach Park. I see Clif Bar is offering samples and I take one. As I walk by one of the booths, a young woman flags me down and tries to sell me on signing up to support her charity. She says that if I do, I could potentially race Ironman Arizona next year again, too. She says it very enthusiastically. I tell her I can't think of a worse prize. In front of me, I overhear two middle-aged men talking. I pick up on their conversation. They are talking about pizza.

"I can't believe Ironman doesn't get hot pizza to the finish line," one of them tells the other. He's airing his frustration. "Let me tell you, I've worked for many pizza shops, maybe four or five. The way you do it is you just keep ordering them, and they'll put them in the oven all day, one after another, so you always have hot pizza being delivered."

I realize there is no pizza to be eaten right now and pass the two men. I continue down through Tempe Beach Park, past the registration tent and through the grassy areas. There are metal gates set up, outlining the transition areas and the bike corral. In a few days this area will be jam-packed with bikes and gear and competitors, but right now it's the calm before the storm. I try to go around the bike corral to the right and hit a dead end thanks to the metal gates. I turn around and go back the other way, following along the gates until I reach the water. I sit down on a bench and eat my breakfast sandwich. There's a breeze and it's nice in the shade. The sun is getting hotter by the minute here in mid-morning, a not-so-subtle sign of things to come. A few days from now, at this exact time, I'll be on the bike course, hopefully somewhere between mile thirty and forty. Right now, it is nice here in the shade. I look into Tempe Town Lake. The water is brown in color. It does not look particularly inviting. The man-made canal collects runoff and, along with it, a lot of dust and dirt. I suppose it's further motivation to swim as fast as I can. I look at my watch. Fifteen minutes until the meeting starts.

The common piece of advice I've received concerning my first Ironman is to "enjoy" my few days here before the race. Check it all out, soak it all in, they tell me. I've been finding that guidance to be confusing. Enjoy what exactly? The main goal of these next three days is to rest and mentally prepare for a 140.6-mile race. I've got a million things left to do. I still have to hit the grocery store, I have to put my bike together. I have to attend this meeting, I have to do the practice swim tomorrow, I have to go to bed early. Sounds . . . fun. Sitting here by the canal eating a sandwich is probably as good as it's going to get.

I take an extra moment to "enjoy" my sandwich and walk back around the bike corral, past the registration tent, to an open field. On one end, adjacent to the Ironman Village, there's a small stage with a digital TV screen. The screen is rolling through product advertisements. I sit down in the grass. Away from the water, the sun feels very hot. I move to the other side of the field, where there are small strips of shade. There are a few dozen other athletes. This meeting itself is not mandatory—just that you attend one of them either today, tomorrow, or on Saturday. A man comes on stage and introduces himself. I don't recognize the name. Seems like he's an employee of Ironman. Or a volunteer. Most likely the latter? I don't know. I look around for someone taking attendance. I don't see anyone. The man with the mic welcomes us all to Tempe and lets us know if we're here for the Athlete Briefing, we're in the right place.

"Now," he says, "we're going to go through what you can expect this weekend." He holds up a stack of papers in his right hand, the mic in his left. He paces across the front of the small stage. Sweat drips down his face in the heat of the day. "And everything I'm going to talk about is right here in the Athlete Guide."

I am greatly annoyed by this. First off, you cannot call a mandatory meeting and not take attendance. I want credit. Second, you cannot say the meeting is very important and then read through something you've already given us to read. Stop. Wasting. My. Time. Please. He flips the guide open and looks down at the first page.

"You guys are lucky," he says, looking back up. "You get to race, you get to have fun, you get to go 140.6 miles, and we cater it all for you!"

I get up and leave after ten minutes, once I have confirmed that he is just going to go through the guide a page at a time. I walk back to Mill Avenue and get an Uber. I stop at Buffalo Exchange and buy a cheap pair of warm-up pants to wear the morning of the race. I realized at the airport last night that I had forgotten to pack them. This is the desert. Don't be fooled by the hot days—the mornings will be cold, in the low-to-mid 50s, which is like the Arctic for my Hawai'i-conditioned system.

I find a grocery store on the way back to the hotel. I'm dropped off there. I buy whole wheat bagels, whole wheat bread, peanut butter, jelly, a Snickers bar, one small bottle of Coke, a bag of pretzels, bananas, lunch meat, sliced cheese, and a six-pack—of Gatorade. I already have the energy bars, rice, oatmeal, and protein powder in my luggage. I call yet another Uber and head back for the hotel. The room is ready and I'm able to check in. It's a normal hotel room. Walk in the door, and the bathroom is immediately there on your right, and past that it opens up into the main room, with two double beds and their headboards on the right side of the room. On the left is a big, flat countertop with a TV on top, and past that a small desk. There's a window on the back wall that looks out into the parking lot. Below the window is a small air-conditioning unit, and in the corner, beyond the second bed, is a reading chair. Between all my gear, the bike, and then my mom and aunt and all their stuff, it's going to be a tight fit, and we'll be lucky if we don't kill each other by the end of the weekend.

I flop my suitcase onto the bed closest to the door. I put the grocery bags on the dresser next to the TV. There's a small fridge in one of the dresser cabinets, where I stash the lunch meat, jelly, and Gatorade. I drag the bike box into the foyer, next to the bathroom door and the main door. This will be the first time I've put together the bike since Danny helped me put it together three months ago. Let's see . . . I know one wheel goes in the front, and the other in the back . . .

It takes me thirty minutes to get it assembled. I'm proud of this. The handlebars are on correctly, the pedals went on without a problem, the tires pumped up OK and nothing got bent or broken during the flight. This is a huge relief, seeing the bike together in one piece. I grease the chain, then take the bike outside and ride it around the parking lot. I adjust the brakes, try out all the gears, and tweak the position of the aero bars. It all checks out fine. I wheel the bike back inside and lean it against the wall across from the bathroom. We will have to move the bike every time we want to open the door, but there's nowhere else to put it. I slide the bike box between the first bed and the wall. It just does squeeze in there. I get the call that my mom and aunt have landed from Philadelphia. I continue unpacking my bag while I wait. I drink a Gatorade and use the foam roller on my legs, back, and feet.

I make two cups of rice in the rice cooker and put it in the fridge for later. I clean the rice cooker in the bathroom sink. It barely fits under the nozzle. I dry it with one of the white hand towels. I eat a banana and drink half a Gatorade, then top off the bottle with water. I plan to drink this, then refill it again. Then I'll have one more and sip on it and then cut myself off so I don't have to wake up in the middle of the night and pee. I open the backpack and sort through the stuff I got at registration. There are two cans of Red Bull in the giveaway bag and two packs of sample protein powder. I throw it all away. I don't want to roll the dice with anything new this close to the race. And I only drink Red Bull with vodka.

In the backpack I find the plastic bags for my clothes. There's a red Run Gear Bag, a blue Bike Gear Bag, a black Run Special Needs Bag, and an orange Bike Special Needs Bag. All of them are thick plastic with white drawstrings. There's a box on each bag where you write your race number with black permanent marker. I lay these bags out on the bed. The colors pop out against the white backdrop of the comforter. Red. Blue. Black. Orange.

I lay another bag I brought with me on the bed, too. This one is completely white. On top of it I put everything I'll need the morning of the race for the swim—my wet suit, goggles, cap, body glide,* soap (defogger), warm-up pants, and jacket.

Then, on each of the four other bags, I lay out corresponding items. Coming out of the swim, I'll need all my bike stuff in my Bike Gear

* I haven't used this on swims in the past. My sister gave me a bottle when I visited last weekend. She said a lot of swimmers use it under their wet suits. It should ease the tension of my suit on my shoulder.

Bag—my bike leotard, bike shoes, socks, helmet, butt paste, and gloves (the small saddle bag on the bike will already have extra tubes and bike tools inside).

I put my running shoes, socks, race bib, and four safety pins on top of the red Run Gear Bag, which I'll collect after the bike. I will run in my bike leotard, so I won't have to change.

Then I lay out the food on the bed: nine GUs, four Clif Bars, and two Bonk Breakers. I split them up among the morning, bike, and run bags. On race morning, I'll add a bag of pretzels and a couple of peanut butter and jelly sandwiches to the bike bag. I put an extra tire tube and a bottle of Coke in my Bike Special Needs Bag. Into the Run Special Needs Bag goes the roll of KT Tape.

After organizing all this my mom and aunt arrive. While they settle in, I go on a jog. It's a short run, three miles, in 25:14 (8:13 minutes per mile). I listen to music as I run. I feel great, completely recovered from my illness. My IT band is fully healed and hasn't bothered me. All my joints feel good, my shoes are broken in and comfortable. All is without issue. It feels good to feel this confidence, and to break a sweat in the evening heat. It feels like I've arrived, and it feels like I'm ready.

November 17, 2017
Tempe, Arizona
2 Days Until the Ironman

Proper planning and preparation prevents piss poor performance.

—The Seven Ps

Because yesterday was a busy day—hitting the ground running with registration, "mandatory" meetings, shopping, putting the bike together, unpacking my big suitcase and repacking it into small bags—today is going to be mellow. I sleep in until nine, eat a bagel with peanut butter and banana for breakfast, drink a protein shake. I watch a little television. I convince my mom and aunt to go out on their own for the day. I go to the hotel gym and use the stationary bike for thirty minutes. I pedal nice and slow, without much resistance, and eat salted pretzels and drink

Gatorade and listen to music. I stretch out for thirty minutes after that, paying close attention to my legs, back, and shoulders. Back in the room I use the foam roller.

It does not get much more exciting than that, unfortunately. Today is all about killing time and fueling up. There's nothing to be gained by doing anything. I only want to stay loose and fresh. I want to make sure I'm consistently snacking and hydrating. I switch back and forth between Gatorade and water and often mix them together. I am not carbo-loading in any scientific or calculated manner. But I am eating things that are high in carbohydrates, like whole wheat bread, rice, and energy bars. I'm making sure to get plenty of protein via the shakes. I know the jury is somewhere in the middle about how much protein you need, but it makes me feel stronger and satisfied.

I'm glad it's a chill day. Tomorrow will be busy with the bike check-in and practice swim, so it's a good time to hang around and think. There are a few things I need to figure out:

1. How will I approach the swim? My shoulder is sore, but if you remember from the Athlete Guide, the bike has hard cutoffs. Every minute more I spend in the water is one less I have for the bike portion. The chance of a flat tire and the fact that I've never ridden more than seventy miles make me think I should allow myself all the time I can. This means doing the swim as fast as I can. But slowing down and taking an extra twenty minutes in the water would make things a lot more comfortable on my shoulder.
2. What will my pace be on the bike? The course is three loops, each about 37 miles, and approximately 15 miles of that is uphill. Some of the uphill is more severe, but as far as I understand, it never gets super steep. It's more of a long, gradual climb. How should I approach this?
3. What's the plan on the run? Since I've practiced the bike-to-run transition many, many times, should I try to go out strong? Or should I ease into it?

I also have to write an e-mail. A lot of friends have been asking me for my tracking information. I sit down at the desk in front of my laptop and start writing. The purpose is to inform my friends, but I'm also talking it through with myself.

Hey hey,

If you are receiving this e-mail, it's because you have expressed interest in following me during this Sunday's Ironman. I appreciate your support. I will most definitely need it.

Here's how to follow:

Download this app on your phone: [pasted link to Ironman app]

Find the Ironman Arizona and type in my name or bib# (1970). There should be a button to get push alerts and track me, or you can just refresh it incessantly. There should also be a map feature that will approximate my location on the course.

I'm not exactly sure what to expect in terms of timing. As many of you know, I've only had three months to prepare, so there's a lot of unknown once I get into the big distances.

Swim (2.4 miles): *I'm hoping to be somewhere between 1:10–1:20. That could change on the fly. I've had a little shoulder soreness in the past couple weeks, so I may not be up for pushing it as I usually would. I'm going to settle in and see what happens. If it starts to bother me, I may chill and settle for 1:20-1:30. If I go any longer than that, you know something has gone wrong. Either I've cramped up in the cold water and am doing breaststroke, or I've been elbowed in the face, lost my goggles, and sank to the bottom of Tempe Town Lake.*

Bike (112 miles): *I'll be interested to see how the bike goes. Most of my training has been in Hawai'i, where it is humid. Phoenix is dry, but possibly windy. I'm not sure whether I'll be at 14–15 mph or 17–18 mph for my average speed. I'll take either. So long as I keep hydrated, well fed, don't have any mental breakdowns, and don't have any bike problems (flat tires, etc.), I feel like I should be able to be in* *those ranges, at least for the first 75 miles. After that, we will see. Any long delays probably mean I've had a flat tire, crashed, bonked, or stopped for a beer.*

Run (26.2 miles): *One thing I've really focused on is bike to run transition, so I'm hoping to come off the bike and get into the run without much issue (all things considered). But, after the first 10–14 miles, all bets are off. Here is where I'll need all of you to mentally send me energy. Like the end of Final Fantasy II, where all the past characters come back to restore vitality in those fighting the battle on the moon, so too will your caricatures appear in my brain and give me strength to keep going. I hope to stay steady somewhere in the 9-min. mile range, maybe a little faster on the front end and slowing down on the second half, assuming no nagging foot, IT band, or knee injuries pop up.*

I've called ahead and told all the breweries in Tempe to make extra beer for Monday.

Thanks for your support! See you on the other side.

—Will

I push send. There I have it. My plan. Laid out, nice and pretty for all the world to see, and for the results to judge. After a while my mom and aunt come back from Scottsdale. They had a good time. We go down to Mill Avenue and have dinner. I get a big bowl of pasta and watch my mom and aunt enjoy a couple glasses of wine. We head back to the hotel around 9:00 p.m. and I'm in bed shortly after. I lie awake for a while, reflecting on how my life has become nothing more than a waiting game, getting through the days in anticipation of the future. The sad part is that I'm not even looking forward to the future—I'm most interested in its passing. My mom and aunt lay down on the other bed, prop themselves up with pillows, put in their headphones, and watch TV on their iPads. I roll over. After ten minutes I get up and pee. It takes thirty more minutes to fall asleep.

November 18, 2017
Tempe, Arizona
1 Day Until the Ironman

There is no terror in the bang, only in the anticipation of it.

—Alfred Hitchcock

I wake up and I feel great. It's a beautiful day in Arizona, sunny and in the 70s, and it's been five days since I've had a drop of alcohol. The sickness is behind me. All the travel is done. The bags are packed. We're one day away. There are only three things left to do before the big dance: drop off my bike, drop off my running and biking clothes, and do the practice swim. By lunchtime today, I'll be in the home stretch. All that will be left to do is rest and relax.

The hotel is four miles from the starting line. In theory, I could call an Uber Large and put the bike in the car. I decide to ride my bike over. It's a nice day. I figure I can take the ride nice and easy and use it to loosen my legs. Then I can do the same with my shoulders on the practice swim. I don't plan to do any other exercise today. In fact, after lunch, I don't plan to leave the hotel room. I will lay out all my clothes for tomorrow, and otherwise I will lay myself out on the bed.

I dress and say goodbye to my mom and aunt, who are still lounging in the other bed. They tell me they will meet me down there for the practice swim. I roll the bike out the hotel door, into the hallway, and out through the lobby.

Arizona is especially nice in the morning. The sun blasts through the open, clear sky but is not yet at full strength. It bathes the land in golden light. The dry air is cool and I breathe it in. I get on my bike. Last night I put on two stickers given to me at check-in. Each one displays my race number. There's one around the main frame of the bike, on the bar below the seat. The other one is on the front of my helmet. I'm wearing the branded backpack they gave me at check-in. Inside are my run and bike bags and my wet suit. With my bike leotard and shoes packed away in my bike bag, I ride in regular shorts, a T-shirt, and flip-flops. It feels wonderful to be riding this way. For so long, I have only ridden with great intensity. Today, I'm just cruising.

I take my time and reach the bike transition area—which is four miles from the hotel and right there with the start and finish lines—in thirty minutes. I had no interest in pushing the pace beyond a slow roll. Now would not be a good time to get into an accident or fall off the bike. When I arrive, there are already many bikes hanging from the racks. Picture the bike corral as a vineyard of bikes: The metal racks are the posts, and the bikes are the grapevines. They run in straight lines through the open field, each in full bloom, with the various colors of the bikes standing out against the green grass. There's a long line to get through the gate. Everyone waiting in line is wheeling a bike. I lean on mine as I wait. The line moves fast and I get to the front in ten minutes. I am met by two greeters—two volunteers—who take my bike from me. They put it up against a clean, white background and take a picture of it. Then they hand it back to me. I wheel the bike through the grass, keeping an eye out for anything that could puncture a tire. There are signs at the end of every row with a range of bib numbers on them. I find my spot, 1970. I estimate that my spot is a twenty-second run from the changing rooms, and a ten-second run from the exit to the bike course. The bikes are stacked very close together and the area is not as big as you would expect it to be for 3,000 bikes. The reality of that number is shocking to me as I look out over the vineyard, as I watch all the athletes tend to their vines. All these bikes will be left here overnight. Can you believe that? This is a very expensive vineyard. I assume they guard it heavily at night. I picture armed guards, pacing back and forth, holding large rifles, maybe someone on top of the grandstand with binoculars, a radio, and a sniper rifle. Most likely, it's a bunch of volunteers who look after it all.

Both the start and finish lines are close to the bike corral. The finish line is a block away and I cannot see it. But I can see the starting line, as well as Tempe Town Lake, from where I stand at my slot. That's where I'll get in the water for the practice swim.

Also next to the bike corral—I can see it from here—is a small grassy area. I walk over with my bags. A volunteer greets me and asks me my race number. She points to two separate sections of the field. Both have neat lines of bags, one after another. The running section is full of red bags; the bike bags on the other side are blue. Like the bike corral, each row of bags corresponds to a range of numbers. I find the sections for 1970 and put the bags on the ground, next to the others. Each bag has a sticker with a race number on it. It's not a high-tech solution by any stretch of the imagination—everyone just leaves their bags on the ground—but I'm not sure what else you do with 6,000 bags.

Tempe Town Lake is a beautiful recreation area encompassing the "lake" itself, the waterfront, and the small parks that have become the bike corral, starting line, and run/bike bag staging area. It's an oasis in the desert, a place for paddleboards and paddleboats, a place for people to come walk along its shore during the early morning or evening. It's beautiful. On the other side is a larger open space called Papago Park. There are a lot of tall cacti there. I will see some of them on the run tomorrow.

Ironically, one thing Tempe Town Lake is not great for is swimming. In fact, swimming is normally prohibited. You can paddleboard on it, but you cannot swim in it. It collects runoff from the surrounding area, resulting in water of questionable quality. It's murky and brown. Of course, water quality is nothing for an Ironman to be concerned about. Tomorrow we're going to swim 2.4 miles in it. Today, we have the chance to jump in and feel it out.

The practice swim is open for an hour and a half, with strict start and finish times. I plan to swim for twenty minutes, stretch out the shoulders. There's nothing to be gained from anything else, physically speaking. But mentally, it's a chance to see how the temperature feels and check out the visibility of the water. It's also a chance for me to have another go in my wet suit and to feel out my shoulder.

I take off my warm-up pants to reveal my jammers. I pull my wet suit from the backpack and hold it in my arms. I stand against the metal gate between the bike corral and the water. There are hundreds of people scattered about the waterfront, stepping into their wet suits and fixing their goggles. Others are already out of the water, done with their practice swim, dripping wet. Even more are in line for the bike corral. I wait another ten minutes until my mom and aunt arrive. I pull the suit over my shoulders, work my arms through, and grab my cap and goggles. I give them my backpack. My aunt looks around at all of us there, changing into our wet suits. She looks at the others dropping off their bikes. She turns to my mom.

"Karen, I don't know who in the hell would want to do this shit."

I head for the water. "Swim fast, don't breathe!" my mom calls out. It's what she always used to say to me before my swim races as a kid—too much breathing slows you down. I give her a thumbs up. There's a concrete staircase with railings that leads into the water. I push my goggles tight to my eyes, then pull the cap on over my head, covering the straps. I walk down the stairs. The last step is underwater. I step down onto the step and the water covers my ankles. I fall forward into the water and start swimming. The water is somewhere in the mid-60s. I feel the initial shock of the cold on my bare feet and hands. I feel it trying to get down my sleeves and down my neck. But the suit holds. With each stroke, the water feels less cold and more refreshing. I try not to think too much about the water. By now, hundreds of people have peed in it.

There's a small wind coming through the canal. There's a small chop on the water. It's nothing compared to the ocean currents I'm used to, but not unnoticeable. I take it very easy, stretching out with each arm. I swim down under the first bridge and follow the buoys that've been set up. It's a small course that makes a small circle. As expected, visibility in the water is very poor—I can barely see the hand in front of my face. When I breathe, I can taste the grit of the water. As I complete a lap on the course, my mind becomes aware of my shoulder. It doesn't hurt, but I notice it. It is certainly still less than 100 percent. I have no doubt that I will be able to finish the swim, though I might have to adjust my expectations. I had hoped to be somewhere in the vicinity of 1:15. I might have to take it easy and settle for 1:30, or 1:40, and raise my expectations on the bike.

I decide not to take a second lap and swim back for the stairs. Outside the water, it's starting to heat up. It's around 11:00 a.m. now. My mom gives me a towel and I dry off. She tells me I looked cute out there in my little wet suit. One of the guys next to me overhears this and laughs. I ask her to stop embarrassing me in front of all the Ironmen. We walk through the Ironman Village, ignoring the vendors who call out for us to come over and try out whatever they're selling. As I leave the area, I feel anxiety try to creep in. Dropping off the bike, my running shoes, and everything else I've kept so close these past few months makes it all feel real. The time is near.

We decide to get an early lunch. My mom got a tip about a place that sells pastrami sandwiches. I think hot red meat covered in cheese might be too much of a stomach risk, so I order chicken parm and pasta instead. Looking back, I'm not sure why I considered fried chicken covered in cheese a better alternative. Must have been blinded by the side of pasta. After lunch, I send my mom and aunt out into Tempe for the rest of the afternoon and ask them to stay out through dinner.

"What are you going to do?" my mom asks.

"Pray," I tell her.

I return to the hotel room. I ensure the thermostat is set at a cool and comfortable 68 degrees. I shower and hang my wet suit and jammers up to dry in the bathroom. I drape the wet suit over the shower curtain rod. I plop down on the bed and turn on the TV. There's not much left to do in the way of preparation. Most of my stuff is staged at Tempe Town Lake. All I need tomorrow is my swim stuff, some food, and the timing chip. It can all fit in my backpack. It feels good to be ready, logistically speaking. Whether I'm completely ready remains to be seen.

I lay in bed for a while, reading baseball hotstove news. I check my e-mail. Today, I received three e-mails from three different Ironman accounts. One is from "Ironman Arizona." The subject is "*Good luck tomorrow!*" Alongside the event date and location—November 19; Tempe, Arizona—there's a photo of a guy running and it has the caption "Good Luck."

The next e-mail is from "Ironman Triathlon." The subject is "*Don't let the Holiday's sneak up on you!*" I notice that Holiday's is misused. I'm sure it should be holidays without the apostrophe. Inside is a link to the 2017 Holiday Gift Guide and this passage: "Check out our 2017 Holiday Gift Guide for unique and fun products that will get you on the podium for the best gift giver ever this holiday season." The last part is ridiculous but that's what it says.

The third e-mail is from "Ironman Store." The subject is "*Will, Life is what you BAKE of it.*" It's a newsletter for items on sale at the online store. There's a link to buy a new Finisher Patch Jacket, a link for Black

Friday Savings, and a link to the Home for the Holidays section of the store, which advertises Ironman cookie cutters, spatulas, ice cube trays, and throw blankets. I ponder my peculiar present, in which a triathlon company sends me an e-mail with such a subject line. It makes me curious. I do a search and count up all the commercial e-mails Ironman has sent me since I started this journey back in August. In total, they've sent me eighty-two.

I wonder what everyone else is doing? I close my e-mail and head to the forums. A couple of people have posted pictures of themselves lying on their hotel beds. Most of them show the person's feet at the end of the bed and the TV in the background. The captions vary, but the notion is all the same: *I'm doing nothing*. Side conversations have broken out. Some people are asking logistical questions, like what time the parking lots open. Others are worrying aloud about flat tires and goat's-head thorns, or the wind on the bike course. I see one conversation about the practice swim this morning. Someone is complaining about the conditions at Tempe Town Lake. They say they weren't expecting it to be choppy, and that they're praying it's not choppy tomorrow. To which one guy replied, "This is Ironman, not Easyman."

Fair enough. I flip through the TV channels and find an old movie, *Troy*. I haven't seen it in a long time. It's kind of a sad movie. All the deaths. All the bloodshed. All the tension that must have existed in life back then. I hate the part when Hector dies. But it's also kind of inspiring. Seeing those guys run on the front lines. Seeing them run into the thick of it with such bravery. Maybe I can take something away from that for tomorrow. I continue watching the movie. In one of the scenes, someone on the front line gets a spear through the face. I try to stop thinking about tomorrow.

I sip on Gatorade and water throughout the afternoon. I drink the first half of the Gatorade, then refill it with water and drink the rest.

Mr. & Mrs. Smith comes on next. I guess it's a Brad Pitt marathon or something. This movie is not inspiring but it *is* distracting. Angelina Jolie seems like a good person. I wonder what she would think of the Ironman. She would probably be a volunteer if they asked her. During the movie I cook dinner. I cook more rice and I eat two cups like it's two spoonfuls. I also eat a turkey and cheese sandwich on a whole wheat bagel. Everyone has advised me not to overeat the night before, but I feel like I have to fuel up. The rice is clean, the turkey is lean, and I digest bread very well. I eat the rice and sandwich and drink the Gatorade as I watch *Mr. & Mrs. Smith*. "You still alive, baby?" You bet I am!

After I wash the dishes in the bathroom sink, I check my texts. I have received several messages from friends. It's like I'm going off to have an operation and no one is quite sure how it's going to go. "Good luck tomorrow!" "Hang in there tomorrow!" "Be strong tomorrow!"

I'm left feeling impatient. It's getting close to seven o'clock and I'm restless. I want to fall asleep before my mom and aunt get back. I plan to get up at 4:00 a.m. If I can fall asleep by 8:00 p.m., that'd be great. I know it's going to take a while to fall asleep, so I decide to get a head start. I turn off the TV and put in my earplugs. With nothing left to do, with the pressure to fall asleep growing every minute I'm still awake, my mind races. It takes me back through all the training, all the steps to get here, back to the days when I didn't have a bike, when my IT band prevented me from running more than two miles. I think back to the day I did my longest ride, seventy miles, and followed it up with a seven-mile run. I think about how destroyed I was afterward. I think back to my longest run, fourteen miles. I think about all the things I'd rather do than run fourteen miles again. Tomorrow, I have to bike forty-two miles and run twelve miles farther than I ever have. The doubt envelops me like the blankets on the bed. Am I ready for this?

Regardless of what happens, I'll be relieved to hear the gun go off tomorrow. From the moment I signed up for this race, I have felt like I have something hanging over me, something to be concerned about, a hurdle that I must clear for my life to move forward. And the worst part is that it's true. It's not something I'm building up in my head, unfortunately, not something I'm embellishing. No. It's actually true. I have the biggest single-day physical challenge of my life tomorrow. No matter how I position my brain, no matter how I think about it mentally, I still have to do it physically. *Tomorrow*.

I have been living my life each day this week, and for the past three months, just to get to this day of reckoning, to take it on, and to get past it, one way or another. Well, here it is. *Tomorrow*.

It made me feel better to see there are others who are nervous, anxious, and full of negative anticipation. I cannot imagine living that way and putting myself in this position time and time again. There's been a lot of talk on the forums about how good it feels after you complete an Ironman, how that sense of accomplishment is "worth all the pain and suffering." I'm not sure how that's possible, but OK—it's something to tell myself. It will all be worth it.

It will all be worth it.

November 19, 2017
Tempe, Arizona
3 Hours Until the Ironman

Come back with your shield—or on it.

—Spartan creed

I'm awake ten minutes before my alarm goes off. It's been one of those nights, when an irrational fear of oversleeping—which I never, ever do—ensured that I woke up every hour. To wake up and see that it's finally 3:50 a.m. comes with a huge sigh of relief, the long wait close to its end. I can get out of bed now. I can rise to meet the day of reckoning. It is time to stop all the posturing. No more meetings. No more practices. No more planning. No more opinions. Today, there will be no more talk—only action.

I immediately crack a Gatorade and take down three large, forceful gulps. The Arizona air dried me out like a prune overnight, and I wake up thirsty, my mouth dry and caked. In the other bed, my mom and aunt are sleeping. I tiptoe around and carefully move the food items on top of the dresser. I decide to take a page out of Bmac's playbook and make a whole wheat bagel with peanut butter and banana. I take out the bagel and break it apart with my hands. The crumbs fall down onto the dark wood. I unscrew the cap from the peanut butter and dip the knife in, the first glob going directly into my mouth, the second and third and thereafter spread on the bagel. I cut the banana into small coins and place them around the bagel, like pepperoni on a pizza. I put two scoops of the chocolate Muscle

Milk protein powder into an empty Gatorade bottle and fill it with water from the bathroom sink. I close the door in the bathroom to shake it so I don't wake up my mom and aunt. I look at the toilet, knowing it would be in my best interest to poop before the race. But I'm not ready yet. I need coffee. I take more water from the bathroom sink and add it to the coffee maker, put in a new coffee pack, and hit brew.

As I'm eating my bagel I double-check my bags. I keep the bagel on the dresser and walk over to take a bite whenever my mouth is empty. Everything I need for the swim—the timing chip, wet suit, cap, and goggles—is in my pack. There's also quite a bit of food. I'm bringing three peanut butter and jelly sandwiches, a bag of Muscle Milk powder, a sandwich-size bag of pretzels, a Snickers bar, and a bottle of Coke. Before the swim I will turn in my special needs bags for both the bike and the run. In the bike special needs, I put an extra tube, the bottle of Coke, and the Snickers. In the run bag I put a roll of KT Tape, in case my IT band flares up. It's a lot of stuff to remember and leaving any of it behind would be a very bad start to the day. Between bites of the bagel and swigs of the shake I check and double-check the bags, mixing in sips of the coffee. I'm hoping it will get things moving.

I forgot to bring an extra pair of shoes, so with my sneakers in my run bag and my bike shoes in my bike bag, I'm left with my flip-flops and a pair of athletic socks. It's not the best look, but it's cold outside and I don't want my toes to freeze. Right now, I don't want to be uncomfortable in any way. There will be plenty of that to come.

I pull on my newly purchased warm-up pants and a gray cotton hoodie. I finish the bagel and the shake and the coffee. I finish the bottle of Gatorade and drink a glass of water. I try to go to the bathroom but all I can do is pee.

To my surprise, the ride to the starting line is not total chaos. The Uber I had scheduled showed up right on time and, from the looks of the app, it seemed like there were plenty of cars around. In fact, it's pretty mellow down by the bike corral. A short line of cars is waiting to get in a parking garage, and there are neat lines of people crossing the streets, creating a small, half-block bottleneck down near the beach park. Otherwise it's very chill. Cars are still able to get through, and there's no major standstill. The driver drops me off a block from the bike corrals without issue. I guess the race is pretty small in the grand scheme of things. There's only three thousand of us. I wonder why.

Bags in hand, I walk to the transition area and go into the bike corral. The sun is still down and there is no light in the sky, just the glow of the orange streetlights that line Tempe Town Lake, and the brightness of the white floodlights set up by the race. It's chilly out, somewhere in the mid-50s—30 degrees cooler than what I'm used to back home in Hawai'i. Many people are dressed Michael Phelps–style, with long warm-up pants and a hooded sweatshirt, the hoods up over their heads, earphones in and cranked up. You can tell they are in, or trying to get in, a state of mental focus (for what it's worth, I look like this, too, only without earbuds). Other people, who no doubt come from cooler climates, are wearing shorts and flip-flops without socks.

The first thing I have to do, before I check the bike and dress for the swim, is drop off my special needs bags. Both need to be dropped off around the corner from the transition area, under the bridge at Tempe Beach Park. Volunteers collect the bags and arrange them into bins, sorted by race number. The run bags will stay right here—this is the start of the run, and the halfway point after you complete the first lap. I'll be able to access the bag on either of those two laps. If my IT band flares up on the first lap, I can stop and tape it. I'm pretty sure it would be too little too late by then, but knowing it's there gives me some mental peace, however false.

The bike special needs bag is a different story. We drop them off here, but after the swim start, they will be transported out onto the bike course. I don't know exactly where—only that we will be able to access them on either the second or third lap of the bike. Again, I don't plan to use mine. There's nothing in there I'm relying on. The most important thing is an extra bike tube. I'm carrying two with me on the bike. If I get a flat and have to use one, I'll stop and pick up the extra so I always have two with me. I thought about putting two or three extra tubes in the bag but decided not to. If I end up needing more than three extra tubes, the best thing I could have in my bag would be a gun, so I could shoot myself.

The Snickers bar and Coke are in there as morale boosters, should I find myself with a massive debt of energy.

The special needs drop-off is very organized. Some volunteers already hopped up on coffee are buzzing around, yelling encouragement and grabbing bags left and right. It's only 5:45 a.m., so I'm not quite there yet. But I feel good and relaxed. It's about an hour until the swim start, and everything's coming together. All I have to do is drop the sandwiches and pretzels in my bike clothes bag, set up my computer on the bike, pump up the tires to race pressure, and stock the cages with water and Gatorade. That will leave me plenty of time to get body marked and stretch out for the swim.

Everything looks good with my bike when I arrive. Both of the tires feel the same as they did the day before, and nothing's been moved or stolen or anything like that. I clip the computer onto the handlebars and rotate the front tire to ensure it's picking up the signal. It works as it should. Time to pump up the tires to race pressure.

A lot of racers have brought their own pumps, but Ironman has also contracted mechanics. They have set up shop in a corner of the bike corral. They've put out a bunch of pumps for athletes to use. I carry my bike over to them, waddling in my socks and flip-flops. I don't want to risk rolling the bike through the grass and getting something in my tire—that would be very, very bad. I lean the bike against the metal fence so it stands up by itself. I grab one of the pumps. I kneel down beside the front tire like a NASCAR pit crew chief, running my fingers along the rim and the spokes and looking for potential problems. It all looks normal. There's a black, hard plastic, twist-off cap on the tire valve to protect it from dirt and grime. It needs to be removed before I can put the pump on. I grab the cap with my thumb and pointer finger and twist counterclockwise to remove it.

The horror of the next second consumes me. *PFFFFSSSSTTTT.* Air rushes from the tire and it drops to the ground.

All around me athletes stop in their tracks. They bend their knees and get down, pivoting like a bomb has gone off, inspecting their tires, searching for the source of the sound.

I look down at my hand and see that I'm now holding not only the plastic cap but half the valve. The valve is stuck inside the plastic cap. It broke off clean with the first turn of the cap, a sign of sudden defection. I don't know how or why—I had removed the cap yesterday and pumped up the tire without a problem. But there it was, in my hand, the air gone from the tire. The other athletes relax when they realize it's not their bike.

"That sucks," I hear one of them say.

Another one looks at me. "I'm sorry that happened," he says.

I'm trying to hold back the emotions, to not let frustration and anger overcome me. Yes, the valve was fine yesterday. No, I've never, ever, ever removed a valve cap and had the whole thing break off. Yes, this is Murphy's Law, something that could only happen forty-five minutes before the start of an Ironman. I take a deep breath. I've got extra tubes here. I know how to change the tire. I need to stay calm and change the tire.

I use the tire wrenches to loosen the outer tire, then pull out the tube. I hold it in my hand and rub my finger over the piece of the value that remains. It's an unbelievably clean break, as if it was cut instantly by a hot steel blade. I don't know what to make of it. I am especially nervous because all of the extra tubes I have are the same make and model, and I bought them all at the same time from the same store. Hopefully, I bought one bad tube and not a bad bunch.

I test the valve on the new tube by trying to break it in half. It seems fine. I install the new tube and put the tire back on. That's an easy thing to write but it doesn't happen so quickly under the hot glow of the white lights, up against the ticking of the clock, with athletes coming and going and gossiping around me.

"That guy over there," someone tries to whisper. "His tire just burst!"

"I would *die* if that happened to me," someone replies.

I say a couple fuck yous under my breath as I work. I pump the new tube up to 110 pounds per square inch and replace the plastic cap. I carry the bike back over to my spot in the corral and take a deep breath. Fixed and done. Now it's 6:15 a.m., thirty-five minutes until the age-group start. I have plenty of time to settle down, stretch, and pre-hydrate.

Gatorade in hand, I head over to the Porta-Potties and pee. I still can't poop. There's not much I can do about it—I can only push so hard.

I've already blown one valve today. I stop off at the body-marking station and get my bib number, 1970, drawn on both my arms. On the back of my left calf, they write my age, 32. The sun is still below the horizon but I'm starting to see rays of light brighten the sky, streaks of red and orange and yellow. I keep sipping the Gatorade. The good thing about having the swim first is that you can drink all you want. If you're not peeing in Tempe Town Lake during the swim, then you're just getting peed on.

I go back to the bike special needs station and beg them to let me access my bag. When I tell them what happened with my tire, they immediately bring me the bag. I take the extra tube out of the bag. I'm glad I have it. This is exactly what it's for.

I return to my bike to dress for the swim. I pull my wet suit out of my pack and put it on the ground next to the bike. Out of the corner of my eye, I notice something weird. It's the front tire again. The tire is pushed out from the rim, and the tube—the one I just installed—is bulging out between the rim and the tire. It looks like a mouth blowing a bubble, the rim and tire the lips, the tube the gum. I'm hit with another wave of shock. OK, I tell myself, it's just offset. You must have not aligned it correctly on the rim. This will be an easy fix. Just see where it's coming off track and push it back into place.

I reach down and put light pressure on the tube with my three middle fingers to see if I can push it back in under the tire. The second my fingers hit the tube, it explodes. *PPPPPFFFFFFFSSSSSSSSTTTTT*. It's louder this time, even more terrifying. My eyes grow to the size of saucers. The tire deflates in less than four seconds.

Athletes walking by hit the deck like it's an ambush. A guy a few bikes down, who is adjusting his brakes, snaps up at the sound and frantically checks his tires. Then he looks up at me with relief.

"Oh thank God!" he says, his hand on his heart. "It's you."

Not everyone is a dick. A couple of athletes come over after the explosion. One of them offers me an extra tube and words of compassion. Another tells me I should take the bike to the mechanical tent. They will be able to help me there, she says. I look over. The line for help at the tent is long. Still in my flip-flops and socks, I pick up the bike and carry it over to the tent.

I check my watch often while I wait in line. It's now 6:22 a.m., eighteen minutes until the start of the Pro group and twenty-eight minutes until the age groups go off. People in front of me are getting their tires filled by the air compressor. I can't help but think I should have priority. But I wait quietly. There's only three people ahead of me. I bite my lower lip. Five minutes later I am called into the tent.

The mechanic puts the bike in a mechanical arm and goes to work. I tell him I think my tubes are defective, that two of them burst. I tell him I'm not sure what happened—only that I'm one exploding tire away from not being able to participate in the race. He roots around for an extra tube in a cardboard box. It's overflowing with bike parts. He comes over and takes off my tire. It's 6:28. I should be OK. I just need to throw on my wet suit and get to the swim start. There should be time.

Halfway through his inspection of the tire, kneeling beside the bike, he stops. He stands up halfway and puts both hands on his knees. He squints his eyes and breathes out audibly.

"Man, I've really got to pee," he says. He looks over at the Porta-Potty line. You've got to be kidding. It's last-call for the bathrooms, and the line streams out from the potties and winds its way through the rows of bikes, at least a hundred people long, no exaggeration.

"Shit, the line looks pretty long," he says. I can tell he's trying to gauge my thoughts on it. Would it be cool to stop and take a pee? Hell no it wouldn't!

The situation is so ridiculous it's hard to believe I'm not on a television show. The tire is blown out, the clock is ticking, and the mechanic has to pee so bad he can't concentrate. Squatting there, next to the tire, he looks in pain.

I'm concerned about time, but also concerned that he's going to rush the repair because he has urine coming out of his eyes. I do not want him to rush. This man is my only hope. I need him to be the best he can be. He looks at me again. He's in pain. I look at my tire lying on the ground, completely apart. I look at the line for the bathroom, a hundred people deep.

"Dude, dude, dude . . . look, go . . . go now," I say in a burst of enlightenment. "Go up to the front and tell them you're a volunteer mechanic. They'll let you cut."

I know for sure that he will be allowed to cut the line. No athlete is going to piss off the mechanic. This is the man that's going to be roving the course later today, helping people with their mechanical problems. What athlete in their right mind is going to deny him a favor? Who would take that chance? Trust me, I tell him, they will let you cut.

He realizes I'm right and hurries off. I see him ask and receive permission to cut the line. It's now 6:31 a.m. I'm still OK. I take a deep breath. I'm still OK. I can still make it.

He returns seventy-eight seconds later. Not that I'm concerned about time or anything. It's just the start of the race, the one I've spent the last three months training for, the one that's cost me thousands of dollars, the one I flew here for, that my mom flew in for. That's all.

Looking relaxed, the weight of the world off his shoulders, the mechanic is back in business. He gets down on his knees with a renewed focus, carefully inspecting the rim and tire. He stretches out the tube and places it on the rim. He tells me my tubes might have been defective, but probably not.

"Most likely," he says, "you did this to yourself."

He pumps up the tire to race pressure and bangs on it. He shrugs his shoulders.

"I think you're all set now."

I give him a fist bump and a thank you. I don't have time for much else. It's 6:37 a.m. There are three minutes until the Pro start. I pick up the bike under my right armpit and run with it through the rows of bikes, trying to keep my flip-flops from flying off. I hang the bike by the seat on the rack, then take off my shirt and warm-up pants. I tie my jammers tight and step into my wet suit, right leg then left, wiggling back and forth to get it over the heel and then pulling it up to my ankle. I spread body glide—which comes in a dispenser similar to deodorant—all over my shoulders, neck, and chest. This will keep the wet suit from sticking and relieve the torque put on my shoulders. I slide my arms into the suit and pull it up over my shoulders. When I zip it up in the back, I feel strong and taunt and elastic, like a superhero—Spiderman or something. The feeling gives me an emotional jolt. Then I get a real jolt. The cannon goes off with a boom, signaling the start of the Pro Division.

I squirt some soap in my goggles, rub it in, and wash it out with water. I run through the rows of bikes to the exit on the far side of the corral. Everyone has been lined up for fifteen minutes now, self-seeding based on speed. Near the front of the line, there is a tall stick with a sign stapled to it. It says 1 hour. As the line goes back, there are other signs: 1 Hour 10 Minutes, 1 Hour 20 Minutes, 1 Hour 30 minutes, all the way back to 2 Hours. You are supposed to gather around the sign that best estimates your time. I want to be up by 1 Hour 10 minutes, or at the very least 1 Hour 20 minutes. But there are a lot of people—3,000—blocking my way down the narrow, fenced-in starting area. It's like trying to get up to the front row of a rock concert. I zig and zag and excuse my way through the line, turning to the side to squeeze through here and tapping people on the shoulder there. I catch annoyed glances from some, but for the most part, people are understanding and allow me to pass. I can see the Pros in the water kicking hard under the first bridge.

I get to a place between the 1 Hour 10 Minutes and 1 Hour 20 Minutes signs just as the 1 Hour folks are heading into the water. I pull on my goggles and then stretch the cap over them, ensuring the back straps are trapped under the cap. If anyone kicks me in the head, it reduces the chances that my goggles fly off. It would take a good kick to knock off both the cap and the goggles. But the way my morning is going, anything is possible (which is ironic, because "anything is possible" is Ironman's slogan).

The long, thick hoard of people is being intentionally bottlenecked up ahead. The idea is to get people into the water gradually, in what's known as a rolling start. The big crowd is slowly funneled into the water a few people at a time, creating space in the water and allowing the faster swimmers to get out in front. Still, chaos is, by definition, unpredictable, and I'm not taking anything for granted.

As athletes jump in up ahead and start thrashing, everything is orderly back in the corral. We calmly step forward when space permits, staying right behind the person in front of us. All around us the crowd gathers, pushing up against the side gates and yelling out words of encouragement. I notice one athlete's cap is out of the ordinary. All the men are in green, and the women are in pink, but this guy is wearing a purple cap.

I ask him how he got the cap. He tells me it was a gift from Ironman, a present for signing up and competing in so many events. He makes fun of himself a little bit. "I'm one of those crazy people you hear about," he tells me.

We waddle forward together until the crowd forces us to part. I watch as people ahead of me go through the gate and down toward the water. I move up, one spot at a time. Here I am, I think. Here's the moment I've been waiting for. All the training, all the planning, it's all behind me now. It's time to get in the water. I'm not sure what will be waiting for me when I get out. Will the tire pop again? Will it hold up over the course of the 112 miles? I can't worry about it right now. It is for situations like this that many people have given me cliché advice: "Don't worry about what you can't control." It might be cliché but right now it is very true. The bike will be what it will be. The tire will either be fine, or it won't be fine. All I can do now is get in the water.

When it's my turn to go through the gate, I pull my goggles from my forehead down over my eyes. I feel them latch onto my face like suction cups. I step through the gate and walk another twenty paces until I reach the staircase that recedes down into the water. I go down the steps deliberately, one at a time. On the last step, my ankles submerge into the water. I bend my knees, swing my arms back, and dive forward. I plunge into the cold water. The Ironman has begun.

When I enter the water, I brace myself for impact. All of the stories I've been told, all of the warnings I've received, they all prep me for aquatic combat. I grit my teeth, tense my muscles. I'm looking out the corners of my eyes for projectiles—feet and elbows are the most dangerous. A blow to the temple from one of those could leave me dizzy, rattled in the water. Just like the practice swim yesterday, the visibility is terrible and I can't see my hand in front of my face or my shoulders to my sides. It leaves a very small window to defend myself against errant feet and arms, and it makes it more than possible that I swim into one accidentally.

I take my first few strokes, my head on a swivel. It's choppy from all the swimmers, but not too windy, and soon it becomes clear that constant defense won't be necessary. The pack spreads out quickly, and there's more than enough room to maneuver if you know how to sight in the water. Sometimes I have to slam on the brakes and swing around the side. Other times I make a diagonal beeline for open water. Sometimes I have no choice but to plow right through.

For inexperienced swimmers, sighting can be a challenge. It requires that they stop their strokes, lift their heads straight out of the water, and look ahead, sometimes awkwardly. This temporary pause takes them out of their rhythm and leaves them vulnerable. The people behind them are likely to run into them, and at the very least they're going to create a traffic jam. For me, my swimming experience allows sighting to take place on every breath. When I turn my head to the side to breathe, I lift from the front, catching a brief glimpse of the road ahead as my eyes break the surface, before my head turns completely to the side. It's quick and without pause. Like a running back finding holes in the defense, I anticipate runways in the large packs and accelerate into open space.

I realize in the first ten minutes that I've either seeded myself too slow, or others have seeded themselves too fast. Physically, it demands that I maneuver through traffic consistently. Mentally, it relaxes me. It feels much better to pass than to be passed.

I breathe every five strokes. One–two–three–four–breathe. One–two–three–four–breathe. One–two–three–four–breathe. I think of my mom. "Swim fast, don't breathe!" It's good advice. But I'm going to sacrifice speed here for the sake of the cadence; it ensures I get into a good rhythm, that my heart rate stays under control, and that I get constant updates on the path ahead. It gives me a pattern to follow. It allows my body to find an unconscious rhythm, to shift into autopilot. Meanwhile, my mind works hard to navigate traffic, to avoid being kicked in the face.

Through my tinted goggles, I can see that the sun is close to coming over the horizon directly in front of me. From the quick glimpses I catch, the sky is beautiful, a mixture of purples and blues and reds and pinks and oranges. But when the fireball comes up above the horizon, it's going to rise right in front of us. Most people will have to look right into it as they tackle the first half of the course. Fortunately for me, and a couple hundred other swimmers, we started early enough to beat it out. That is, we will reach the turnaround before it comes over the horizon.

This is why some racers over-seed themselves. Even though they belong in the back, they want to get in the water earlier, to have more time to complete the swim and to get as far as they can before the sun incinerates the first half of the course. There is no question about it—it's an advantage to swim the course when the sun's still down, before it blinds the way. Sighting in the face of the sun would be significantly more stressful, even with tinted goggles. That is one reason why you have two-hour swimmers mixed in with the one-hour crowd. The strict cutoff times are another. You have to hit certain checkpoints by certain times of day, and those times of day are the same for everyone, regardless of whether you start the swim at 7:05 a.m. or 7:25 a.m. The sooner you get in the water, the softer the cushion.

The sun is still down when I hit the halfway point. Only now, getting a grip on how much farther I have to go, does it really hit me that I'm feeling good. The first half I said to myself, "OK, keep it steady, see how you feel." Now, it's time to accept that I feel great. My shoulders, though not 100%, are not holding me back. The combination of the body glide and the cold water is keeping the soreness at bay. Maybe this is an opportunity for me. Both my mind and body are on the same page, telling me I can speed up, go faster. After all, this could be it for me. I could get out of the water and find my tire is again flat. I could have problems with it all day. I could miss the bike cutoff time. I could commit suicide during the marathon. There are so many unknowns left, so many things that could derail my day. If I go after this swim, if I show what I can do, at least I'll have that. If I only finish one event today, at least I could say I went after it. At least I'd have something to show for all I've been through.

I kick harder as I make a tight left turn around the buoy and start on the back straightaway. The course is straight, right back down where I came from, and the field is now officially spread out. I'm able to locate long stretches of open water, a couple hundred yards at a time, separating the packs. When I enter these gaps, I turn my effort up another notch, staying in my same rhythm—one–two–three–four–breathe—but pulling down harder and faster with my arms and kicking my legs more intently.

With everything working for me, I fly through the open water. I approach and then overtake groups in front of me, navigating my way through them, shooting out the other end into the next gap. One–two–three–four–breathe. I'm transported back to a time when this activity dominated my athletic life. The freshwater, even though it's brown and dirty, feels clean and cool as it runs across my hot face.

I know I'm getting close to the finish when I go under the first of three bridges. It's a great feeling mentally, to know I'm almost there, and to know I feel great. Physically, it's a shot of life. I can hear the crowd on the bridge when I raise my ear to the sky to breathe. I'm amazed at how, in those moments, that sort of thing can offer so much support. All I can think is that they're all watching me. To think they might be looking down at me motivates me. Maybe, if I go faster, I can impress them. Maybe they'll point at me and say, "Look at him go!"

Imagining myself as the star sends adrenaline through my system. The stairs are now in sight. I give everything I have, bearing left at the end of the straightaway and making a diagonal beeline for the far wall and the staircase. Everyone around me is going as hard as they can. This makes me push harder. We bump into each other, jockeying for the best position, for the straightest path to the staircase. I stay strong in my lane and refuse to let anyone push me aside. I think back to my dream where I kicked someone in the face. I feel my heartbeat flutter. I pull down hard with my arms and kick my feet. I imagine a mountain of water behind me. I pull ahead of the people around me. I feel my hand touch the smooth concrete. I grab the railing and pull myself up onto the staircase.

I jog up the stairs and I glance at my watch. Approximately 1 hour and 5 minutes. It gives me a jolt of confidence. I belong here, I think—at least here in the water. But I'm quickly humbled at the sight of the bike corral. You haven't done anything yet, it reminds me. You have completed 2.4 of the 140.6 miles. Congratulations, you're a big bad swimmer. You're 1.7 percent of the way there.

This reality check is given an exclamation point when I reach the top of the stairs, where I am accosted by a wet-suit stripper. It's not what you think. Not even close. In fact, I'm the one taking off my clothes.

Groups of volunteers meet racers as they come out of the water. They are doing their best drill sergeant impressions, moving with extreme purpose and yelling out commands. My volunteer has a well-practiced process of getting me out of the wet suit as fast as possible. I lock eyes with her and follow her commands: *You! Here! Turn around! Zipper!* She spins me by the shoulders and grabs the zipper at the base of my neck. She rips it down to the base of my butt. She puts her hands under the wet suit on top of my shoulders. She shouts in my ear: *Arms!* I feel the suction of the wet suit as I tug my arms free. She pulls the wet suit down to my waist. *Sit down!* I drop to the ground. *Lay back! Feet up!* She rips the wet suit from my waist and down to my ankles like she's starting a lawnmower. My legs recoil as the wet suit comes free of my feet. *All right! Get up! Go! Go! Go!*

All the while the crowd is pushing up against the gates and yelling out. *Go! Go! Go!* The woman stuffs the balled-up wet suit into my arms like a football and sends me running down the path, a couple tenths of a mile up and around the changing tent toward the bike bag area. As I run, volunteers radio my number and progress to their counterparts. When I arrive at the bike bags, a volunteer is waiting for me. She signals me over to my bag. I grab it and run toward the men's changing tent. Inside, everyone is in a state of partial nudity. People who are wearing a tri suit only have to wrestle their dry socks onto their wet feet. But many have to do a more extensive change, myself included. I sit down on one of the plastic chairs and pull off my wet jammers. Predictably, they get stuck on my ankles, and I have to lean over and fuss with them. It wouldn't be a public locker room if someone wasn't hopping on one foot with their nuts hanging out. Everyone is trying to get their wet clothes off and their bike kits on as fast as possible. The combination of wet skin and dry garments makes me feel like I'm dipped in glue.

There's no time to be shy or embarrassed. Besides, no one cares. Everyone has their own problems to worry about. I get my bottom leotard on and sit down to empty the rest of the bag. A wave of fatigue comes over me as my body recovers from the swim. I am not the only one. It's noticeably quiet in the changing tent. The only people talking are the volunteers. They want to assist us. One comes up to me. *Water? Gatorade? Need help with your shoes? Anything? Anything I can do for you? Anything at all?*

I wave him off and stuff my wet clothes into the bike bag. I've got my shoes on, my bike jersey zipped up, and my helmet on. Into the three pockets on the back of my jersey I stuff three peanut butter and jelly sandwiches, the bag of pretzels, four Clif Bars, two Bonk Breaker bars, and six packs of GU. It's a hell of a lot of stuff and I can feel the weight of it wobbling around, hanging from my lower back. I stumble toward the tent exit. A volunteer takes my bike bag—which now has my wet swim stuff in it—and leads me out the door to another row of volunteers. Six of them are standing in a line and wearing disposable gloves. I walk up and three of them gather around me. They all put their hands on me and rub sunblock on my face, neck, arms, legs, and calves. It's hard not to feel like a rock star. I stand as they rub in the lotion, like I'm a little kid and my parents are trying to make sure I don't get sunburned. When it's all rubbed in they send me off down the chute. I put on my sunglasses as I move along.

The jog through the corral to my bike takes only fifteen or twenty seconds, but it's drawn out by the anticipation of the moment. If the tire is flat again, I know my day is done. I run through the rows and past all the expensive, fancy bikes en route to mine, which can barely hold air in its tires. As soon as I turn down my row I start looking for signs that the tire has popped or deflated. To my surprise, no part of me wants it to be flat. I've come too far to let something this stupid stop me. Please, don't let me go down this way.

I arrive to find it in perfect condition—both tires are rock hard and ready to go. This is an incredible morale booster for me, a huge sigh of mental relief. My shoulder held up, my tire is fixed. The war is far from over, but I've won the first few battles.

I pick up the bike and carry it across the grassy area to the transition exit. I cross the grass and put the bike down where the pavement begins. I check my watch. It's been ten minutes since I finished the swim. I push the power button on my bike computer and watch it boot up. I mount the bike, clip into the pedals, and start off. I see the stopwatch on the computer begin to count the time. It's crazy to think about how—best-case scenario—I have a six-hour ride ahead of me. I look up. People are lined along the metal gates as far as I can see. The crowd roars as I pedal through the narrow chute toward downtown Tempe.

The first thing I do, before I even make it out of the bike exit lanes and onto the main course, is start chugging fluids. I've got a bottle of Gatorade and a bottle of premixed electrolyte water. One advantage I have over people who are trying to win the race, or people who are determined to break a certain time, is that I'm not worried about stopping to go to the bathroom. I will flood the Arizona desert if I have to, so long as it means I don't get dehydrated. The last thing I'm worried about is a couple-minute bathroom break. I drink a quarter of the Gatorade and almost half of the electrolyte water before I exit the corral and transition onto the city streets.

It doesn't take long to settle in on the bike. It feels great to have one sport down and to set off on the second. It's a sign of progress, something to celebrate, if only for a moment. I realize I have 112 miles in front of me. It always comes back to those 112 miles. The stress-inducing reality is that I haven't ridden that far in my training, not even close. I tell myself to stay focused in the moment, to take it one lap at a time. One hour at a time. One mile at a time.

I want to average 16 miles per hour. This means I will have to ride closer to 17 miles per hour during my actual ride time, figuring I will take a couple 3- to 5-minute bathroom breaks that will bring down my average over the course of 6 or 7 hours. If I get another flat tire, I will have to make up even more time, assuming I'm able to fix the flat. I'm calculating all this very generally, keeping in mind that averaging 15 or even 14 miles per hour will still get me there before the cutoff. It's 8:30 a.m. I have 9 hours to complete 112 miles.

For nutrition, the plan is to eat twice per lap, or once every 18 miles. One "meal" will be a GU gel, and the other will be something more substantial, like a bar or a peanut butter and jelly sandwich. Aid stations are approximately every 15 miles, and I plan to drink about 40 ounces of liquid between them. Half will always be Gatorade. Half will be a combination of plain water and electrolyte-infused water. Regardless of how I feel—whether or not I'm hungry or thirsty—these will be my unbreakable commandments. I will identify two aid stations that will serve as my bathroom/rest stops, preferably one near the start of the lap and one shortly after the climb. These will serve as mental checkpoints, a way to cut up the course. I will focus on making it to the next aid station. I will try not to think about the big laps or the whole 112 miles. The goal of my first lap is to feel out the course. How fast does it ride? Where are the fast and slow sections? I want to take advantage of the course and meet my speed goal with the least possible effort. I know the course is generally flat for the first ten miles, followed by a gradual seventeen-mile climb to the turnaround point. I'm not sure how slow the climb will be, or how fast the downhill will be. I don't know what the wind will be like on the uphill. This first lap will tell me a lot about how to manage my efforts.

I come out of Tempe Town doing between fifteen and eighteen miles per hour at any given point. People line the street on either side. All of them clap their hands and many of them wave their arms over their heads. Some of them hold up poster-board signs. I blank it all out and it becomes a blur as I blow by. Once out of the city center, a half mile down the road, the packs of spectators and their cries of encouragement are gone. Now, it's just me and the road and a couple dozen of my fellow competitors. There are several turns as the course weaves out of town. Some require I slow down. It makes it hard to get into a rhythm. I am still feeling the aftershock of the swim. My throat is scratchy, presumably from the murky water. When the wind comes through my helmet I can feel that my hair is still wet from the swim. Soon, it will be wet with sweat. The sun is growing stronger by the minute and I can feel its heat warm my body.

Although everyone has some way to track their own distance, either in the form of a bike computer or a GPS watch, Ironman still does the courtesy of putting up mileage signs every so often. Just three miles in, I come across my first sign: Mile 40. I stare at it as I pedal past. It takes me a while to understand. The sign represents the mileage marker for this point on the second lap. Right now, I'm on mile 3. It will be another two and a half hours—37 miles—before I pass this sign legitimately. It's a buzzkill coming off the high of the swim, a stern reminder of the scope of what's to come. Thank you Ironman.

I pass the sign and try to find a cadence. Out of nowhere the rumbling starts. At first, I think it's just gas. Then I realize it's not just gas. I feel strong pressure in my stomach. My morning cup of coffee had a long fuse, a three-hour delay. It's not five miles into the race and I'm planning my first pit stop. This isn't a reflection of effort or willpower. This situation is nonnegotiable. I've seen what happens. I've watched too many YouTube videos. I've read too many headlines. I will take my bathroom breaks seriously.

I turn onto McKellips Road. Over my right shoulder, I can look back and see the Tempe skyline, a small hill called A Mountain, and the buildings of Arizona State University in the distance. Directly beside me is a farm field. Ahead of me I can see the overpass for the Pima Freeway. I cross under the overpass and see the first aid station up ahead on the right. Volunteers are lined up in a row for a couple hundred feet and hold out Clif Bars, Gatorade, water, and other snacks for riders to grab as they go by. I pedal all the way to the end, where there is a row of Porta-Potties. I do my business quickly. It's mostly gas coming out, after all—a little pressure that needs to escape. I jog back to my bike, thank the volunteers, and ride away. I know there is an aid station at the very top of the hill—the top of the Beeline Highway—right at the turnaround point. It's twenty miles from here. That will be a good place to stop again, before I come back down the hill.

I continue down McKellips Road. Farm fields are on either side. It's very dry on the left, yet very green in the fields to my right. They must irrigate one side and not the other. A mile or two more, and I pass another sign. This one is for Mile 80. I have more than seventy miles to go before I reach this point on the third lap, five hours from now. Thank you Ironman.

Past mile ten, I make the turn onto the Beeline Highway and start the major uphill climb. We are officially "out of town" and in the desert. I can see the dry, brown land and the green shrubs, and the outline of peaks in the distance. The Beeline is a divided highway with two lanes going in each direction. The city has closed down the southbound lanes for us to ride in. On the way up the hill, we ride in the right lane, and on the way down, the left. Traffic whizzes by in the northbound lanes on the other side of the median. The divide is narrow at some points. Most of the time it is a small strip of land with dried, yellow grass and green shrubs.

I take a deep breath and try to keep a consistent rhythm. This hill is the cornerstone of the course. It is very gradual and looking ahead there is no end in sight, not even a false summit, just endless road that climbs the hillside. It goes on for approximately ten miles, carving through the dried, sunbaked Sonoran Desert landscape, exposed to notoriously high winds that blow down and across the valley. When the winds blow, they often bring with them the small thorns called goat's-heads. These goat's-heads are blown onto the course. They are like little land mines—run over one, and my tire will surely go flat.

I keep my eyes glued to the road in front of me, looking out for anything that might pose a threat to my tires. I'm surrounded by other riders. They go on as far as the eye can see in front of me, up the hill. Many people have bunched up together. Some of them are wearing the same bike jerseys and look like they're part of the same clubs back home. A lot of them cheat, riding nose to tail, drafting off each other. I try to keep my righteous anger at bay, funneling any and all frustration into my legs. The number of people within my eyesight is more than a hundred. All of us are headed up the hill. No one is coming down the hill yet.

The wind is consistent and gusts often. It's not the apocalyptic scene that many forewarned about in the online forums, but it's certainly as advertised, consistent and nagging. The forecast calls for winds of 15 to 20 miles per hour with elevated gusts. Between the wind and the uphill grade, the 16 or 17 miles per hour I was able to pedal in the first 7 miles becomes 13 or 14. I begin to worry. Riding at this speed leaves me little room for error. I could be in danger of missing the cutoff.

A mile later, a pack of bikers comes flying down the hill on the left-hand side. Wow, it's the Pros! That didn't take long—they are already 10 or 15 miles ahead of me. The first guy is way out in front, followed by four or five others a half-minute behind. They're all tucked tightly into an aero position, their heads covered by fancy, aerodynamic helmets, their legs cranking as they go by like speeding cars.

Seeing them gives me a burst of adrenaline. I switch gears. I pedal faster. But I quickly realize that I'm not a Pro cyclist—staying right here in the 13 to 14 mile per hour range on the hill is the best bet for me. If I go any faster, I will run out of gas later today. My hope is that the downhill allows me to make up enough time, and that I don't have any mechanical issues going forward. The front tire looks and feels fine. It seems like the mechanic did a good job. Still, my eyes sweep the road ahead with the utmost paranoia.

The hill continues and gets steeper. The sun beats down and the wind blows across the road. I begin to be overtaken by large packs of riders. Probably slow swimmers who are experts on the bike. It's one of the worst feelings in the world, being passed. The natural reaction is for my cadence to increase, to want to go faster and keep up with them. I'm tempted to push myself and forge ahead. But I know that would be a foolish move. I remind myself what Drew and Bmac both told me: "Run your own race." I can't get caught trying to keep up with others. I need to stay within my comfort zone and stick to my plan. This is not easy in reality. It sucks to be passed. It sucks to feel slow. But I have a plan. This pace is the plan. I need to stick to it.

I push away the temptation and the adrenaline and remain smooth and easy within my boundaries—*chug, chug, chug*, like the Little Engine That Could.

As I slog up the hill, the wind changes directions. It's blowing directly downhill now, right in my face, and it's a morale killer. My speed drops to 12 miles per hour. My head drops down to look at the road. People are passing me with regularity. I take a deep breath and focus on turning the crank over, one foot at a time. I look up and see that many people have once again began to draft off each other. There is a group of five riders huddled together in a 3 x 2 formation. Other solo riders sneak in behind them, dipping in for a few minutes and then dropping back when they see one of the riders look back. It pisses me off.

The officials, who roam the course on motorcycles looking for various violations, like blocking and drafting, are nowhere to be found. I consider self-policing. Maybe yelling out something like, "Hey, have some pride you pussies!" But then I remember these people are Ironmen, and they do this for fun. I think of Drew and Bmac again. Run my own race. I'm not trying to win here. What these people do has no impact on me whatsoever.

I take a deep breath. The wind continues to blow straight down the course. When I reach down for my water bottle, I lean too far and swerve like a drunk driver. I can feel the weight of the sandwiches and bars shifting around in the back of my bike jersey. The sun is intensifying by the minute, and for the first time I become aware that I'm sweating. I see beads of water on my legs and arms. I can feel that my jersey is damp. I can feel the sweat on my forehead and down the side of my face. I feel a pain in the side of my neck. I take my left hand off the handlebars and feel the left side of my neck, then the right. Both sides are rubbed raw, kissed by the wet suit. As I ride, the sweat drips from my hair and the side of my head, finding its way down my neck and into the abrasions.

The bright side is that the farther I go up the hill, the nicer the scenery gets. Off to my left, I can see a large open space of saguaro cacti, and in the distance the outline of the mountains. I'm careful not to gaze off into the distance too long. I need to make sure I'm keeping my cadence up, and I also need to watch the road for anything that might cause a flat tire—trash, glass, potholes, goat's-heads, and rocks.

I've given up worrying about what everyone else is doing. I took a big, fat chill pill after that last pack of cheaters. Now I've come to enjoy watching other riders go by. I can tell a lot about a person in the short time it takes them to pass me. I can tell their age because it's written on the back of their left calf. I can see the type of bike they are riding, the gear they are using, and the branding on their bike jerseys. I can tell who spent big money. I can tell if two people are from the same bike club. I can often tell where people are from. I see one guy with an O'ahu saddlebag. I wave and say aloha as he passes. We ride side by side for long enough to exchange a few words about where we live on the island. Small world.

My musing comes to an end halfway up the hill. My back is really starting to bother me. It's not hard to figure out why—I literally have five pounds of food hanging from my back. I reach behind and pull out a Clif Bar with my left hand. I tear off the top with my teeth. I hold the bar in my mouth as I remove the wrapper and stash it in my back pocket. It's important to use my left hand for grabbing food and water. My right hand needs to stay on the back brake, in case I need to slam it on. If you slam on the front brake with your left hand, you will introduce your teeth to the pavement. I take a bite of the bar. It's soft and chewy, like it has been warming in an oven.

Eating is the last thing I want to do. Despite all the talk about cold beer and hot pizza, none of it motivates me at the moment. It's hot, I'm exercising, and my stomach is unsettled. But I need to start getting rid of some of the weight, and eating at least one bar per lap is part of the plan. I sit up straight and try to stretch out my back. On the side of the road, I see my first flat tire. It's a man in a red jersey, and he's got his front tire off, holding it up for inspection. Dear God, please don't let that happen to me. I think about the people this morning who watched my two tires explode. Now I understand their reactions. *I would die if that happened to me!*

I keep my eyes glued to the road in front of me, looking for shiny objects. I stuff the second half of the bar into my mouth, chew it as best I can, and wash it down with water. It sits like a log in my stomach.

The last mile up the hill takes forever. It seems steeper than the rest of the hill. Maybe that's just my imagination. To combat it, I take a page out of my trekking playbook, a strategy I use when I'm hiking up a big hill: I put my head down and try to focus only on the ten yards directly in front of me, nothing more. It helps me to break things down into small pieces, into single steps. My legs burn as the hill crests and I reach a plateau. I see a bunch of signs warning of the turnaround up ahead. I see an aid station on the left-hand side after the turnaround. I'm happy to see it. I need to get off and stretch my back. And I need to use the bathroom again. I follow the cones and slow down. When I get to the end, I stand up on my pedals and make a relaxed U-turn around the final cone.

A feeling of accomplishment comes over me, the first measurable milestone complete. We're not even twenty miles into the race yet, and I'm only halfway through the first lap, but it feels so much more than that, conquering the hill for the first time. Two more uphills to go, I tell myself. I park my bike with a volunteer, who hangs it on the rack. I throw out the trash in my pockets and head for the Porta-Potty. I pee, which is a good sign—I'm hydrated. Then comes the rest of it, a burst of gas and splatter. Ugh. I reach for the toilet paper, but there is none. I look around. Not a single square of toilet paper. But there is an empty energy bar wrapper on the ground.

What happened in that Porta-Potty—what I was forced to do—I will not repeat. It is with a lost sense of innocence that I return to my bike. A volunteer offers me half a banana. I eat it immediately. I see a table with a bunch of other goodies, including Clif Bars and salted pretzels. If that's the case—if every aid station has these food items—there is no reason to carry all this food with me. No reason whatsoever. I pull the food from my back pockets and start putting it onto the table. Three Clif Bars, two Bonk Breaker bars, a big bag of pretzels, six GUs, and three peanut butter and jelly sandwiches. The volunteers stare at me like I'm an exotic creature.

"Did you bring *all that* with you?" one of them asks.

"Yeah," I say.

She looks at the other volunteers and laughs. They all start laughing. "Why?! We have so much food here!"

Stop it, I think.

"It's my first triathlon," I tell her. "I wasn't sure."

"Oh . . . bless your heart."

I smile. What else am I going to do? Punch her in the face? I tell her I'm going to take one of the peanut butter and jelly sandwiches, the two Bonk Breaker bars, and the six GUs. The rest is hers, I say. She wishes me luck and offers water and Gatorade. I take both. I open the water and put in an electrolyte tablet. I watch as it starts to dissolve and bubble. I hand her the empty bottles from my bike, hop on, say thank you, and head down the hill. I feel a lot lighter now. Unfortunately, I can tell the damage has been done to my back. I can tell it's going to ache all day.

Coming up the hill, I could see that the way down would bring mercy. But it's not until I start going down that I realize how fast it rides. Coming up, I averaged a little more than 13 miles per hour. On the way down, I turn into a bullet, reaching speeds in excess of 25 miles per hour. This builds my confidence that I can still make my sixteen-mile-per-hour goal. Not only is the downhill a great way to make up time, it's a great time to rest. I shift up to the highest gear and it still takes minimal effort to turn the cranks. At one point, I look down and catch myself going 31 mph. Woah woah woah. I stop pedaling and let myself coast. I have no business going that fast. My front tire could explode. Someone could come up behind me and cut me off. A cat could run into the road. I want to go as fast as I can, but you have to be alive to finish the race.

I reach the bottom of the hill and head back through the town section of the course. It's relatively flat again, and I'm able to pedal at 16 miles per hour, sometimes more and sometimes less, depending on the turns and the wind. I decide that the two aid stations I stopped at on the first lap will be the two I stop at on the next two laps. They are nicely spaced, one at the start of the lap and one at the top of the hill. Coming back into town, I start to see spectators again. Some ring cowbells. Others blast music through stereos. Some call out to me. One middle-aged woman blows me a kiss. Then on the edge of town I see something horrific, something that entices me to stop playing around: a girl sitting on the curb, her head wrapped in a white bandage that's no longer white—it's red, soaked with blood. Her eyes look black and she's staring down at the ground. I see her bike next to her. It looks all right. I don't know what happened. A lot of things can happen out here.

The crowd thickens as I ride into the center of Tempe. The turnaround is a very narrow, small area, and up ahead I see some riders having to put their feet on the ground to make the tight turn. I slow down and let the other riders around me go first. Seeing that bleeding girl reinforces my caution—I'm not taking any chances. I make the tight U-turn and start off on my second lap. I hear my mom yell out my name.

"Wiiiillllll!"

I can't see her, though. There are too many people in the crowd and I don't have the chance to look up for long. I look at my computer. Over the first 37 miles, I averaged 17 miles per hour. Most of that is thanks to the downhill. Not bad. Not bad at all. It's right where I want to be. I feel good. I'm hydrated. I'm getting food down. My legs feel OK. I'm not sitting on the curb with a bloody cloth around my head. I don't have five pounds of food in my back pocket . . . anymore. There's a big uphill but then a big downhill. I'm . . . OK.

The second lap begins. Right away my stomach starts up again, and at the first aid station, I poop. It's short and sweet—a quick splattering and blast of gas to relieve the pressure. I'm in and out in two minutes. But the lift I received from completing the turnaround is gone now. I feel the pressure rebuilding in my stomach, like a storm brewing at sea. I become aware of a pain in my ass—quite literally. Sitting on the bike is uncomfortable, the hard seat unforgiving on my undercarriage, putting it all to sleep. Everything's tingly, or numb. It's hard to tell which is worse.

There's more wind on the second trip up the hill. My cadence slows and people begin to pass me, just like the first lap. Only the course is more crowded now, and I'm consistently swarmed by packs. The swim is done, which means everyone is on the bike course, the slowest swimmers just coming down the hill for the first time. I am sure many of them will eventually catch me, given I'm stopping twice per lap and given I'm now, admittedly, all of a sudden, struggling. It's not just one thing. It's everything, all at once.

It's strange how quickly things begin to pile up, how quickly I fall into a bad place. Just seven miles ago I was OK; now I'm spiraling downward out of nowhere, misery attacking from all angles. My back hurts and encourages me to switch positions often. I lean over the aero bars for a while, then change to sitting upright, trying to find a comfortable place to remain. Nothing doing.

Meanwhile the seat continues to take its toll on my undercarriage. The seat. My back. My butt. My penis. My neck. The sun. The wind. My stomach. It's rumbling again. I can feel the energy drain from my legs. I take a drink of water; it makes my stomach simmer. Gas bubbles try to push their way out. I have to squeeze my sphincter together to prevent disaster. My head starts to droop toward the ground.

Then my mind gets in on the game. It reminds me I'm not yet halfway through the race. I stand up on my pedals to stretch out my legs and my back. The wind takes advantage and billows into my chest. I sit back down. My butt hits the seat. Pins and needles return. I feel the gas bubble in my stomach. It's ready to burst. I'm not going to make it to the aid station at the top of the hill. I need to pull over *now*.

I see the Porta-Potties up ahead on the right. If you showed up late and missed the preview, now's the time to go back and read the prologue of this book. Please don't make me go through those moments again—no man wants to re-explain how he got caught with his hand down his pants. After the bathroom ordeal and after all the cream is applied to my undercarriage, I grab a Gatorade and a water and mount my bike. I merge back onto the course and into the steady stream of bikers, an endless current in both directions. It's now midday or thereabouts, a bright sunny day, which here in Arizona is a nice way to say it's hot as hell. Off I go up the road, up the big hill, toward mile 50. I'm officially miserable. I watch my bike computer as my pace slows to less than ten miles per hour. It's almost identical, in both timing and feeling, to my seventy-mile practice ride, when I had my head down at the stoplight.

I reach down for my Gatorade bottle and chug the rest of it. I almost run into someone while I have my head back drinking but I don't care—I'm not going sit back and watch myself "bonk" out of the race. I fish around in my pockets and bring out a caffeinated GU. I wash it down with water. I put my head back down and grind it out. I begin to motivate myself with my mind. *I feel better*, I tell myself. *I can get through this. Just a few more miles up this hill, then a lot of downhill. At least make it to the third lap. Don't let everyone be right.* I think of all the people who have doubted me. Mr. I'm on Another Level comes into my mind. *Fuck that!* Adrenaline courses through my system at once, little bolts of lightning throughout my body, like Thor picking up his hammer.

Immediately I notice my legs feel better. There's more energy coming to them. It's unbelievable, something you have to experience to understand, how your body can take such a beating, be at its limit, and then bounce back when you give it what it wants, what it needs, physically and mentally. Not much has changed; everything is still uncomfortable. But just enough has changed. My perspective has changed. I'm back in control. My pace increases and returns to normal. I bury my head and pedal, deliberately with new confidence, until I see the sign for the turnaround.

When I reach the top of the hill I don't congratulate myself—the war is far from finished. But I do let my guard down for a minute, so the adrenaline can recede until it must be summoned again. I stand up on the pedals. I shake my hips side to side. Good god. It will be a miracle if I can still have kids after this race. I take it slow through the turnaround.

When I pull into the aid station, I notice something: Riders are optimistic. We are only halfway through the course—we've biked about fifty-five miles—but we have completed the hardest half. We're done with two uphills, and there is only one left to go. Hearing the riders talk about this makes me aware of it, and it brings a smile to my face. It reinforces my confidence. I walk around a bit to get the feeling back in my undercarriage, then head for the bathroom. I only pee this time—a good sign, however misleading.

I switch out my empty bottles for a new water and Gatorade. Oh hail thee, sweet Gatorade! I owe it my life. What they distribute here on the course is the Endurance formula, with double the sodium and triple the potassium of a regular Gatorade. I know it's what saved me on the last uphill—that and the caffeine in the GU. Its taste is sweet and concentrated, and it makes my tongue feel tacky. But it's the nectar of the gods as far as I'm concerned. I set off down the hill, happy to be starting the second half. When the steepest part of the hill is over, I eat one of the Bonk Breaker bars and suck down another GU. A few minutes later my body responds to the nutrition.

Paranoid after that spell on the uphill, I decide to increase my liquid intake. I gulp down the entire Gatorade on the descent and as I make the turn back toward town, I approach an aid station and decide to grab another on the go. It's a good setup. They have an area before the aid station where you throw all your trash—you literally throw it into a backstop they've created—then a lineup of volunteers holding out items for you to take so you don't have to stop. It's exciting for me, because up to this point, I've always had to stop and use the bathroom. Now I can get one on the fly.

I throw the empty bottle onto the ground. It slides across the pavement and comes to a sudden stop when it slams into a huge pile of other plastic bottles. I ride past the volunteers holding out bananas and Clif Bars. Beyond them I can see the row of Gatorades. I lift my right hand from the handlebar and point at one of the volunteers holding a Gatorade. He looks at me and we lock eyes. He's young, probably in his early twenties, maybe even younger and in college. His unkempt, black hair is spilling out from under a baseball cap. I close in on him. He looks at me, and I look at him. We ready for the exchange. He extends his arm, holding the bottle out away from his body. He stands like a statue. I stare at the Gatorade, ready to pluck it from his hand. I reach out my hand.

I'm expecting no resistance, no movement on his part. But at the last second, he turns, opens his chest, and comes toward me, like a quarterback handing off on a run play. All of a sudden, my guy thinks he's Tom Brady. It happens so fast. I reach out to grab the bottle. Instead, it grabs me. The collegiate volunteer pushes the bottle into my hand with such force that I bounce off the exchange, my left hand unable to control the handlebars. I swerve left, then hard right in an attempt to correct course. I barrel off the road and onto the rough shoulder, into the crowd of volunteers. I scream. "Woah!"

The sea parts as people dart and, in one case, dive out of the way. I wrestle the handlebars like I'm trying to choke a squirming snake. I'm trying to gain control. I feel the rough road of the shoulder under my tires. I'm narrowly missing people as they spin out of the way. I see daylight to the left and pull hard back toward the road. I emerge from the crowd, miraculously, without hitting anyone. I look down at my right hand. My wrist is sitting on top of the handlebar grip. Clenched between my fingers like a baton is the Gatorade.

I turn and look back at Tom Brady with scorn. What the hell, man! His eyes look like saucers and he's covering his mouth and nose with his hands. The rest of the volunteer crowd is going nuts. They have their arms in the air. They're cheering.

"Awesome, man!"

"Way to save it!"

"Go! Go! Go!"

I breathe a sigh of relief. That could have been bad. That could have been very, very bad. I twist the cap from the Gatorade and take a long drink. I look down at my computer and see that my pace has slowed significantly. I refocus and ramp it back up to sixteen miles per hour. There's no time to dwell on it. The only option is to forget about it and keep going. I decide that, for the rest of the bike, I'm going to get a new Gatorade only when I stop to go to the bathroom. Only when my feet are safe on the ground. I pass back into Tempe town and the spectators begin to cheer. There are many bikers coming and going. No one has any clue I just avoided a hospital visit. Crashing is now my greatest concern, right up there with a flat tire.

I make the tight turnaround and once again hear my mom call out, “Wiiiillllll!” I still cannot find her. There are hundreds of people. I don’t want to get caught looking and risk crashing into something, or someone. The second lap took me two hours and twenty-five minutes. I do a quick overview of myself and assess my state of the union. My lower back aches, and thanks to the seat, I’m numb from my waist to my knees. But I feel like I’ve survived something, and there’s only one lap to go. I try to think of it that way. Only one lap to go. I try not to think about how big the lap is—thirty-seven miles.

At the turn coming out of town, I see a guy on the side of the road, vomiting. Both hands are on his knees. I can see the pulse come up through him, starting in his stomach, culminating as his shoulders go back and his head goes forward. Orange-colored vomit comes streaming out. It drips off his lips as he spits. The orange is from the Gatorade. It looks like he pedaled just far enough out of town, away from the crowd, before he decided to let it fly.

Not too far past that, before I get to the Beeline, I pass the Mile 80 sign. This time, it’s for real. Thirty-two miles to go. When you’ve already gone 80, 32 might seem like nothing. But I remind myself that, at 16 miles per hour, it’s still two hours of riding. Plus, I have to go up the hill again. I have to avoid a flat tire. I have to avoid crashing. I have to avoid the bonk, which is coming after me more and more. I can feel my performance declining. On sections where, before, I was able to go 16 or 17 miles per hour, I’m now struggling at 14. I pull up to rest and coast on a small downhill. When I do, a man passes me. I look at his calf as he passes. He’s 68 years old. Here we are, 80-some miles into the race, and the 32-year-old is being passed by the 68-year-old. *That’s* why they write your age on the back of your calf—for moments like this. Thank you Ironman. I make up a story about the man. He’s a former navy SEAL. He was involved in a government-sponsored steroid testing program.

I make the turn onto the Beeline and fuel up—Gatorade and GU. The wind is still howling straight down the hill. It blows through the holes in my helmet. It wraps around my sunglasses. The bike gets heavier as the road tilts and I start the climb. I do whatever I can to make myself comfortable. I move around on the seat. I clench my teeth. With gravity pulling my weight downhill, the pressure on my undercarriage worsens. My back cries out for me to stand up on the pedals and stretch. When I do, the wind blows against my body and tells me to sit down. It's a repeat of the previous lap, only this time, I have thirty-some more miles of wear and tear on my legs. I bend over the aero bars and lower my head toward the road. The pedals become hard to move. The sun, high in the sky, bakes the land. The thought that I still have to do the marathon creeps into my head. I push it away. It comes back. I push it away again.

I know what I need to do. I learned my lesson last lap. I already gave my body what it needs physically. Now, I have to take control of my emotions and give it what it needs mentally.

I cycle through thoughts of my friends and family. I think of them all, watching me on the tracker, rooting for me. Don't be a pussy, I tell myself. Don't let them down. They're all watching you. They're all rooting for you. I think of my mom and aunt, waiting down at the transition area. They flew all the way out here to see you, I tell myself. That's how much they love you. I think back to all the training. I think about my girlfriend, who supported me through all of it. I think about Mr. I'm on Another Level. My legs burn. I think about my dad. He's gone, but it feels like he's right here, riding alongside me.

Tears start coming down my face, out the bottom of my sunglasses. I want to scream. The emotion streams through my body. I pedal with a renewed intensity. It feels like therapy, like I'm grinding an axe. I get down into the aero position, into the "pain cave." The harder I pedal, the better it feels. My hands clench the aero bars as my friends come in and out of my head. Some of them tell me that it's all right, that I have nothing to prove. Others offer me motivation.

"Come on Willy," I can hear Bird say. "Get your gumby ass up the hill."

I think about what my dad would say. I hear him say it. The tears keep coming. I have to blink my eyes rapidly to get the water out, so I can see clearly. I keep pedaling. I take control of my breath. Past the ninety-mile mark. Up the hill. The closer I get, the more obtainable it seems. Stay with me here, Dad, just a little bit farther, please don't leave me.

It takes me forty-five grueling, ball-busting minutes to reach the top. I wheel my bike into the arms of a volunteer at the aid station and drop to the ground. I sit on my heels, elbows on my thighs, head between my knees. I wipe my eyes. I take a very deep breath. It's done. I stand up and shake out my legs. My muscles burn intensely, but there's a sense of accomplishment I can't ignore, and a sense that I was helped up the hill.

I come back to reality. We're not done yet. It's all downhill from here . . . until I reach the bottom. Then I have to run twenty-six miles. It's hard to get excited or celebrate, given that reality. But I will be forever grateful to get off this bike, to get off this bike seat, to have the feeling in my penis return. I don't care how far I have to run after. No amount of distance can intimidate me at this point. I'll run fifty-two miles—no, a hundred miles—if I can just get off this bike.

I eat half a banana and refill my water and Gatorade. I poop in the Porta-Potty. It's entirely liquid. I rinse my hands with water (no soap!) and get back on the bike. I unwrap an energy bar and take a big bite as I pedal away. Over the next couple miles, on the way down the hill, I pass several riders in distress. I had been riding with my head down the whole way up. Now, coming back down, I can assess the carnage.

The third lap is when everything changes. At this point, if you did an overview of the course at any given moment, you'd see people throwing up, people fixing bike tires, and people being carted off in ambulances. Many people are losing their concentration or running out of luck. Some have crashed into each other. Those who went out too hard are now losing their lunches. The people who didn't eat or drink enough are now bonking. It's officially a shit show.

As I descend, I see a continuous line of riders coming up the hill. A lot of them are in bad shape, and not even their fancy helmets and expensive bikes can save them. It goes to show that you can't buy your way through the Ironman. It's not the car—it's the engine. I see more riders pulled over, fixing flat tires. The memory of my two flats this morning is not gone. Far from it. Seeing the people standing next to their bikes serves as a reminder. Some of them are trying to fix the flat on their own, stretching out new tubes in the bushy median. Others sit still, looking demoralized, presumably waiting for the mechanic to save them.

I look at them as I pass but, as I don't want to become a part of the crumbling world around me, I keep my attention on what's in front of me, watching out for anything and anyone, riding defensively. I'm content to coast down the hill. There is no reason to rush. It's 2:30 p.m. The cutoff is 5:30 p.m. The only way I miss the cutoff at this point is if I crash or have a maintenance issue. My mind wants to celebrate. I tell it to stop immediately. This is a very hard thing to do, but it's the right thing to do. Now is not the time to lose focus, not when I've come this far. There is still so much that could happen. Don't let your guard down, I tell myself. One flat tire, and all of a sudden things aren't so peachy. Remember this morning? You clearly do not know how to change a flat tire.

I am more focused in the last ten miles than I was at any point during the ride. As you might imagine, it's the part of the ride that seems to take the longest. When you've ridden 105 miles, I think things get skewed. You might think of those last seven miles as nothing, a drop in the bucket. But seven miles is seven miles. I have to sit there and turn the pedals for another twenty-five minutes—your average person's workout at the gym. I remember the advice I learned in Kona, about how the end of the bike is the time to take in nutrition for the run. I eat my last energy bar, another GU, and drink the rest of the Gatorade. I look down at my computer. Six miles to go. Five. Four. Three.

Now I can celebrate. Even if both my wheels fall off, I can still carry the bike to the finish in time.* I come out of the aero position and sit up on the seat. I take a deep breath. I look around at the riders next to me and smile. They smile back. We all know what's coming. We cruise into town with a kind of relaxed coolness, as if we don't have to get off the bike and immediately start running a marathon. The wind is blowing, but I feel so relaxed that I'd just as soon take off my helmet and let my theoretical hair down as I would complain about it. I make the final turn and head straight into downtown Tempe. The crowd roars for us as we come in, ringing bells, holding up signs, shouting. Lost in the celebration are the people who are making the turnaround and riding away from the finish, just starting their third lap. Unless they have saved their best for last, they

* Looking back, I'm not sure if that's legal or not. But at the time, it was good enough for me.

will not make the cutoff time. I am so glad I am not them. *I would die if I was them.*

I bear to the right and go past the turnaround. I hear my mom again: "Wiiiilllllll!"

This time, I see her! She's standing beyond the turnaround, at the entrance to the transition area. She jumps up and down and waves. I give her the thumbs up. To my surprise, I really mean it. The despair of the final ascent is firmly behind me, a distant memory. My muscles—and my mind—have recovered, and there are many positives to drive me forward. I hit my time—it took me 6 hours and 57 minutes to ride the 112 miles, an average of 16.1 miles per hour. I avoided a flat tire. I am about to get off this concrete bike seat. I am, all things considered, feeling OK physically and upbeat mentally. I have proven to myself that I can get through tough moments. Despite the incessant diarrhea, the torturous numbing, my inexperience on the bike and the emotional breakdowns, I have accomplished all my goals. I feel confident. It's 26.2 miles to the finish. What can stop me now?

The bike-to-run transition is much more chill than the swim-to-bike. There's no wet suit to strip, and no clothes to change. I pedal slowly down a long chute, eventually reaching the same place I came out seven hours ago. Seven hours! A bunch of volunteers are waiting and they instruct me to dismount. They take my bike from me and point toward the grassy area with all the run bags.

Go! Go! Go!

I start to jog. It feels so good to be off the bike. My body breathes a sigh of relief. Feeling in my butt and groin return. I find the red run bag with 1970 on it, then head over to the changing tent. There are a lot of chairs set up outside. Everyone seems equally happy to be off the bike. There's a lot of lounging going on, leaning back in the chairs and making small talk. There's an aura of "we're almost done" in the air, even though we have a marathon to go. I change my socks and put on my shoes. I pin my bib number across the front of my jersey, using a safety pin at each of the four corners. On the front is my number, 1970, along with my name,

Will. I put my hat on my head and clean off my sunglasses. They have sweat and dust on them from the bike ride. A volunteer comes over and gives me a cup of water. I choke down a GU and wash it down with the water. Off I go down the chute: 114.4 down, 26.2 to go.

The course follows a path along the canal of Tempe Town Lake for two miles, then turns around and comes right back. You run past the transition area on your left, keep following the canal down for a couple of miles, cross over a bridge, run along the canal on the other side, then turn around and come back the way you came. You take a short detour through Papago Park before meeting up with the route you came in on, crossing back over the same bridge. Instead of following the canal back, you cut through town and run on Tempe's streets to the transition area. That's one lap. Then you do it again. It's a pretty course, with a view of the canal throughout. It's cooling off here in the late afternoon (it's about 3:15 p.m.) and it will continue to get nicer as the evening sets in and the sun goes down.

The amount of times I've practiced the bike-to-run transition pays off immediately as I trot off and find my rhythm in the first half mile. The path along the canal is slammed with spectators, and it's easy to feed off them coming out of transition. Subdued spectators are sitting under tents. People are cheering and holding signs. Some families have set up a series of signs with different quotes of encouragement. There's a group of guys wearing Speedos and spandex short-shorts that line up and form a tunnel for me to run through. It's a complete zoo, but it's just what you want when you're at this point in the race. Overall, I feel good. My legs are tired, of course, and my abs are crampy and tight, and my lower back still hurts from carrying all that food, and I'm still having digestive issues, and I'm worried about my IT band. But in this world of triathlons, that's a good report, all things considered. I'm steady in my form and pace. I complete the first two miles in 17:01, a sub-9-minute-per-mile pace, and the first 3.9 miles in 34:05, for a total of 8:44 minutes per mile.

Then it hits me in a hurry. I realize the cramps in my abs are not cramps. They are—once again—digestive-related, and I need to stop right away. Luckily, there are a lot more aid stations on the run than the bike course, one almost every mile. I won't have to "stop and take a dump on the side of the road" like that one lady in London.

I stop just short of the four-mile mark. I scramble to get in the door. When I go to get out of my clothes, I realize there's a problem. I have pinned the bib number to the front of my jersey, two pins holding it on either size of the zipper. I can unzip the jersey, but I cannot take it off without ripping the bib number—the paper still holds the two sides together. Now I see why everyone else attached their bib number to their pant line and not across their chest. Whoops.

I try to take the jersey off like a T-shirt. I get the top part over the back of my head. My elbows bang into the side of the Porta-Potty and I shuffle my feet to regain my balance. The sweat acts like superglue, gripping the material to my chest, back, and arms. In my fatigue, I can't pull it off, and I become short of breath in the hot, overheating Porta-Potty. The smell of baked feces makes my stomach turn. I'm running out of time. I need another plan. I reach under my jersey and stretch the leotard down as far as it can go. The straps dig into my shoulders as I yank down on the bottom. It barely comes below my butt. I just sit down when it all comes out. The relief is overshadowed by the pain of the straps digging into my shoulders. It was a risky move—what if the leotard had ripped? Why didn't I just unpin the bib number? No time to second-guess now. I step out of the Porta-Potty and back among the spectators. A few of them look at me curiously. Probably because the Porta-Potty was shaking. I remove my bib from the front of my jersey and reattach it to the back. The spectators clap for me as I run off.

From there, I regroup on my plan. The fact that there are aid stations every mile makes it easy to break down the course. If I focus on running nine-minute miles between them, I can stop at each aid station for one or two minutes to use the restroom, stretch my back, and get something to eat and drink. There's no need to run through them. It's 4:36 p.m. I have until midnight. I have plenty of time to reach the finish. Just watch your step, avoid twisting your ankle, I tell myself. Take a deep breath and keep on chugging. And for Christ's sake, don't do anything stupid. If you feel your IT band start to act up, stop, walk, and let it calm down. Don't let anything get away from you.

The strategy slows me down significantly. I cross the eight-mile mark in 1:21:49, a pace of 10:14 minutes per mile. That's OK. In fact, I feel really good about it, considering I'm actually running. Right now, there are so many people walking that it's extremely tempting to walk myself. I have to weave in and out of them on the path along the canal, groups of people walking together, chatting like they're on an after-dinner stroll. This confuses me. It does not appear, from their composure and demeanor, that they are exhausted or fatigued. It looks like they never planned to run at all.

I keep running, sticking to my plan. If I have to walk later, so be it. But my legs are holding up so far. I didn't do all that training to stroll along the canal. I want to leave a little more on the course. The only exception is at the aid stations. I come out of my run and slow down to a walk as I approach the tents. I stroll through the aid station, one tent after another offering different kinds of nutrition. I pick up a cup of water and a cup of Gatorade. I have noticed that sometimes the Gatorade tastes good and other times it is poorly mixed and tastes like jet fuel. More often than not, I dump half a cup of water into the Gatorade. Every other aid station, I eat a half a banana, a handful of salted pretzels, or a mini Clif Bar. Once an hour, I eat a GU from the back pockets of my jersey.

I drink and eat and walk until I reach the end of the aid station. I stretch my back for thirty seconds before I start running again. By this point, seven or eight aid stations in, I'm very well hydrated. My energy feels good. My head feels good. I'm still pooping every few miles, but it's been better without the pressure of the bike seat on my backside, and my legs are hanging in there. This is not true for everyone and it is becoming more and more common to see struggling athletes pulled over on the side of the course. Some have their hands on their knees. Others walk in circles with their hands on their hips and their heads tilted back. Others lay down on their backs, their knees to their chest.

Just as on the bike course, the run course takes pride in messing with you. Before one aid station, as I approach mile nine, I see a sign that says Mile 20. It's for people on the second lap. Seeing it takes a scoop out of the confidence I have built, the sense of accomplishment I was enjoying. Mentally, it's an awful thing to compute. I'm not yet halfway through. I have another eleven miles until I reach this sign for real. Then I'll still have six miles to go. Thank you Ironman.

These signs cause all sorts of problems for people—some direct, some indirect. By this point, there are so many people on the course that the volunteers don't know who is on what lap. You run by the same aid station twice—how are they to know whether it's your first or second? One way is to ask. As I walk through the next aid station, my hands on my hips, I overhear a volunteer trying to make conversation with another athlete.

"Hey, great job!" she says to the girl, handing her a cup of water. "Are you on your second lap?! Are you about to finish?!?"

The girl becomes very upset. She lets out a big sigh of frustration.

"NO," she says, snatching the cup. "I know I look like I am. Because I look like shit!"

Holy smokes, get me out of here. I try to ignore any and all fuming participants and stick to my plan. One aid station at a time. Drink. Snack. Stretch. Pee or poop. It takes me two hours and eighteen minutes to close in on the end of the first lap.

The junction where those on their second lap head to the finish line and those on their first lap veer off for another lap is by far the most wicked and sadistic twist the race organizers have up their sleeves. There's basically a big fork in the road. Side by side are two signs in the center of the fork. One says, "To the finish line." The other points in the other direction and says Lap 2 or something. I can't take much more of this emotional abuse.

I see a guy in front of me bear toward the finish line at the fork. I want to throw a rock at the back of his head. I'm jealous that he's about to finish. He turns and looks behind him. I can hear him yell to the volunteers on the side of the course.

"Is there anyone behind me? Is there anyone behind me?!"

"No," someone yells out. "The finish line is all yours!"

He wants to make sure he's properly spaced away from everyone else so he can have his glory and finish with the full attention of the crowd. Or so I gather. I lose sight of him as I bear in the other direction at the junction. I pass through the transition area and start back along the canal. There are even more spectators than when I started. There are posters and stereos and lots of hand waving and dancing. At the end of a long line of spectator tents I see my mom and aunt standing in the grass along the pavement. They call out my name.

"Wiiiilllllll!"

I slow down to a walk and stop in front of them. I stand on the path at the edge of the grass. "Hiiii."

My mom's face flashes anxiety, like I'm about to miss my train. "Will, keep going!" she yells.

"It's OK, Mom. I can spare thirty seconds."

She gives me a hug. "You're doing so great!"

She tells me the app predicts, based on my current pace, that I'll finish around 8:00 p.m. I look at my watch. That's two and a half hours from now.

"I might slow down a bit. I'm getting tired."

She tells me she will be at the finish line before eight, in case I get in early. I assure her that I will not. I wave goodbye and continue on, down the canal, to the next aid station.

I wasn't lying to my mom—I am getting tired. My cardio and energy levels are fine, and I'm not losing my breath. But the pavement is taking its toll, and my legs are starting to wear down. I'm growing more aware of the bottom of my feet with every step. The entire way is paved concrete or asphalt, either a sidewalk or a road. I am paying very close attention to my left knee and the IT band, preparing to stop and stretch at the first sign of discomfort. So far, so good. I take down another GU, some pretzels, and a Gatorade/water combo at the aid station and continue on.

The sun is setting now and the sky looks pretty. It's a glimpse of something calm and beautiful in a day otherwise filled with fire and fury. Streaks of purple, pink, and orange dominate the paint-by-number sky, the lights of Tempe's tall buildings beginning to glow in the twilight. I can feel the dry desert air turn cool, the heat of the day subsiding. I take my sunglasses from my face and I put them on top of my hat. I lift my head and take a deep breath. It's been a long road, I think, and I'm almost there.

I run along the water. For a little while, the picturesque sunset takes my attention away from my body, providing a mental escape. Reality soon returns. The pounding of the pavement is the only sound I can hear, even though I run past many tents with loud music. I sound like a horse going down a cobblestone street, my form getting lazy and my feet slapping the pavement. Time-wise, I'm still doing OK, averaging nine minutes, more or less, between aid stations.

I pass a guy wearing a University of California Berkeley jersey, which sticks out to me because one of my old roommates went there. He looks like he's doing OK, running just a little slower than I am.

I reach the next aid station near mile sixteen. Ten miles to go. For the first time, the idea of finishing seems tangible, though ten miles is still a long run. I drink a cup of water and wonder how many people on earth have never run ten miles in their life. I take a minute of extra time to stretch out my back. I touch my toes. It's tighter than ever. Who knew peanut butter and jelly sandwiches were so heavy?

I run out of the aid station and continue along the water. Halfway to the next aid station, I see the guy from Cal again. He's ahead of me. How did that happen? He must not have stopped at the aid station. I pass him again and continue on, crossing the bridge and past the seventeen-mile mark. From the bridge I can look out and see down the canal to the main area of Tempe Town Lake, where we swam this morning. Only nine miles to go. I push away the thought that I can count on two hands the number of times I've run nine miles in my life.

I stop at the next aid station, and then the one after that. It's as repetitive as it sounds. The bottoms of my feet hurt badly now. I can feel it spreading up to my ankles and knees. I want to think about the finish line, about the possibility that there might be hot pizza and beer waiting for me. But I think only about reaching the next aid station. One at a time, one after another, and the rest will take care of itself. I stand at the edge of the aid station, drinking water and stretching my back. A steady stream of athletes goes in either direction on the two-way path, a quarter of them walking, a quarter of them running. The rest are somewhere in between, shuffling along, their feet barely coming off the ground. I eat half a banana and some pretzels. Everything hurts, but I know if I stop for too long, it will hurt even worse. I take off from the aid station and a quarter mile along I see the guy from Cal again. I realize we are the tortoise and the hare. I'm going hard between aid stations and stopping to rest. He's keeping it slow and steady right through the stations.

I confirm my suspicions. I stand drinking a cup of half water, half Gatorade when the guy from Cal cruises into the station. He slows to a walk to grab a Gatorade, chugs it, and then starts back into his run, leaving the aid station in less than twenty seconds. I catch up with him five minutes down the path. I pull up next to him. I run alongside him for several strides. He looks over at me.

He says, "How you feeling?"

"Ready to be done," I say. "Just going aid station to aid station."

"Only six stations to go!" he says.

He's right! I pull ahead of him and beat him to the next. Near the station I see the sign again: Mile 20. Holy shit. I'm back here and still in one piece. It's not six miles to go—it's six aid stations. Six cups of half water, half Gatorade. A couple handfuls of pretzels. I can do this!

When he arrives, he finds me and says, "Five more to go!" He yells it loud so everyone can hear. I can see a feeling of confidence rise from some of the other runners. I see nodding heads and I hear clapping hands. This reveals which runners are only on their first lap. They are the ones that do not clap. Suddenly, I'm overcome with perspective. Five aid stations. Five miles.

The run course is more or less flat except for one notable, extended hill in Papago Park. On the second lap, it falls between miles 22 and 23. On the first lap, I attacked it. I wanted to get it over with as soon as possible. This time around it gets the last laugh. As much of a lift as I received from the camaraderie at the previous aid station, there's no denying my continued deterioration. Each stride forces my teeth together. The bottoms of my feet are killing me, my legs have had enough, my ankles are weak, and my knees can no longer take the pounding. There's a small—very small—hint of pain in the side of my knee. I know that feeling all too well. I don't need any more convincing.

Here on mile 22, for the first time outside of an aid station, or the two minutes I spoke with my mom and aunt, I stop running and walk. It feels naughty, wrong even, at first. But then common sense takes over. It's only 7:15 p.m. I have five hours to go four miles. I could crawl and still make it.

I look around. Everyone seems to concur. There are more people walking up the hill than running.

It feels great to slow down. Finally, I can look around and see what there is to see. I can see the Tempe skyline across the water, lit up and shining bright in the clear night. I can see a couple stars. I notice the people around me. I see different types of walkers. You have the people who are happily walking because they want to be walking. You have the people who are walking but don't want to be walking. They look like their shoes are filled with concrete, having to deliberately lift and move them as they stomp along. I am somewhere in between. Sure, I would like to be running, ideally. Do I care? Am I distressed by the fact that I'm walking? No. Not at all. I'm four miles from the finish line.

Walking brings other benefits, too. I can have more than a passing conversation with other athletes. I walk next to a guy from Los Angeles and he tells me he's done a couple of Ironmans before, and that the challenge is good. He doesn't think he'll do any more, though. He says it takes up too much of his time. Plus, how many can you do before you've done enough? I tell him it's my first triathlon. He looks at me with concern.

"But you're on your second lap, right?"

"Yes," I say. "Are you?"

"Yes," he says. "If I wasn't, I would jump off this bridge."

I'm not quite sure we're on a bridge, but the guardrail and the sloping hills of the wilderness beyond make it look like we are. Plus, it's dark, and we've traveled 130-some miles, so who cares. We have a laugh. The pressure is completely off, the uncertainty eliminated by our imminent finish. At the top of the hill, we start jogging and run to the next aid station together. We talk about Los Angeles. I tell him a story about the summer I spent the fourth of July at Playa del Rey. The closer we get to the finish line, the more interactions like this take place. People have realized they're going to make it, and the sense of relief makes everyone friendlier. For those of us who are not concerned about time, we already feel like winners. I already feel like I have done it. All that's left is a formality, to tie a bow on it by crossing the finish line. Perhaps this is what some triathletes hate about the new brand of competitors, the indifference, the idea that you would be content just to finish, that you would not push hard all the way through.

At the aid station just beyond the 23-mile mark, the volunteers are trying to encourage us. It's 7:38 p.m.

"If you go hard, you can finish before 8:00 p.m.!"

One girl looks at her watch and takes off running. The guy from Los Angeles and I look at each other. He tells me he's going to take off. I wish him luck. I need to use the bathroom. I've still been drinking water and Gatorade at every aid station. There's no poop anymore, only pee—my stomach has fully settled, finally, after all these hours. I am relaxed as I use the Porta-Potty. I come out and stretch my back. Soon, I will experience the rush of the finish. Right now it is calm. There is anticipation in the air, one that coaxes us into a contemplative silence. Everyone is keeping to themselves, preparing for what's to come.

I run by myself to the last aid station before the finish, somewhere past mile 25. As I stand drinking my water—no more need for Gatorade at this point—my mind flashes back to Kona. I remember the announcers, watching the first-place guy come in. "He's getting pretty!" It makes me wonder what I look like at this point. I take my sunglasses and put them in the back pocket of my jersey. I take my hat off my head, run my hand through my hair, and put my hat back on. That's about as pretty as I get. The volunteers smile as I set off.

"Congratulations!" they call out. It sends a shiver down my spine. It's hard to believe. I'm really here now.

I jog toward the infamous fork, one sign pointing toward another lap and one toward the finish line. It's wonderful—beyond wonderful—to bear to the right and follow the arrow toward the finish line. I can see the lights up ahead and I can see the course funnel down to a long, narrow chute. People are lined up on either side of the chute, leaning over the metal gates, banging on the sides of them. It fills me with energy. Sore legs? Hurting feet? Not right now. The adrenaline soars through me, in a much different way than it did on the bike. Back then, it was intense and emotional, uncontrollable. This is different. It's a shot of caffeine, a shot of life, a sugar rush.

I clap my hands as I run through the chute. It's the only way I can think to burn off some of the adrenaline. My heart is pounding. I look up into the grandstand and at the people along the course. The crowd reacts to my clapping and enthusiasm. It's as if they all know me; I'm part of the family. At some point the path turns from pavement to carpet. Straight ahead, just a city block in front of me, is the finish line. A ramp leads up to and under a framed portal. It's my exit from this journey, from the last three and a half months. It's my last few steps as a regular athlete. From here on, I will go by a different title.

I run on the black-and-red branded carpet that leads under the square, black-and-white branded archway. Above my head I see the ticking clock—it's 8:09 p.m., 13 hours and 14 minutes since I started. I make sure to step on the head of the Ironman logo as I cross the finish line. I don't see him, but I hear Mike Reilly call out my name.

"From Waimānalo, Hawai'i, Will McGough, you are . . . an Ironman!"

Will McGough takes shelter from the sweltering heat on his cross-country bike ride through Nicaragua in 2016. The journey was 450 miles but spread out over ten days. COURTESY OF WILL MCGOUGH

November 19, 2017
Tempe, Arizona
1 Minute After the Ironman

Coming down is the hardest thing.

—Tom Petty

When I cross the finish line, a volunteer immediately takes me by the arm, as if he's going to walk me down the aisle. He wants to make sure I'm not going to fall over, that I have my wits about me. I feel fine. My adrenaline is pumping from coming down the finish chute, from hearing the crowd and realizing that it was, finally, all over. I am so happy to be done.

"Are you OK?" he asks. "Can you stand?"

"Point me to the podium," I say.

"You're five hours late."

He walks me back to a second set of volunteers. They hand me my medal and what they call a "finisher's T-shirt." It's a T-shirt you only get if you finish the race. It has the middle-finger cactus on the back. They encourage me to stand up against an Ironman-branded background and they take my picture. After, another volunteer wraps an aluminum-foil towel around me. I take it willingly. I'm cold now that I've stopped moving. The heat is pouring from my body. I hear the towel crinkle as I pull it over my shoulders. I continue down a side chute and come to an open field with a couple of tents. Under those tents are a variety of food offerings. In the center tent are big stacks of pizza boxes. Hot pizza???

Not so much. As the man at the village predicted a few days ago, the pizza is cold. But I don't care. I'm in love with the idea of pizza. I couldn't think much about food during the race due to all the digestive issues, but here now, with it in front of my face, I don't hesitate to ask for a slice of plain. The volunteer hands it to me on a paper plate. I look around for beer but there is none. There are athletes sitting in the grass. There are not many chairs at all. It's all right. I'd rather stand. I don't want to sit down when I know I have to get right back up. When I sit, I want it to be for good. I look at the pizza. I am intrigued by it—I want it—but I cannot take a bite. My mind is ready to eat, but my stomach isn't. Not yet.

My mom and aunt are waiting for me outside. It's a challenge to carry the pizza on the plate, hold the T-shirt, hold the towel around me, look for my mom and aunt, and put one foot in front of the other. I was confused by the volunteer's question when I finished. "Can you stand?" Dude, of course I can stand—I'm a goddamn Ironman. But now, five minutes after finishing, I can already feel my body letting its guard down. It's amazing how once you let go mentally you begin to fall apart physically. The fatigue is building like a wave out on the ocean. It's coming.

I take small steps through the crowd that gathers outside the gates at the athlete exit. I wait there until my mom and aunt find me. My mom runs up and hugs me. Her excitement contradicts my state of shock. It's hard to believe what I just did. Still, it's great to see them and have them hug me. The feeling of success is coursing through my body and mind. On top of that is a huge sense of relief. It is really over.

What do I want to do, my mom asks. Do I want to go out? Do I want to crush six beers? I don't know. I don't know what I want to do. I don't quite have a grip on what I'm feeling yet. I feel like I just woke up, like I'm still shaking off the night and processing this new reality into which I've woken.

Besides, there's still work to do. Even when the Ironman is over, it's not over.

One of the worst parts is that, after you finish, you then have to collect your bags and bike. I never want to see that bike again, but alas, after thirteen hours and 140.6 miles, I'm heading back to the bike transition area, carrying the pizza on the white paper plate, bouncing side to side as I waddle through the uneven grass.

I arrive at the transition area and collect my bike bag. Inside is my still-wet wet suit. It's been sitting in the sun all day, inside the bag, and stinks. My run bag, which has my nasty bike socks and sweaty helmet in it, is in no better shape. My morning clothes bag isn't too bad—it just has my warm-ups in it. I take these three bags to my bike. I hang the bags on the handlebars and push the bike through the field. This time, I am not concerned about rolling it through the grass. Now that the race is over, I can guarantee I will not get a flat tire. I use my right hand to push the bike and my left hand to carry the pizza. I meet back up with my mom and aunt. They have called an extra-large Uber. We stand on the street corner, a block down from the finish line. I can hear Mike Reilly calling out names. There are dozens of people rolling their bikes through the streets and along the sidewalks. Most are wearing their medals around their neck. We wait for the Uber. My mom makes a joke and tells me that a real Ironman would ride his bike back to the hotel. The thought of sitting on the bike seat again makes me cringe. A guy passes me and nods his head at my bike.

"Howzit?" I know immediately by the way he says it that he's from Hawai'i.

"Aloha," I say.

He stops to talk with me. I stand there holding my bike. He looks at it.

"That's awesome, brah, congratulations," he says. "You did the race on a classic bike."

I'm not sure what he means by this. It must be some sort of triathlete joke. The SUV pulls up. My mom holds the pizza as I take off the front tire and lift the bike into the back of the SUV. The driver becomes concerned about the grease on the chain. She makes me take the bike out, lay down a towel, and put it back in again. A simple request and a minor inconvenience, but one that draws a huge exhale on my part. Good god, just get me out of here.

In the car, I look at the pizza. I want it, but I do not want to eat it. I can't. My stomach feels closed off, shut down for business. All the Gatorade and energy bars and GUs have taken their toll. I feel queasy, like I have a hangover. I'm alive but not quite functioning. The taste of food is intriguing. The thought of actually eating it is not. When we arrive at the hotel, I remove the bags from the back and then the bike. I put the front tire back on. I roll the bike through the automatic double doors and into the lobby. The man behind the front desk gives me a thumbs up while making his face pose a question.

"How'd it go?"

I return the thumbs up and a smile. He smiles. I roll the bike down the hall to the room. My mom holds the heavy hotel door open for me and I roll the bike into the room. I let go of the handlebars and allow it to roll right into the dresser. It falls over against the wall, the front wheel turned sharply, the handlebars hitting the wall.

I decide I cannot eat the pizza. I ask my mom and my aunt if they want it. They look at it and shake their heads. I throw the pizza into the trash can under the desk in the hotel room. I'm sad about it; disappointed even.

I try to keep moving, knowing that the soreness will come and that I might crash at a moment's notice. I unzip my bike jersey and take off my leotard. There are deep, red rings on my thighs where the elastic of the leotard has dug in all day. It is by far the longest I have ever worn it. I use what's left of my strength to rip off my wristband. There is a ring on my skin where the wristband sat. It protected me from the sun and the dirt. The line is white and clean. The rest of me is grimy and red. When I take off my socks I see my feet are the same way. It looks like I'm wearing white socks. I get into the shower. I put my head under the showerhead. All I can taste is sweat. I run the bar of soap over my legs. I stand and let the hot water hit me in the chest. The hot water erases the chill. It feels good to get clean. The more I relax, the more I realize I'm a ticking time bomb. The adrenaline is gone. I don't have time to linger. I get out and wipe the steam from the mirror. I look into the mirror. My face is sunburnt, along with my forearms, the lower half of my thighs, and both calves. I look at myself in the mirror. You son of a bitch. You really did it.

While I can still stand, I decide to FaceTime with my girlfriend. I go outside and sit on a bench beside a cactus. She had watched my progress on the tracker and answers the phone with congratulations. I try to relay to her what I have been through, but I cannot. It seems so far away. She's happy I didn't kill myself. "How's your butt?" she asks. We laugh. Then she gets serious.

"You didn't . . . like it, did you?"

"Don't worry, hunny," I tell her. "It's all over now."

This makes her happy. Back inside, it takes a few minutes for my mom to convince me that, despite feeling sick, I should go to the hotel bar to try to eat something. I want to eat very badly, believe me. I've been dreaming of the post-race celebration for months. I order a cheeseburger, wings, and a beer. Compared to the bike seat, the bar stool feels like a king's throne. I recap the race with my mom. She tells me she saw many people suffering, and that she was worried about me out there. She says she is proud of me, that she doesn't know how I did it. I tell her I'm not so sure either. I wonder aloud how many people didn't finish. She says many people—both men and women—were escorted off in tears when race officials enforced the cutoff and closed down the bike course. I tell her I can't blame them a whole hell of a lot. I would be in a much different place right now if that had been me. To go through all that training, all that travel, all that pomp, to swim and ride all that way, only to be told you're not good enough.

It feels good to remind myself over and over that I was good enough. The bartender brings me my beer and sets it down on the dark wood bar. She does not use a coaster. I take a napkin from the stack and wrap it around the base of the glass. I hold up the beer to the light. It's golden and clear. This is it, the post-race beer I've been dreaming about the past four months. This is my gold medal.

I take a gulp of the beer. The satisfaction is underwhelming. It tastes off. I ask my mom to try it and she says it tastes normal to her. I try it again. Ugh. I rub my tongue on my teeth. My body is rejecting the beer. I've only taken a few sips when my food comes. The bartender puts the plate of wings and the cheeseburger and fries in front of me. I know before I even take a bite that I'm not going to be able to eat most of it. I eat two wings and half the cheeseburger, mostly to appease my mom, who insists I should eat something.

"Mom, that's all I can eat."

"Are you sure? Try one more bite."

We go back to the room and already I'm starting to feel sore. But I can still walk normally, for now. I lay down in bed and look at my phone. I have dozens of text messages from friends and family. Bmac sent me a video clip of myself finishing. I have no idea how he got it. He seemed to be very proud. Drew sent me a bunch of congratulatory texts. Turns out, some had been texting me all long, while I was biking and running, encouraging me to keep going, telling me they were watching me on the tracker, rooting for me. My sister, for as much grief as she gave me, was my number one cheerleader throughout the day, posting my progress on

Facebook. She's very proud of me, perhaps even impressed. It feels good to have done what I said I was going to do. What would these messages have said if I had missed a cutoff? I'm glad I don't have to find out.

To lay in bed feels wonderful at first. But the longer I lay there, the more restless I become. My legs especially—they want to keep moving. My mind continues to search back through the memories of the last seventeen hours. I had forgotten all about the two flat tires. I don't think I even told my mom about them. I prop myself up with pillows, take out my notebook, and write down everything I can remember about the race. This takes a long time. After a while I look over and see that my mom and aunt have fallen asleep with books in their hands. It's 1:00 a.m. when I turn out the light.

November 20, 2017
Tempe, Arizona
1 Day After the Ironman

New beginnings are often disguised as painful endings . . .

—Often attributed to Lao Tzu

I'm startled awake at 9:00 a.m. Holy shit, I had the craziest dream! I was in this ridiculous event where I had to do a long swim, bike 112 miles, and then run an entire marathon back-to-back-to-back. How insane! I throw off the covers and swing my legs to the side of the bed. There were people who tackled you to take off your wet suit, people throwing up and crashing everywhere. I even cried during the bike part. How absurd! Then, when I crossed the finish line, some guy on a microphone yelled out that I was Superman. No. Ironman! He said I was Ironman! Ha ha!

When I put my feet to the floor, my body lets me know it wasn't a dream. The bottoms of both my feet are sore and sensitive to the touch. Every muscle in my legs call out for me to lay back down in bed. But now I'm curious. I push up with my hands on the bed and rise to my feet. I'm unstable and stiff, like a robot that needs oil. I take a step. I feel the soreness in my feet, my hips, my calves, my quads, my hamstrings, my shins, my knees, my ankles and, of course, my glutes. My butt is bruised, sensitive to the touch. It is more comfortable to tilt my feet back and walk on my heels. I try to walk on the sides of my feet, but that hurts my ankles. I hobble around the hotel room, wincing with every step, like I'm walking on a bed of tacks. I stop at the foot of the bed and try to bend over and touch my toes. It doesn't go well—I almost fall forward. I stand back up straight. My mom and my aunt are still asleep in the other bed.

I shuffle on my heels across the carpet to the bathroom. I raise my arm to flip on the light switch. Ow! My shoulder cries out, sore and swollen. I don't dare lift my arm over my head. With strong thuds, my heels land on the tile floor as I head for the toilet. I turn around and face the wall. I pull down my pants. I reach out and grab the towel rack and, like I'm doing a squat, slowly lower myself down onto the toilet seat. My legs begin to shake and tremble, and the pain shoots through my quads. Halfway down they give out. I fall and smack down on the seat. The impact makes a loud noise and sends a shock wave down my legs, nightmares of the hard bike seat flashing to the forefront of my memory. Ow.

It takes me a long time to get off the toilet seat, but I do, using first the sink and then the towel rack to get up. It feels so surreal, even just a day later, to think I did all that. Was it really me? It's like someone took over my body for the day and is now handing it back to me in twelve pieces. I put both my elbows on the sink and lower my head to the faucet. I turn on the water with my left hand and cup my right under the faucet. When it's full, I bring it to my mouth and drink it. I do this several times. I'm incredibly thirsty. I feel my stomach rumble—in a good way. I'm ravenous.

It's a far cry from last night, when I had absolutely no appetite. That might have been the most disappointing part of the whole experience. After the race, I imagined myself going to the nearest bar and drinking as much beer as they would sell me. That's been part of the deal for me all along. Exercising this much gives you a free pass to gluttony. To exercise for thirteen hours only to discover that your body is rejecting beer is simply cruel.

Today, though, will be a different story. I'm starving. I come out of the bathroom and find the leftovers in the fridge. I use my heel method to walk to the lobby. I'm walking like I'm recovering from two broken legs, and people in the halls look at me with concern and compassion. I'm pretty sure they think I'm disabled. *Good for you*, their eyes say. *Keep trying.*

Maybe this is a preview of what it's like to be old. I locate the microwave in the lobby, heat the food, and waddle back to the room. I eat the cheeseburger, side of fries, and remaining wings sitting propped up in bed. My mom and aunt are still asleep in the other bed. I put the plate on the bed next to me and bring my computer onto my lap. I'm curious to see what's happening on the forums. A lot of people have posted photos of themselves at the finish line with their medals. Some put out messages of congratulations to everyone who competed. A few people lost things in the transition areas and are trying to get them back. Then there are a few morbid posts. Apparently there was a big crash out on the Beeline that sent at least one man to the hospital. It wasn't the same accident as the one that left the girl with her head bandaged and bleeding—that was a different incident on a different part of the course. I take big bites of the cheeseburger as I read and digest the reality of it. Sure, I'm sore, but I probably shouldn't complain, all things considered.

I want to eat more. Much more. And I want beer. But first I have to take the bike apart and pack it back into the box. I fly out early tomorrow, and I don't plan to be in any shape to do it tonight. I can barely stand up straight or walk, but somehow, I need to get this thing apart and packed down. I take my time and move slowly, deliberately. I work quietly. Pain and soreness shoot upward from the bottom of my feet, first to my calves, then my knees and upper legs. I grit my teeth and flip the bike upside down, on its seat and handlebars. I hobble around the bike like a drunk circling a campfire. I take off both tires and wrap them in cardboard and newspaper. I lay the bike down. I kneel next to it and unscrew the handlebars. I use the bed to help myself stand up. My legs scream with soreness. The one thing I have going for me is that, unlike on the way here, I don't care if the bike makes it back in one piece. I wrap the gears and the body as best I can and shove it into the box. I fit the tires in around it and throw in more crumbled newspaper. I close the top and seal the lid with packing tape. I sit down on the bed to rest. I put both hands on my knees and push myself back onto my feet. I grab the box by its end and drag it into the corner. I go around the other side of the box and push it fully into the corner, between the bed and the wall. I collapse facedown on the bed, exhausted.

My mom stirs in the other bed. She picks her head off the pillow, takes out her earplugs, and looks toward me.

"Will, do you need any help?"

Later that day, I meet a friend from Scottsdale at my favorite bar in Tempe, Casey Moore's Oyster House. It has a beautiful, laid-back, wrap-around patio and is in a residential neighborhood. The house is said to be haunted. I get out of the backseat of the Uber, pulling on the top of the door to pry myself out of the car. I try to walk as normally as I can in spite of the overwhelming soreness. I feel like a ninety-year-old man who got up from his chair and whose only goal is to find another.

I find my friend sitting on the patio at a table. She says she has a surprise for me and pulls out a big, party-size bag of my favorite chips, Doritos.

"We've got to fatten you back up," she says. "You're a shell of what you were."

I tell her it's the best gift I've ever received. The beers go down easy. One. Two. Three, just like that. Why not. I've earned it—certainly after last night's disappointment. I can finally celebrate. I can finally toast my accomplishment. For the first time, I can reminisce about the experience with the knowledge that I am worthy, that I did conquer it. There's nothing left to nag at my mind, to worry about in the future. These beers are my first taste of victory.

I sit happily on the padded seat, my legs extended. So long as I'm sitting on a soft surface, I'm comfortable. I can drink the beer and eat the food and have a conversation, and I forget all about what happened yesterday. But when I get up to go to the bathroom a stern reminder is delivered. I can't walk correctly. I can't sit on a hard surface. I can't defend myself if I'm jumped by an eighth-grader. Yesterday, I was everything. Today, I am nothing.

Afterward I meet up with my mom and my aunt for dinner at Pedal Haus Brewery on Mill Avenue. I can pick out other athletes at the tables and the bar because they are still wearing their race wristbands. I no longer care to investigate whether or not they're drinking. I order a double IPA, a flatbread pizza, and a meal-sized portion of mac and cheese. I order another beer before the food comes. When the pizza is brought out, I immediately send it back to the kitchen to be reheated.

"I'd like this pizza as hot as you can get it," I tell the waiter. "It's very important."

When he brings it back, the cheese is practically bubbling.

"Excellent," I tell him.

Back at the hotel room, I eat the entire bag of Doritos. I chew the chips carefully—I burnt the roof of my mouth on the pizza—but I eat every single one. My aunt looks over at me from the other bed. She's curious to see what I'll consume next. I lick the nacho cheese off my fingers. It's nearing midnight. Sorry Auntie, this show is over. The curtain is closed on the Ironman. I start to get up to go brush my teeth. My legs wobble as I try to stand. It's either the beer, or the 140.6 miles I traveled yesterday. One or the other.

The next morning I am still very sore, but significantly better than the day before. I still feel all my leg muscles when I walk, and my feet and ankles cry out with every step. But I don't feel ninety anymore. Today, I'm seventy or seventy-five. I put the bike box on top of my rolling suitcase and push it around the airport. I say goodbye to my mom and aunt in the terminal. They tell me they are proud of me.

"Are you going to do another one?" my aunt asks. "'Cause if you are, I'm going to have to have your head examined."

I thank them for all their help and support. It really did make a difference having them here with me. I pay $150 to check the bike, go through security, and find my gate. On the plane, I start chatting with the person next to me.

"What were you up to in Phoenix?" she asks.

"Well," I say, "I did this race thing."

"Like a marathon?"

"That's part of it," I say. "It's a triathlon called the Ironman."

She nods her head with familiarity. "That's the one where you swim, right?"

"Yes, and bike."

"How far do you go?"

I tell her the distances.

"Woah," she says, "you must be really fit!"

"You know," I say, feeling good about the compliment, "it wasn't so bad."

She looks at me. "You must be, like, kinda insane to want to do that sorta thing."

I smile at the woman. "Not really. I just wanted to try it."

"I would never do anything like that," she says.

"What do you do for fun?"

"Watching Netflix is more my speed." She starts to laugh.

I decide not to tell her how much Netflix you can watch while training. I'm able to doze off for a couple hours. I wake up every once in a while to shake out my legs. They're crammed up against the back of the seat in front of me. When we land in Honolulu, I use that same seatback to pull myself up out of the row. The woman sitting next to me notices my limp. She blocks the aisle and lets me go in front of her. She smiles as I pass.

"Looks like you had a lot of fun," she says.

November 29, 2017
Waimānalo, O'ahu, Hawai'i
10 Days After the Ironman

> *Let another praise you, and not your own mouth; a stranger, and not your own lips.*
>
> —Proverbs 27:2

I head to Mexico tomorrow for nine days on a work trip. I fly from Honolulu to San Francisco, to Mexico City, and then to Tuxtla, in the state of Chiapas, where I'll spend a week before continuing on to Villahermosa in Tabasco. A couple of days ago I realized I was out of Ambien, and since I never leave home without it anymore, I made an appointment to go back and see my doctor for a refill. I have to do this every couple months. You know, that whole controlled substance thing. It's the same doctor I saw back in August, when I first started training. I'm excited to gear up for my red-eye flights. I'm more excited to report back about how I did in Arizona.

I am completely healed from a superficial soreness standpoint. I can walk without a limp now. It's a good thing, because I returned home to a full schedule. It was the week of Thanksgiving, and I had an old friend come in from Seattle for the weekend. We ate and drank and went scuba diving. It was the perfect celebration. Now he's gone and I have a few days to relax and catch up with myself. And, with other Ironmen.

Right after the race, the forums were filled with celebratory and congratulatory exclamations and messages. Others expressed their disappointment about not meeting their desired times or, in other cases, of not finishing at all. Of the 3,269 competitors who signed up, 2,236 finished, meaning 1,033 either did not finish or did not start the race (for whatever reasons). I had a chance to look at my performance as it compared to the rest of the pack.* I was 170th overall in the swim; 1,695th in the bike; and 722nd in the run. In terms of total time, my 13:14:10 put me 941st out of 2,236 finishers. Guess I'm not that great a biker. But in the big picture, not bad for a guy who started training three months ago.

I had heard triathletes—specifically Ironmen—talk about the "victory lap," but it's not something I could fully appreciate until I got here to the other side. It's just what it sounds like—returning to real life, among all the normal people who knew you were training for an Ironman, encountering and updating them on how the race went. My doctor. The guys at the tri shop. The grocery checkout clerk. Anyone I interacted with over the last few months who was aware of my plight, who I annoyed with stories of my training. I get to go back to all these people and tell them the good news. Yes, it's largely—if not entirely—egotistically motivated, especially in the case of informing those who I suspect were skeptical of my chances.

* My rankings differ slightly depending on whether I look them up on the Ironman website or the Ironman app. These numbers are from the Ironman app. My numbers on the website are actually a little better.

Speaking of, Mr. I'm on Another Level from the tri shop? I'm excited to tell you he did not finish the race in Arizona. He quit on the bike course. Ahem.

I know, I know—I'm bragging. I'm not normally this way. I don't think most Ironmen are, either. I know triathletes can be annoying when they talk about their training, or what kind of power wattage they need to average in their next race, but one thing I've noticed is that Ironmen, despite the stereotype that they are full of themselves, aren't big braggers. They will represent. They'll wear event T-shirts. They might snicker if you bring up the fact that you're running a 5K. Then, of course, there are the tattoos. But beyond that kind of stuff, I haven't met too many accomplished triathletes who run around bragging about what they've done. Gordon Haller. Drew. Tommy. Bmac. Mimmo. They speak of their feats modestly. Which is surprising. After 140.6 miles, you'd think you would have earned the right to gloat.

So far, I've tried my best to stick to the facts and not oversell my accomplishment. I did mention it to one of my colleagues, who I do business with over e-mail but rarely see in person. I wrote something about my life getting back to normal after the Ironman last week. He wrote back, "Omg, you *really* did it? That's amazing!" He italicized the "really" and everything. Thanks, mate. Not that you doubted me or anything!

Mostly, the reactions have been voluntary and unprovoked from friends and family. I received a lot of nice messages from those who had been following along from the beginning. Other participants came home to similar celebrations. For example, one woman who was active in the online forum came home to find her foyer decorated with streamers and large banners. She posted photos of it. The banner was huge, stretching across the entire room, with "Congratulations" written on it. All of her friends and family had signed it or written a note. The caption was, "Came home last night to find this poster waiting for me! We truly have some amazing friends!"

Another woman commented on the photo: "My friends did something similar, and since a few of them didn't really 'get it' about IM, it meant the world to me. So nice!"

The "didn't really get it" part of that last comment got my attention. It compelled me to ask her what she meant. She wrote back and explained:

Your friends before the race: That's so intense, so complicated; Hope it's worth it; Are you sure you need to do that?

Your friends after the race: Congratulations, we are so proud of you!

I certainly had doubters in my life, but because my training was so short and sweet, and because everyone close to me knew—or strongly figured—that I would not be taking up this lifestyle permanently, they all bore with me. Those who didn't quite understand my plight didn't have the chance to become fully annoyed because before they knew it, it was done. Other athletes with longer training periods don't have it so easy. A longer training time frame means more opportunity cost; more missed events, birthday parties, and nights out. Those closest to you are most affected by it, and undoubtedly the happiest to see it end. Now that it's over, friends who may have been skeptical before are suddenly cheerleaders—happy you succeeded, happy it's over, and hopeful you'll never do it again.

But hey, what are friends for?

When I arrive at the doctor's office, the nurse leads me back into one of the examination rooms to take my vitals. She has me stand on the scale. I weigh 171 pounds, more or less the same I weighed at the beginning of August. That's strange, considering I've slimmed down noticeably. One of my friends told me the other day that I'm the skinniest he's ever seen me. That's saying something—we've known each other since grade school. But whatever I've lost in shape I've apparently gained in lean muscle, because even though I've slimmed down, my weight is the same.

I sit down in the chair next to the scale. The nurse places the little clip on my index finger. She watches the screen. Her expression changes from mundane boredom to genuine concern. I ask her what's wrong.

"Are you feeling OK?" she asks me.

"Yeah," I say. "I feel fine. What's wrong?"

"Well, nothing, it's just . . . do you usually have a low pulse?"

"It's usually resting in the low sixties," I tell her. "I've been athletic my whole life."

"OK," she says. "Well . . . it's at forty-six right now."

I sit up and turn around to see the screen. It does indeed read forty-six.

"Let's try the other finger," she says. She takes another clip from the machine and hooks it onto my opposite pointer, so now each hand has a clip on the pointer finger. We watch and wait. It again lands in the mid-forties, fluctuating between forty-six and forty-seven. She goes out to get another nurse. I feel fine, but now I'm nervous. Do I really feel fine? I stand up and shake my legs, run in place a little. Yeah, I feel great. The nurse comes back with another nurse. The new nurse says she wants to manually take my pulse. She places two fingers across my wrist and looks down at her watch. The corners of her eyes wrinkle as she concentrates. After fifteen seconds, she looks at the other nurse, then back at me.

"You feel OK?" she asks. "You're sure?"

I nod my head. "Yes," I say. "I really do."

"The doctor will be right in."

They hurry out. I've been to this doctor a handful of times over the past year and never once has he "been right in." I've always had to wait at least ten minutes in the little room. I usually kill time by playing with the ear microscope, reading the laminated public health announcements hung on the door, or snooping through the drawers. Sometimes I lay down on the wax paper with both hands behind my head. But today, it's not two minutes before the doctor bursts through the door. As soon as he enters he pulls back his momentum. I'm sitting in the chair beside the examination table. He smiles.

"Will! It's you!"

The nurses come in behind him and he turns to them. "It's OK," he says, "Will's an Ironman. He's in better shape than all of us."

He motions for the nurses to leave and they close the door. He comes over and shakes my hand.

"Did you think I was dying?" I ask him.

"We don't get too many people with a low heart rate like that," he tells me.

"But I'm good, right?"

"It's completely normal for someone like you," he says.

We chat for a few minutes about the race. I had seen him at the beginning of my training, and now at the end of it. This meeting here closes the book on the experiment, medically speaking. He prescribes me the Ambien and we shake hands. See you in a few months, I say. OK, he says, goodbye.

I walk to my car. Maybe that's why Ironmen don't brag openly. Maybe, little by little, it all speaks for itself.

I drive home past all my usual, previous running routes. Walking into my apartment I see my bike in the box, pinned between the head of my bed and the wall, the top of the box sticking out above the mattress like a headboard. I have yet to unpack it. Maybe it will never be unpacked. I certainly don't want anything to do with it right now. These next two weeks are dedicated completely to rest. It was fortunate that Thanksgiving fell directly after Ironman Arizona. I've never experienced such a guilt-free eating experience. It was nice to have the holiday off from work, too. I could ease back into normal life and catch up with friends. I went to the beach a few times, had a beer with the sunset. It was nice to relax and not feel compelled or obligated to go for a run or a ride. I don't miss that part.

That said, I'm glad I'm going to Mexico and that my schedule will pick up again. I'm not sure what I'd do with myself otherwise. I don't miss the workouts or the looming anticipation, but I do miss the mission of it, the sense of purpose. It's not that I cannot or will not get this fulfillment from other areas of my life—I always have, and I will again. Transitions are what they are, though. My life has been a certain way for the past hundred days and now it will be completely different. Going through that kind of change is always a process.

Rest assured I am not the only one feeling this way, experiencing what I'm calling "The Comedown." It's been a week since the Ironman and many triathletes are expressing similar feelings. Resting and relaxing are apparently not things triathletes do well. Imagine that! There have been many posts about it online. Most people report they are overwhelmed by the amount of newfound free time.

One woman lamented on social media: "It's only been one week today that I completed IMAZ and I'm bored. So why not redo [my] restroom, that will keep me busy for a couple of weeks." Along with this, she posted a bunch of photos of her bathroom being renovated, the toilet ripped out and all the walls bare. Someone commented that he decided to replace his water heater because he now "has too much time and energy" on his hands and doesn't know what to do with it. Others speak of filling their time with heavy cleaning and organizing.

"So now that it's over is anyone else like well now what??" one woman bemoaned. "Not that I'm in a rush to start training again but it's kinda like what now? What's next??"

Indeed, this time of recovery seems tough for triathletes. On one hand, they enjoy it, basking in the accomplishment, refueling. Many people spoke of the joy of unabated eating, indulging in pizza, beer, pancakes, and all the other things they denied themselves leading up to Arizona. I am also guilty of this. But indulgence in food alone cannot fill the huge hole. Now what? Do I get a new hobby? It's almost as if I can't remember life before Ironman. What the hell did I do with all this free time?

For many, this perplexing question, and the post-Ironman blues in general, entice people back for more. What's the best way to fill the void of training? More training. As some talk about Arizona 2018, others are already making plans for Ironman events in 2019—Santa Rosa, Boulder, Texas. Some athletes say they aren't going to do a full-length Ironman next, but instead will do other, shorter events. And even those who express disinterest in another Ironman make it clear they won't be couch surfing. One man said he was going to pass on Arizona 2018 "to save the 800 bucks plus all the extra food I ate the last few weeks." He said maybe he will do Arizona 2019, but for now, he will focus only on biking. "It will be nice to get my sprint and hill climbing legs back," he wrote.

This "what now?" syndrome is part of the "comedown," the process of recovery. For some, it begins right after the race, either when you cross the finish line or when you realize you won't. My comedown from the Ironman began the day after the event. I was in no position to have any rational thoughts post-race. The time between when you finish and when you go to bed is nothing more than a state of shock. Crossing the finish line was an emotional moment, a feeling of relief like none other. My body was reeling, trying to figure out what had happened. It was running diagnostics tests, figuring out which muscles took the hardest beating. Meanwhile, my mind, the true engineer of the day, was being pulled in two directions—excited about the accomplishment, but overwhelmed with what it took to get there, trying to process all that took place over the course of those thirteen hard-fought hours. Immediately, it was trying to figure out if what happened was good or not. It felt good mentally, having conquered it. But was it good physically? Did I enjoy it? Did it really happen?

The next day is when the rest of your life begins. The physical aspect headlines the afterlife, the soreness being at the top of the list, followed by periods of insatiable hunger, and a general fatigue that can last for weeks. None of these address what's happening upstairs, though. It doesn't speak to how your psyche is handling the aftermath, how it is adjusting to the realization that this thing, which had been the centerpiece of your life for so long, is now over. There is a need to reflect on this, and to reflect on the experience of the race. There is a need to process what happened. There is a need to share this with others. Now, this seems very obvious on the surface. You just did this crazy race; of course you are going to want to tell all your friends and family about it over the course of the next couple weeks, over happy hours and dinners. You'll tell them about the times you felt strong, the times you thought you were going to die, the near misses and how it felt to cross the finish line. You'll give them the highlights, as much as they can handle, because what you'll find out—what I've found out—is that people are only going to be so interested. There's only so much they can relate to. They will sit through the highlights, but I've found these simple retellings of the race are not always completely satisfying to the triathlete. Your friends are going to look at you funny when you talk about your wattage output on the hill.

But other racers will care, and this is where the support of the community plays such an important role in recovery. Not only do racers tell their stories to their friends and family, but they also write up reports for other triathletes—people they've never met—to read. In the days after the event, the forums filled with what they call "Race Reports"—detailed accounts of a person's experience on race day. There seems to be a format to it. First, you describe your day. The reports are filled with the practical information you'd expect—I had a great swim; I had a flat tire on the bike;

my knee hurt on the run but I pushed through. These events are typically described in admirable detail. Then, at the end, most people evaluate their own performances and let the community know whether they are encouraged or heartbroken about it. I'll admit, some of the race reports from people who had a rough day were tough to read. They dive into the emotional aspects of the day, and how the person thinks those emotions will impact them going forward. They wax poetically about what the experience meant for them, and most importantly, they try to put it in perspective as it relates to their overall triathlete career. Some are long; some are short and sweet. Even when they are brief, they still leave you feeling like therapy is the answer. For example, one person wrote this:

> *As I have settled in over the last couple of days I have had time reflected* [sic] *on how my race day did not go as planned. I have to admit that I am taking it harder than I thought. It is so frustrating not being able to perform at the level I know I am capable of. I was thinking to myself while I was out on the course suffering with stomach issues and cramping that this nutrition thing has always been a stumbling block for me and that I should just focus on Olympic distance events where race nutrition is not a factor. I thought I was OK with letting it go and moving on but the angst is growing. This afternoon it came to a head and I realized I can't move on until I conquer this demon. Now I do not know if I should sign up for IMAZ 2018 or another race. I would love to do another Ironman in the Spring but I have the Boston Marathon in April that I need to focus on. Then a family trip to Cancun in the beginning of June. So, I am not sure I can afford the time to go far for another race but waiting until next November for another shot at redemption seems so far away.*

It reads like a letter to a personal friend. Trip to Cancun? Cool! Yet 99.9 percent of the people reading it are complete strangers. This is a typical race report, although it is on the short end of the spectrum. Some go on and on for pages and pages (I guess I'm as guilty as anyone here and now). Even the best triathletes partake. The winner of Ironman Arizona, Lionel Sanders—who finished second at Kona—did one on his personal website. From the looks of it, he writes one after every race he does (nearly a dozen per year). He describes his efforts in each of the three sports. Accompanying the words are graphs that show his power-wattage output. I wanted to paste the whole thing here, but my proofreaders told me it bored them to tears, and plus, we ran into some copyright concerns. You'll just have to give it a read for yourself.* Be warned—it's dry—but it's quite interesting to me on a couple levels. For one, it might be the only sport I've seen where the champion shares the secrets of his success in such a detailed manner. If you're an aspiring competitor, it does give you candid insight into his approach.

"I remember last year thinking my power meter was broken because 320w felt so easy!" he writes. "This year I couldn't even hold that for an hour! The final third of the bike was quite excruciating. The wind was strong, it was starting to heat up, and I had nothing left in my legs. For the final hour I averaged 254w, and in the end I averaged 292w for the entire bike ride. Last year I averaged 315w for the entire ride."

So, that seems helpful, I guess. For me, it's not the words so much as the graphs—that's where I glaze over. But it's important to see and understand, because it's the reality of the community. And if you think analyzing the power graphs of the winner is bad, imagine digging into reports from people who finished 2,341st, or whatever.

Another part of the comedown for athletes is to analyze how they felt about the specific race in terms of its organization and execution—in other words, what they got for their time, effort, and money. As competitors reflect on their races and write their reports, all the memories come flooding back, the good and the bad. The good are mostly celebrated internally, or laid out in the race report. The bad are aired out like drying laundry, strung up across the balcony for all to see and consider. Complaints voiced about the race were all over the map. Some pertained to the behavior of fellow competitors, and others to the organization of the race:

- Not enough seats in the athletes' food area post-race
- People did not seed themselves correctly on the swim

* Visit lsanderstri.com. He also wrote a race report for Kona, if you feel so inclined.

- Sponsor tents played music too loud
- Finish line clock displayed the time of day instead of the race time
- Bad riding etiquette—drafting, blocking, or passing and then slowing down
- People being blatantly paced by friends or family on the run (which is illegal)
- Serving pretzels at the aid stations instead of potato chips, which are easier to eat
- Dirty Porta-Potties and a lack of toilet paper
- Gatorade dilution differed from aid station to aid station
- Too much dust on Mile 2–3 of the run
- Glitchy tracker app
- Lack of lights on the run course after dark
- Poorly trained volunteers who handled bikes improperly
- No sponges on the course to wipe face, nose
- Aid stations breaking down too early

I can relate to the sentiment behind some of these complaints. Each athlete has paid thousands of dollars to be there, including an $850 entry fee. For that price, you expect a certain level of professionalism. You expect the bathrooms to be well stocked, the volunteers to handle your bike properly, the aid stations to stay open, the course to be well lit, and the rules to be enforced. Things like "too much dust," "no sponges," "Gatorade dilution," "music too loud," and the whole "pretzels versus potato chips" thing—which was commiserated by several people—are more subjective. Given the scope of the day, and the intensity involved, it seems silly to let some dust and loud music derail you, much less the lack of potato chips. But when emotions are high, little things blow up into big things. I saw that firsthand on the course.

When I get home, I receive an e-mail from Ironman asking me if I want to purchase the FinisherPix package. This is not the first time I have been presented with the opportunity to buy my race photos. Ironman began advertising photo packages to me the moment I signed up for the race and continues to do so here in the aftermath. When registering for the race, I was offered the photo package for $99, which would include a collection of digital images (no hard copies). Now, after the fact, I can buy them either individually or in bulk: An individual digital photo costs $28.99, and then there are a couple options for packages that cost between $99 and $129.

I considered purchasing the package when I signed up for the race, but it's a lot of money for digital photos. I decided to wait to see what the pictures looked like before buying them. I'm glad I did. Scrolling through the album FinisherPix prepared for me, I see a couple of photos are not of me—they are of a completely different person, some guy who is way older. Weird. There are good shots in there, including one of me coming out of the water, one of me in the aero position on the bike, and one of me running, looking strong. There were a few others of me crossing the finish line that were serviceable. They are by no means incredible, well-timed shots—it's clear they were taken by an automatic camera. But I guess they are nice memories of the day. I suppose they would be nice to have later in life. Maybe I'll buy the $99 package for nostalgia's sake, if they can take out the photos that are not of me. I contact FinisherPix via e-mail to see what we can do.

"Hi, some of the photos in my file don't appear to be me. Is that possible?"

"We apologize for any inconvenience. Regarding the photos in your gallery which show other people than you. Those are athletes which crossed the timing mat together with you or at least very very close to you. This is one of the external factors which we can't influence. Nevertheless we can delete those photos out of your gallery manually if you forward us the picture Ids. Thank you."

OK. This other guy couldn't have been "very very" close to me, because I'm not also in the picture. But, all right. Maybe this is a good thing.

"Thanks . . . does that mean the package costs less, because there are less photos?"

"The package costs will not change. We can still delete pictures you do not want to purchase if you forward us the photo IDs."

Wait, what?

"I don't understand why the photo package wouldn't be cheaper given that there are less photos?"

I never receive a response from FinisherPix. I wonder if anyone else is having this issue? I go online to the forums to find out and yes, yes they are. One woman wrote that she purchased the photo package ahead of time, only to find out upon their delivery that half the photos were not of her.

In response to my story, where I relayed that I had the same problem and that FinisherPix said it was something they couldn't control, she opined, "I think it is something they can control but they have a monopoly on the IM circuit so their give a shit button is completely off."

Others report no problems, and others report more of the same problems. Over the next few days, I see a lot of comments from people saying they did not receive any photos of themselves running. The theory is that no photos were taken after dark.

I found this all fascinating. I don't expect Ironman or FinisherPix to be perfect. I don't expect them to take perfect photos of me in such a chaotic environment—that would be very difficult. But, come on. Is it too much to ask for someone to stand by their performance? A customer buys the advertised package beforehand, and then half the photos they get are not them? That's how you do business?

I don't buy the photos, but I screenshot a few of them from the online gallery. Then I use "Paint" to crop them and print them out. They still have the copyright written across in green letters—that's something I couldn't get rid of—and they are very small and low quality. Supposedly, they send you the larger, high-resolution version after you buy them. Yeah, right. I'm sure they do!

Seeing the watermarked versions in my photo album is actually quite fitting. I shake my head whenever I look at them. They help me remember the whole story.

January 25, 2018
Waimānalo, O'ahu, Hawai'i
67 Days After the Ironman

We rejoice in our sufferings, because we know that suffering produces perseverance; perseverance, character; and character, hope—and hope does not disappoint us.

—Romans 5:3–5

It always seems impossible until it's done.

—Nelson Mandela

Today I ran my old three-mile Waimānalo loop in 21:37 for a pace of 7:12 minutes per mile. It's the first time I've run the loop since my training ended in November. I spent the first part of December on the road for work, and I didn't even consider going to the hotel gym. I traveled around for the holidays, partly for work, partly for pleasure—Philadelphia, Asheville, New Orleans. Then I drove to San Diego and spent a few days there before returning to Hawai'i. I ate and drank a lot. After the New Year, I got back to my normal active routine—light cardio at the gym, body weight training, hiking, surfing, swimming, and the occasional run. I haven't touched my bike. It's still in the same box it came home in from Arizona, between my bed and the wall. It's the closest thing I have to a headboard.

To get out on the run today and see that I've still "got it" feels good, although I would hardly call it a pleasurable experience. Despite running at a fast pace, my body did not feel happy about it. I still feel sluggish and my muscles still don't feel 100 percent. My shoulder is still sore from time to time when I surf. Drew and Bmac and everyone told me it would take several weeks, if not months, to recover fully. One timetable on the Ironman website said that triathletes should take three to five days off for every hour of racing. For me, thirteen hours times five days of rest per hour equals sixty-five days of rest.

On a day-to-day basis, I don't think about the Ironman much. My bike in the box blends in at this point, part of the decor. Once in a while I see the medal hanging in my closet. Mostly, I'm reminded when I'm driving and see bikers along the road. The sight brings back flashes of a former life, and I look out the window at them with nostalgia, a hand pressed against the window. Since I've stepped out of that world, it's been surreal to look back. Once you stop doing three-hour rides and fourteen-mile runs, you wonder how you did it in the first place. Did I really do that? Kind of like looking back on school. Did I really do homework every day? Did I really take all those tests? I guess I did. Damn, that must have been a grind! All those tests! All that studying! It's hard to believe I did it.

One thing that always helps me remember and believe I did the Ironman is my bank and credit card statements. Participating in the Ironman Arizona cost me approximately $3,013*—and that does not include the $850 entry fee I had waived as a media member, the couple hundred dollars I spent on extra food over those three months, or the opportunity cost of my time.

Something I've done in the last couple of weeks, in the spirit of tying a bow on my experience, is stay in touch with Gordon Haller, the winner of the first Ironman, and to chat with Ian Emberson, another of the original competitors. I got along well with them, and both were candid with me about their roles and experiences in inventing and participating in Ironman. They were very upfront about their feelings of watching it grow after the fact, once they were out of the picture, financially speaking. But it wasn't until I had gone through the process that I could really connect with them.

I had been interested in how Ironman went from nothing to something, how it evolved into the behemoth it is today. I wanted to learn from them how Ironman had changed. Before, we could only speak in theory about it. I could only listen to their stories. But now I had my own point of reference and my own stories to share. We were on the same page. Now I could fully understand what they were telling me about the evolution that Ironman has gone through in the past forty years.

* See appendix for a price breakdown.

In contrast to the regimented workouts that triathletes meticulously follow today in preparation for the Ironman, the first Ironmen were free swingers. Hell, Haller found out about the Ironman only two and a half months before it took place. He wasn't exactly training for it. Emberson had to borrow a bike. For those first fifteen—guys who all ran in the same circles among different clubs on O'ahu—it was less about organized, preplanned workouts and race preparation and more about the fact that they actually felt like going for a swim, bike, or run.

"Many times back then, I would step outside and think, 'It's a great day to go ride a hundred miles,'" Haller said.

Today, athletes of all abilities train specifically for the Ironman. It has become a rite of passage, and an accomplishment to be had. It started as a single event forty years ago, one day once a year. By comparison, these days, there are about forty full Ironman events throughout the world, and that does not include all its other branded races, such as the half and short-course races. Compare that to before, when it was a once-a-year whatever, some silly and crazy thing a couple of guys did because they had a very unique definition of the word "fun."

"It was about hanging with your buddies," Emberson said. "It wasn't about winning, not about where you placed. It was about doing the event and the experience. In my day, we would never go out and train ahead of time."

Here in 2018, that's obviously not the case. There's a pro circuit that exists solely to sort out who's the best, and age groupers push one another to new limits each and every year. For the age groupers, it's more than common to come across people who are taking up an Ironman not because they think it will be fun, but rather because they want to prove to themselves they can do it. This was relayed to me over and over again by competitors, both publicly and privately. Is it admirable? Sure—no question. But it does mark a strong detour from the original vision.

"Some people do it to get it done, not because they love the distances," Haller said. This echoes what the hipster triathlete at the tri shop told me several months ago, when he explained why he gave up on Ironman—because of people like me. Back then, I thought they were just bitter, mean store employees. It makes more sense to me now. There has been a switch in the reasoning, a change in the motivations. For those with a pure love for the activity, those changes have brought mixed feelings.

Granted, many people today still approach the Ironman from a perspective of "just finishing." But from what I've observed, that casual description rarely comes with a genuine love for the three sports. Quite the contrary. In fact, when I ask Ironmen why they compete, why they decide to go through the pain and suffering it takes to "just finish," they have a hard time providing a concrete answer. Very rarely—once in a blue moon—does someone say, "Because I love to swim, bike, run!"

Instead, people typically tell me slight variations of the same story. That they "like the challenge" is a common answer. Or, that they like seeing how far they can push themselves.

Over time, I have come to realize that those responses are generalized and oversimplified answers to a complex question. Each athlete no doubt has their own personal drive behind why they want to see how far they can push themselves, and why they choose athletics as a way to manifest this challenge. Buried within each person is a point of deep motivation that drives them through the pain and suffering. The variation I hear the most surrounds the idea of proving something, either to themselves or as an example to others. Here are some of the responses I received from competitors when I asked why they do it:

> *"Because training for Ironman is easier than raising two teenage daughters. It's my therapy. Plus, I've never slept so amazingly in my life! Kind of cool overhearing my daughters brag about me to their friends."*

> *"Setting a positive example. This will be my 2nd. I did my first when my daughter was 18 months, she is now 3 and this is for my son who is 12 months. I work full-time, train, and still have enough time and energy for my family. Letting them know that you can do anything you want in life. Yes, it's hard. Yes, sometimes you just need to take reason out of it, and realize we are capable of amazing things."*

"Teach my kids to set high goals, work hard and achieve greatness. That and I like Oreos and want a tattoo."

"Because I'm running from this girl. I'm maintaining a 200lb loss. And after a near death experience (OKC [Oklahoma City] bombing) I realized life was short and I want to live as much as I can. Training is living to me!" [posted previous photo of herself]

"As a child I was bullied and never chosen to be on any sports teams. Also, during cancer treatment I was told by a loved one that I was being a wimp. No more wimp for me. It's a neener neener to all those bullies, and to prove to myself I'm not a wimp. I'm a badass 50 plus year old woman!"

"IM training, while hard, lots of tears, pain, sweat, smiles, feeling proud, accomplished . . . all those emotions . . . but most importantly for me it has a place in my heart. I love it. When I hear IM . . . I hear dedication, motivation, discipline . . . don't stop . . . always give your best."

"Prove to myself that I am strong and can do anything I put my mind to."

"I'm racing for my youngest brother Ryan. He was 28 when he left us and it's coming up on his 10th anniversary. 4Ryan."

"Four generations of Alzheimer's in my family . . . They say that consistent exercise is a good way to protect yourself from Alzheimer's. There's nothing like training for an Ironman to make sure you consistently exercise . . . and just because I can."

"I'm doing it because I have 4 kids ages 9, 9, 7, and 5 and they make me proud every day. I want to do something to make them proud!"

"I'm doing this for my family!!! Setting an example of what hard work, determination, some tears and 'falls' will get you. I won't 'win the race' but I will finish it, hopefully with a smile!"

On the other side of the coin, family was the exact reason Emberson stopped competing in Ironmans. He competed in the first four from 1978–81, then split the scene.

"Eventually I said, 'What the heck am I doing this for?' I've got a family," he explained. "This is crazy."

He joined back up six years later to "experience" the tenth Ironman in 1988, and to his surprise, things had changed drastically. He noted a big shift in the competitors and their mentality. They were stiff, he said, nervous—a stark change from the carefree inaugural events.

"I thought they were all going to pee their pants at the start," he said of the athletes.

It's true. After reading the message boards and comment sections of articles these last few months, and being around athletes in Kona and Arizona, it is very obvious people get very worked up over the Ironman. I can't tell you how many times in the month leading up to the Ironman Arizona someone made a post expressing nervousness or negative anticipation. The course. The weather. The water temperature. The unknown. It drove a lot of people nuts.

So it once again begs the question: Why? People say they are doing it so they can prove to themselves that they can do anything, or prove to others that anything is possible. The irony is that racing takes up so much time and effort, there is little room to apply those learned skills elsewhere. And it's interesting, because there are so many ways in life to push yourself, so many ways you can feel accomplished. You could learn to play the piano. You could learn a new language. You could join a weekly running club. These would all be reasonable quests for personal renewal, and fantastic examples of accomplishment that would inspire others. In fact, it stands to reason that those feats would be even more inspiring. Is completing an Ironman really as inspirational an accomplishment as it's made out to be? All right, it impresses people, but is it inspirational?

I'm not so sure. All my friends have congratulated me on my accomplishment. All of them have made reference to how "insane" I am. None of them have signed up for the Ironman. None of them have bought a bike or a gym membership. If anything, I think my stories have made them feel sorry for me. They're concerned about the "why" part of it—why I felt the need to do such a thing. They express shock and disbelief at the distances involved. They conclude that they could never do it themselves.

One example happened over the Christmas holiday. I was at an annual get-together of family friends in New Jersey, outside of Philadelphia, and one of them, about my age, praised my efforts.

"Will, I can't *believe* you did that," he said.

"Yeah, it was crazy," I said. "But you could do it, too, if you wanted."

"Will, I could *never* do that."

"Don't you go to the gym five times a week?"

"Yeah, but . . . I could never do *that*!"

I've lost count of how many conversations like this I've had. In the beginning, it bothered me. How do you think I did it? What am I, some superior being? As someone who worked really hard for it, I appreciate the sentiment, don't get me wrong. But hearing my friends tell me over and over again that "they could never do it" bothered me. I don't agree that I'm special, or more talented. I'm just a regular dude who did what was necessary. I grabbed my friend by the shoulder.

"*Yes you can!* You might not want to, but you could, if you wanted to . . . right? Say it!"

"Will, there is no fucking way I could do it," he said.

And it was in this, the reactions from people after the fact, that I discovered the big reveal of the Ironman experience, the great lesson that people learn once they've done it: No matter how insane something sounds, if you want it and if you go for it, you can do it. It doesn't matter how tall the staircase is—you can climb it, step by step. Ironman teaches determination. It teaches perseverance. It's a great exercise—pun intended—that prepares you for other challenges in life. It shows there's a process to everything. Only after you've been there and done it can you look back and see that it was not a heroic achievement at all. It was a series of small steps, one after the other, to get where you wanted to go.

In this way, Ironman's competitors learn that life has no limits. We can do whatever we want. It's not going to be easy, and it will not happen overnight. But it will happen—whatever it is—if we want it and if we work for it.

It's not hard to understand how this feeling of invincibility can become addicting—hence, the strength and commitment of the Ironman community. More relevant on a day-to-day basis is that the workouts become addicting. Leading up to the Ironman, you exercise so much that you get to a point where you cannot go backward. For me it became a mental trap. How am I ever going to enjoy something again in my life? I cannot simply enjoy a workout or a hike or a swim? It has to be fire and fury or I feel incomplete?

Seasoned triathletes have echoed—and embraced—this sentiment of training as a continuous, addicting black hole. I found a series of articles on Ironman's website dedicated to the idea of "repeats." That is, doing a second Ironman after your first, or your fifth after your fourth. In a column entitled "Repeats Part V: You Might as Well Face it You're Addicted to Tri," two triathletes make the argument that a triathlete's "addiction" to his or her training is not so far removed from an actual addiction:

> *Recently, I got into a heated argument over beers with some fellow triathlete friends: were we* addicted *to triathlon/endurance sports, or did we just* really, really like it*? And what's the difference, anyway? It only became an argument given my tendency to get defensive and I protested against the term's pejorative connotations. Wasn't "addiction" reserved for drugs and alcohol and other destructive behaviors? . . .*
>
> *. . . Whether substance or behavior oriented, addiction causes states of tolerance and withdrawal: The body eventually incorporates the stimuli (training) into its sense of "normal." This leads to tolerance, where increasingly larger amounts of the stimuli are required to achieve the original effects. ("Must go longer . . .") Then, when the stimulus retreats, we experience symptoms of withdrawal: anxiety, irritability, and intense cravings . . .*

Her colleague continues:

. . . I'm trying to picture a world where I'm not training or racing, and am catapulted to an apocalyptic landscape. It's cold, windy, jagged, and very, very gray. And that's not even the worst part—I didn't bring my trail running shoes!

IRONMAN training is tightly woven into my lifestyle. It has become part of who I am, for better or worse. I crave my morning workouts, and good luck dodging my wrath if you make me miss one. The more intensely I pursue my triathlon goals, the more single-minded I tend to become about them. (Imagine my wife's joy about six weeks from a race—thank goodness she and my family routinely remind me there are other things to live for that don't involve finisher's medals.)

Does all that mean I'm an IRONMAN addict? Could I walk away from the sport if I really wanted to? I can only respond with, "Why would I want to?" . . .

Don't schedule that intervention just yet. IRONMAN training has made me a better me. *I'm healthier and have more energy now than I can ever recall, which allows me to be more productive at work and at home. I have two careers and still come home at night feeling excited and upbeat. I've incorporated weekly spin classes with my wife into my training so she's more directly involved in the journey. While we do have to delicately schedule events, we rarely miss important milestones. Sometimes we blow everything off just for a nice afternoon together. But my morning workouts remain. Or else.*

What's wrong with a little healthy addiction? Who cares if the lines between passion and obsession get blurred? I'm sorry, but "everything in moderation" or "easy does it" just ain't in my vocabulary. It's more like "Go big or go home"—except for us, of course, it's "go long, and then go home."

One night, while sitting on the couch, I show my girlfriend the above passages.

"Hunny, how would you feel if I did another one? If I became part of this community?"

"How would you feel about finding a new girlfriend?" she wonders aloud.

Contrast that with my sister, who is now convinced that I should race more.

"Let's run the Boston Marathon in 2020," she tells me over the phone. "That gives you two years to qualify."

"I don't know, Kris," I say. "Do you think a marathon by itself would be too easy for me?"

"Go fuck yourself," she says before hanging up.

Over time, I have come to understand and appreciate the mentality of people as they reach this fork, as they mull over the idea of signing up for another. There is a difference in perspective between people who have already done an Ironman and people who have not yet done one. If you ask someone who is training for their first, they usually answer that they "want to see what it's all about"—a plight not unlike my own.

People who have already done one and are training for another, however, sing a different tune. They are the ones who say they "like the challenge." Probably because of how accomplished it made them feel. Personally, I think when people say they "like the challenge," what they really mean is they "like having completed the challenge." They decide to go back for more—or not—because of all the reasons listed: They learned a lot about breaking through barriers, they can't go back to normal workouts, and, generally speaking, it's become the centerpiece of their social calendar. Or their anti-social calendar—however you want to look at it.

The biggest fork in the life of an Ironman exists at the junction of these two worlds, with the answer to a simple question that I've been asked a hundred times since I crossed the finish line: "So . . . are you going to do another one?"

For me, the answer is very simple. For others, we see it is much more complicated. One woman compared the predicament of an Ironman to the pain of childbirth.

"Ironmans are like pregnancies," she wrote in the forum. "We forget the pain and have more kids!!!"

Another person said, "Funny how it hurts so bad . . . but for like three days and then you want to do it again."

Yeah . . . about that.

Sitting here two months later, I feel accomplished, but I don't feel as fulfilled as I thought I would. You would think, after all it takes, that I would feel extra fulfilled. Yet in reality, I feel the same amount of fulfillment as I'm used to getting from a myriad of other activities, like hiking or snorkeling or hitting the gym for an hour. Don't get me wrong—I'm glad for the experience, pumped to have completed it, and grateful to have come out the other end in one piece. I met some very interesting people. But I absolutely do not feel the need to do it again. If "lesser" things have filled me up completely in the past—activities I could do and then walk normally after—why would I go down the Iron-brick road again? Variety is the spice of life. I don't like the idea of revolving my life around one activity (even if it is technically three sports). I want my life to be a full bouquet of twelve different flowers. I want to try this, and try that, and I don't want to feel guilty about it. I don't want to live on a regimen, where each day's worth is determined by the number of miles or the amount of wattage.

But hey, who am I to tell you what to do with your life? One of my friends, who owns a small business here in Hawai'i, told me the other night he thinks perseverance is mankind's greatest trait. If that's the case, then triathletes could be considered some of the world's most well-equipped people. I told him I thought that was one hell of an insight. Maybe he should sign up for a race and see where he stands?

"Interesting idea," he said, holding his hand up to the bartender for another round, "but I think I'm good."

The End

Appendix

GLOSSARY OF TERMS

5K: Refers to a five-kilometer run (3.1 miles). It's a very common race distance in the running world.

Age grouper: An amateur athlete competing in a triathlon.

Bonk: Slang term for when athletes hit a wall on the course and find themselves devoid of energy and unable to continue.

Brick workout: Refers to a workout consisting of two back-to-back sessions of different sports. For example, a run that immediately follows a bike workout.

Nutrition: General term used to describe food and drink athletes take in before and during the race. Typically refers to a mix of energy bars, gels, and sports drinks.

Pain cave: Name used to describe physical and mental aspects of being in the aero position on the bike for an extended period of time; usually associated with being pushed to the brink.

Race report: Name for a recap of the race and performance written and shared by triathletes post-race. They can vary in length from a paragraph to several pages.

Special needs bag: A bag in which athletes can place supplementary items they wish to access while on the course. These bags are in addition to the T1 and T2 bags. For the Ironman, athletes are permitted two special needs bags, one for the bike course and one for the run course.

T1: First transition between the swim and the bike.

T2: Second transition between the bike and the run.

Taper: Generally refers to the few-week period before a race when athletes reduce their training workload in hopes of allowing their muscles to recover.

LIST OF COSTS TO COMPETE IN THE IRONMAN ARIZONA

- Ironman Arizona entry fee: $850*
- Round-trip plane ticket to Arizona: $648
- Cost to transport bike to Arizona: $300
- Five nights in a hotel in Tempe: $520
- Running gear (shoes and socks): $189
- Bike and bike accessories (tires, pedals, bike computer, trainer): $915
- Swimming gear (wet suit, goggles, jammers): $272
- Gym membership: $78 (three months)
- Training events (Waikīkī Roughwater): $91
- Total cost: $3,863

*Comped by Tempe Tourism.
Note: Does not include cost of extra food consumed at meals, or athlete food consumed during training (energy bars, gels, Gatorade, etc.).

WORKOUT LOG

Date	Exercise	Scope (Distance/ Mileage)	Place	Workout Time(s) (Minutes: Seconds)
31-Jul	run	6	Waimānalo	47:03
1-Aug	run	unknown	Waimānalo	34:36
2-Aug	run	unknown	Ala Moana Beach Park and Magic Island	26:13
4-Aug	run	unknown	Wichita, Kansas	41:33
8-Aug	bike/run	16/3	YMCA Kailua	60:00; 26:04
14-Aug	bike/run	17/4	YMCA Kailua	60:00; 31:08
15-Aug	swim/bike	30 minutes/ 16	YMCA Kailua	30:00; 60:00
16-Aug	swim/run	unknown	Sherwood Beach	27:34; 17:16
18-Aug	bike/run	32.8/2	YMCA Kailua	120:00; 16:17
21-Aug	bike/run/ run	16.46/3/2	YMCA Kailua	60:00; 23:09; 22:47
23-Aug	bike/ elliptical/ swim	14.86/1.5/ unknown	Parc Hotel Gym	60:00; unknown; 9:50
25-Aug	bike	4 or 5	Waimānalo	20:00
26-Aug	bike	40.6	YMCA Kailua	146:82
28-Aug	swim/bike/ run	1/17.07/1	YMCA Kailua	30:28; 60:00; 8:20
29-Aug	bike/run	18.13/1	YMCA Kailua	60:00; 8:13
30-Aug	run	little less than 2	Ala Moana Beach Park and Magic Island	15:00
31-Aug	swim	unknown	Ala Moana Beach Park and Magic Island	35:00
1-Sep	bike/run	18/2	YMCA Kailua	60:00; 16:15
4-Sep	swim	2.4	Waikīkī Roughwater	79:08

Date	Exercise	Scope (Distance/ Mileage)	Place	Workout Time(s) (Minutes: Seconds)
5-Sep	run	3	Waimānalo	24:11
6-Sep	bike	18.67	YMCA Kailua	60:00
8-Sep	bike/run	18.14/2	YMCA Kailua	60:00; 17:38
11-Sep	bike	unknown	Trainer	118:00
13-Sep	bike	unknown	Trainer	90:00
14-Sep	run	2.43	YMCA Kailua	23:28
15-Sep	bike	unknown	Trainer	60:00
18-Sep	bike/run	unknown/ 2.75	Trainer	60:00; 25:00
19-Sep	surf/bike	unknown	Waikīkī/trainer	60:00; 60:00
21-Sep	surf/bike	unknown	Waikīkī/trainer	90:00; 30:00
22-Sep	surf	n/a	Waikīkī	90:00
23-Sep	bike	unknown	Trainer	30:00
24-Sep	run	2.75	Waimānalo	23:58
25-Sep	bike	unknown	Trainer	15:00
27-Sep	run	unknown	Volcano	33:23
29-Sep	run	4.35	Samoa	40:42
30-Sep	run	4.35	Samoa	41:15
3-Oct	run	unknown	Samoa	51:35
6-Oct	bike/run	unknown/ 2.75	Trainer/ Waimānalo	120:00; 21:36
7-Oct	run	6	Waimānalo	45:24
9-Oct	bike/run	unknown/6.8	Trainer/ Waimānalo	180:00; 52:52
10-Oct	surf/swim	unknown	Waimānalo/ Waikīkī	2 sessions
11-Oct	bike/run	unknown/4.9	Trainer/ Waimānalo	120:00; 38:04
13-Oct	run	11.19	Kona championship course	91:37
15-Oct	run	3	Waimānalo	23:51
16-Oct	bike/run	28.86/3	Waimānalo	101:30; 21:50
17-Oct	weight training/ run	unknown	Kailua	20:00

Date	Exercise	Scope (Distance/ Mileage)	Place	Workout Time(s) (Minutes: Seconds)
18-Oct	run	7.4	Waimānalo	57:18
20-Oct	bike/run	70.42/6.8	Waimānalo to Lā'ie; Waimānalo	291:50; 58:14
22-Oct	run	13.92	Waimānalo	107:34
23-Oct	bike	unknown	Trainer	60:00
24-Oct	bike	10.99	Waimānalo	41:11
27-Oct	run	unknown	Kaua'i/ Princeville	35:00
28-Oct	run	6.77	Waimānalo-Kailua	50:41
30-Oct	bike/run	29.50/3	Waimānalo-Kāne'ohe/ Waimānalo	99:55; 21:58
31-Oct	bike	14.07	Waimānalo	46:05
2-Nov	swim/run	approx 1; 3.73	Ala Moana Beach Park and Magic Island	31:52; 28:00
4-Nov	bike	unknown	Trainer	70:00
5-Nov	run	8.07	Waimānalo	60:01
6-Nov	bike	21.87	East Side O'ahu	75:00
7-Nov	swim	unknown	Ala Moana Beach Park	45:00
8-Nov	bike/run	unknown/3	Waimānalo	120:00; 22:03
9-Nov	swim	1	Ala Moana Beach Park	27:26
11-Nov	run	4.05	Washington, D.C.	36:57
14-Nov	bike/swim	7.5	YMCA Kailua	30:00; 15:00
16-Nov	run	3	Tempe	25:14
17-Nov	bike	5	Tempe	30:00
18-Nov	bike/swim	4/unknown	Tempe	30:00; 20:00
Note: Does not include warm-up mileage or time.				

Index

Page numbers in **bold** refer to captions and photographs.

Acknowledgments

A special thanks to Bmac, Drew, Tommy, and Bird—if those are in fact your real names. Your help, insight, patience, and inspiration were appreciated. Thanks to Kristin, for giving me hell but also for seeing me through; to S.H., for supporting me and putting up with me; to Gordon Haller, for inspiring me; to Ben and Alex, for reading the early manuscript and being wonderful people; to my Mom and Aunt, for coming to Tempe; to the triathlete community, for doing what you love.

About the Author

Will McGough is an award-winning international travel writer and the owner of Wake and Wander Media. He graduated from Virginia Tech a long time ago and has written for a variety of adventure and travel publications. He also guides trips and splits his time between Hawai'i, Colorado, and the road.